MW00998665

UNLOCK THE FEAR

How to Open Yourself Up
to Face and Accept Change

UNLOCK THE FEAR

How to Open Yourself Up
to Face and Accept Change

Gail Caissy

INSIGHT BOOKS

PLENUM PRESS • NEW YORK AND LONDON

Library of Congress Cataloging-in-Publication Data

Caissy, Gail A.
    Unlock the fear : how to open yourself up to face and accept
change / Gail Caissy.
        p.   cm.
    Includes bibliographical references and index.
    ISBN 0-306-45989-2
    1. Change (Psychology)   I. Title.
BF637.C4C35   1998
155.2'4--dc21   98-12428
                                                                     CIP

ISBN 0-306-45989-2

Insight Books is a Division of Plenum Publishing Corporation
233 Spring Street, New York, N.Y. 10013

http://www.plenum.com

An Insight Book

10 9 8 7 6 5 4 3 2 1

Printed in the United States of America

To my husband, Laurence

Preface

Almost a decade ago, I was standing in front of a class of graduate students at a local university and teaching a course on change, technology, and the future of education. The "future" had always fascinated me, and the phenomenon of change and how it was shaping the future was something I found equally interesting. Countless times, I discussed change and the impact it was having on our civilization with students, colleagues, and others. But it wasn't until I suddenly found myself in the midst of a period of great personal change (with the accompanying stress, loss, and shattered dreams) that I realized how powerful and profound a force it really was. At that point in time, change was no longer an esoteric idea to be studied and discussed in psychology and university classes but rather a very real and overpowering force I had to deal with in my own life.

During the past few decades, change has become an increasingly pervasive force in our world. While it continues to permeate almost every area of modern life, the accelerated rate at which change is occurring over time is forcing us to adapt to more and more of it. Throughout our history, we have always had to deal with personal change in our lives such as marriage, death, illness, and becoming parents. But today, changes occurring continuously and simultaneously in technology and society are compounding the kinds and increasing the number of changes we have to deal with. The result is that there are too many changes and not enough time to adapt to them.

Millions of people today are overwhelmed by too much change and their lives are negatively affected by their inability to cope, as mine was. In an attempt to contend with an avalanche of change in an already busy life, I became totally overwhelmed by it. When I realized what was happening, I set out to read and learn whatever I could about coping with change to help myself deal with it. While there were books available on mastering organizational change, implementing corporate change, becoming a change agent, changing one's behavior, change in the form of life transitions, and experiencing growth through change, there were none on how individuals actually deal internally with change and how they integrate it into their lives on a personal level. I never found a book to read on the nature of change, the effects of change on people, adapting to change, or strategies for managing change.

Despite the fact that there were no books written specifically on change as a phenomenon, I was determined to learn about why it had affected me in the way that it did. So I resorted to reading books on topics related to change (stress, loss) and on specific change events (death of a loved one). I also read through many articles, journals, books, and psychology texts for any bits of information I could find about change, which I tried to piece together in an attempt to make some sense of things.

Being an educator and researcher by training, in the aftermath of those difficult years, I felt compelled to do something with what I had learned. Thus, I decided to collect my notes as well as my thoughts, observations, analysis, and personal experiences and write a book on what I had learned and discovered about change in the hope that others might benefit from it. Much of the material presented in this book is based on my original thoughts and/or analysis, particularly ideas found in Chapters 1 through 4 and Chapter 8.

In writing this book, I also wanted to call attention to the urgent need for more research and focus on this topic. Change is so central to our lives at this time in our history and will undoubtedly continue to be so in the future. Therefore, studying change as a phenomenon with more intensity and with a greater sense of urgency is crucial so that we may learn as much as possible about it and how it affects us individually and as a society. Only then will we be prepared to deal with it in a positive and beneficial manner as we embark on life in the twenty-first century.

Acknowledgments

I extend my deepest appreciation to the following people for taking the time to review the manuscript: Robert Kamman, Ph.D, Charlotte Minich, Elizabeth MacDonald, Richard Roik, Josephine Tenden, and Laurence Tosetto, Ph.D. For his assistance during the production of this book, I also express my gratitude to my editor Frank K. Darmstadt and others on the staff of Insight Books who made this book possible.

Introduction

*I*n response to the question of what he felt would be the greatest problem in America in the year 2000, Carl Rogers, the well-known psychologist, responded:

> It is not the hydrogen bomb, fearful as that may be. It is not the population explosion, though the consequences of that are awful to contemplate. It is instead a problem which is rarely mentioned or discussed. It is the question of how much change the human being can accept, absorb and assimilate and the rate at which he can take it. Can he keep up with the ever increasing rate of technological change, or is there some point; at which the human organism goes to pieces? Can he leave the static ways and static guidelines which have dominated all of history, and adopt the process ways, the continual changingness, which must be his if he is to survive?[1]

There is no force more pervasive in our society today than change. It touches every aspect of our lives and every sector of society. It transforms us in ways we could never have imagined. It drives us forward in new, previously unknown directions, leaving its indelible mark in its wake.

Having to cope with change is not something new to humankind. Life is constant change and adaptation. Since the beginning of time, people have always had to deal with change in their lives. But in past millennia and centuries, most of the changes people faced were those of a personal nature: changes experienced as a result of the natural life cycle. Birth, death, and marriage are among them. In those times, there was little technological or societal change in a person's lifetime. And when these changes did occur, they came about very slowly over long periods that allowed people time to adjust.

Today, people still have to contend with the same traditional changes their ancestors did, but they face many additional ones brought about by ongoing societal change and numerous technological innovations. As we enter a new millennium, the time it takes for changes and new developments to occur in the world is no longer measured in centuries or decades but in years, months, weeks, and days. Technological and societal changes have become so widespread and powerful a force today that they not only generate and introduce many new changes to people's lives in themselves, but they increasingly drive the number and affect the nature of personal changes people have to contend with as well. People today face a staggering number of changes in their lives, a growing number of which are out of their control or imposed without their consent. They include changes in their jobs and workplace, in their homes, in families, in personal lives, in society, in the marketplace, in medicine, politics, communications, business, industry, entertainment, and so on.

Many people recognize, albeit on an unconscious level, the benefits and wonders that change has brought to society: electricity, telephones, microwave ovens, computers, reproductive freedom, vaccines, and a safe water and food supply. Would we ever want to go back to a time when there was no electricity, no antibiotics, or no rights for women? Would we ever want to go back to a time at the turn of the last millennium when the average lifespan of a human being was thirty years? Change has indeed fostered growth and progress, opportunity and innovation, improvement and prosperity in our society, making our lives easier in so many ways. But while recognizing that change is necessary for progress and personal growth, many people find it difficult to accept and deal with change in their own lives. Most people don't want to pay the price personally for progress and growth. Somehow they hope that progress will come but change will pass them by.

But the benefits of change and progress do not come without a price. As it sweeps through our lives and society at an increasingly rapid rate, change causes great upheaval, turmoil, uncertainty, and disorientation. It brings stress, loss, shattered dreams, and problems, many of them unanticipated or previously unknown. For these reasons, many of us find change disturbing and frightening.

Our natural reaction to change is predictable: ignore it, avoid it, or resist it. It is easier to deal with the known, the old and familiar than it is to venture into unknown, uncertain, and unfamiliar territory where we may feel insecure and uncomfortable, make mistakes, have failures, and suffer pain. Rather than see change for what it can become, we have become accustomed to viewing it in terms of what it takes away, especially when it takes away something meaningful to us. It also takes time and effort to adjust to change: time and effort we have less and less of. Unlike our ancestors, people today do not have the long periods of time needed to adjust and cope with change, particularly when an increasing number of changes they have to contend with are out of their control.

We are living in an age when the amount of change we are capable of generating and creating as a society is becoming almost limitless. Every day, millions of people, individually and collectively in companies and institutions around the world using a profusion of research, developments, and information, produce new knowledge and technologies, which in turn grow and multiply exponentially. However, the ability we have as humans to absorb and adapt to change does not increase at the same rate. Human capacity to adapt to change has evolved over hundreds of thousands of years and is limited by the rudiments of biology. As a result, we find that our ability to generate change fast outpaces our ability to absorb and adjust to it.

Over twenty-five years ago, in his best-selling book *Future Shock*, Alvin Toffler warned that the pace of change in our high-tech information society would escalate faster than our ability to absorb the change and that most people were grossly unprepared to deal with it. Toffler defined the distress of both physical and psychological changes that arise in individuals by subjecting them to too much change in too short a time as "future shock."[2]

Clearly a man ahead of his time, Toffler predicted we would soon reach the point where we would be adversely affected by too much change and warned that we must take measures to prepare for it. It is incredible as well as most unfortunate that over twenty-five years after he issued this warning, little has been done to heed it.

In the opening quote of this chapter, Carl Rogers poses some of the most important questions in modern times, and yet his questions about change and its effects on humans also remain largely unacknowledged, unaddressed, and unanswered. Considering the ubiquity of change in society today, the speed at which it is accelerating, and the impact it is having on our lives, it is astounding to learn how little it has been studied, written about, and researched in modern times. We find ourselves on the brink of an era of hyperchange, and yet we know so little about change, how it affects us, the nature of change, how to adapt to it, how to live with it, and how much we can tolerate before we "go to pieces."

Unfortunately, while this is the case and while far more research needs to be done before we can truly understand change and come to terms with its effects, the reality is that we have to cope with change in our lives here and now. We have no choice. Today, the inability to adapt to change can not only adversely affect our physical health and mental well-being, but it can also put us at a disadvantage in the job market, workplace, and society. In our rapidly changing world, change is inevitable. Whether we like it or not, or want it or not, change is here to stay. It is the dominant force of our time. We cannot escape it. We cannot hide from it. It is at the core of our postindustrial society and it continually fuels the growth of the high-tech information revolution. We have to face it and learn to live with it as best we can.

People undergoing significant personal change in their lives experience a wide range of emotions, thoughts, and behaviors. They don't feel "normal" or as they usually do, and they wonder when they will feel like themselves again. They don't know what to expect in times of change and they don't know how best to cope. They want to know how long their feelings will last and what they can do to deal with their circumstances.

This book is about how adult individuals deal internally with change, how they adapt to it, and how they integrate it into their lives on a personal level. The book is divided into three parts, each with a specific theme or focus. Part One, titled Understanding the Nature of Change, provides the reader with an understanding of the nature of change itself by examining how change affects people and their lives, why people fear change, and how people react to change. The sources of change in modern times are discussed and various kinds of change are identified. Change as a process is examined and a step-by-step overview of how people adapt to change is given.

Part Two, Companions to Change, provides the reader with an awareness of factors often associated with change. Individual chapters address the topics of stress, loss, and shattered illusions and mistaken beliefs. The relationship they have to change is discussed and an explanation of how they affect people undergoing change is provided. Part Two also contains a discussion of how experiencing change can lead to personal growth and development.

Part Three, Strategies for Managing Change, provides a wide range of strategies to help the reader cope with change and learn to live with it more comfortably on a day-to-day basis. Strategies can be applied to a specific situation of change a person may be facing or simply may prepare the reader to be more adaptive to change in general. A chapter on getting help and support in times of change is also included.

One final note: the pronouns he and she are used interchangeably throughout the book. This was done in order to eliminate the need to repeatedly use the terms she/he or they. Unless otherwise specified, what is said about one gender regarding change applies to the other.

part one

Understanding the Nature of Change

chapter one

Change, People, and Progress
A Historical Perspective

Change has always been with us. Since the beginning of time, it has played a vital role in shaping our world, our society, and our destiny. Throughout history, change has been a constant catalyst for technological advancement and progress in our civilization and culture, and it has been a primary agent in directing our individual lives and personal growth.

In past millennia and centuries, most of the changes people faced in their lives were those of a personal nature: changes experienced as a result of the natural life cycle such as birth, death, marriage, aging, and disease. There was little technological innovation or societal change within a person's lifetime. When changes in these areas did occur, they happened slowly, easing into society over long periods of time with minimal impact on people's lives.

In recent history, however, change has become much more pervasive and powerful. Today, not only do people have to contend with all of the same personal changes their ancestors faced hundreds or thousands of years ago, but they also have to deal with myriad others their ancestors never knew—changes generated by rapid and ongoing technological and societal change. Technology and society are new sources of change for people in modern times. To develop a better understanding of the impact that changes in these areas have had on our culture and lives over time, we now undertake a brief historical review of some technological and societal changes that occurred in the past. We consider the reactions people had to them as well as the impact the changes had on their lives at the time. We also learn how the nature of change as well how change occurs is itself changing.

Major Milestones in Human History

Man has been on earth for about a million years now. Through his evolution over time, he has constantly sought to make life easier and to improve the quality of his life. In the quest for improvement, he has developed and created many new things and processes, many of which involved making changes to the status quo. A number of these new inventions and discoveries were so significant they changed his life forever. They had such an impact at the time they were developed that they permanently changed the way things were done. From each discovery made in history, there was no turning back. These significant changes, which occurred over time, became milestones by which we study and assess the evolution and history of man. They became a measure of his progress. We now briefly highlight some of the major milestones in the history of humankind.

In prehistoric times, people lived as hunters and nomads. In order to survive, they were constantly on the move searching for food. They hunted animals and searched for roots and berries. Large groups of people could not live together in the same place because no one geographical area was able to supply enough food to sustain more than a few people at a time. People were preoccupied with safety and were constantly on the alert for danger (wild animals) or adversaries (strangers). Subsistence and survival were the goals of people living in these times.

By about 3000 BC, people had learned how to grow their own crops and food and how to domesticate and raise animals. This ability to grow crops and domesticate animals changed the way people lived significantly. No longer was it necessary for them to move continuously looking for food because they could grow their own. That meant that people could build permanent shelters and remain in the same place for long periods of time. As a result, their lives became more stable. They began to have neighbors. Because they had fixed shelters, defense and security were easier to provide. Living in groups made it easier for people to look out for each other. It also meant they could trade their crops or animals with others for goods, animals, or crops they did not have themselves. People began to weave cloth and make pottery and they traded them for food that others grew. An early form of specialization of work began to develop. Villages and towns began to spring up and the development of civilization began.

At about the same time as agriculture was developing in approximately 3000 BC, writing and record keeping also began. This meant that events in history could be recorded in written form rather than be transmitted in oral form and records on any number of things could be kept. Writing provided a new means of communication for humankind and as a consequence gave people access to knowledge. They could record important events, communicate ideas, keep track of their possessions, and thereby leave a lasting record of their lives for future generations.

About 2700 BC, the wheel was discovered. This revolutionized transportation as it was then known. Until that time, people and animals were used to transport things. Because this was the case, things could not be transported long distances over land and only a limited number of things could be transported because of the great physical burden placed on a person or animal. Once the wheel was used to build carts and other forms of transportation, the physical burden was reduced and a larger number of goods could be transported over much greater distances. Thus, trade was more viable and became more widespread. Transportation and trade routes began to develop as a result.

Skipping ahead a few thousand years, we move to the 1440s to another great development. It was during this decade that Johannes Gutenberg invented the movable-type printing press. Until that time, books and records were copied by hand or printed with wooden blocks. This was done by the small number of people in the population able to read and write. By 1455, the first books were printed with metal movable type. The invention of the printing press meant that many identical copies of a book or document could be produced. It allowed mass dissemination of information as a means of communication and education. People who wanted access to knowledge had to learn to read and write. Thus, the idea of education for the common people as opposed to education for a small elite in society became desirable and possible. Learning to read and write became important for anyone dealing with printed media. Providing this kind of education for people who until this time in history had used only oral communication and learning was indeed revolutionary. By the year 1500, there were over 1,000 print shops in Europe and over fifteen million books in print.

The development of the printing press had another ramification. Before the printing press, people were out of touch with anything that happened beyond their own immediate environment. With the development of print media, they could read or hear about things going on outside their immediate geographic area and in other places in the known world.

The next milestone in human history we examine is the arrival of the industrial revolution in the late 1700s and early 1800s. The industrial revolution was made possible by the development of mechanical inventions (power-driven machines) that could do work that people previously did by hand or with the help of simple tools. The harnessing of steam as an energy source (the steam engine) to power these machines as well as the use of natural resources obtained from distant places were novel to the process of producing goods. Since machines were able to replace human strength and muscle power, people were no longer needed solely for their physical strength in the workplace. With the advent of mass production in factories, weavers, artisans, and craftsmen were less in demand and for the most part their livelihood became obsolete.

The industrial revolution greatly changed the way people lived. Because jobs were available in factories, towns and cities quickly sprang up around them. People moved to cities and towns to get work. Because mass transportation had not yet been invented, ordinary people had to live close to where they worked. Thus, during the industrial revolution, cities and towns grew rapidly as waves of people began migrating from rural to urban settings. The predominantly rural way of life was changing significantly. Specialized work became more and more common because people no longer had to grow their own food and raise their own animals to survive. They were able to work in factories and industries and were able to buy food as well as other goods they needed with the money they received as wages. This was the beginning of the transformation of a rural, agricultural society to an urban, industrial one.

Transportation networks (land, rail, water) also quickly developed and expanded in order to ship raw materials to the industrial centers as well as finished products to their designated markets. The development of steam as a source of power in the 1800s was important for both industry and transportation (trains, ships).

The development of electricity in the 1800s is another creation that had a tremendous effect on the way people lived. Electricity provided a more portable or easily transported source of power and it could run machines and tools in industry. Electricity provided a means of supplying light to people's homes and to the streets, replacing gas, kerosene, coal oil, and candles. Having a source of light available twenty-four hours a day meant that the day didn't have to end when it became dark and factories didn't have to close down at dusk. Electricity led to the development of appliances that ordinary people could use in their homes (iron, vacuum cleaner). Many of these appliances automated jobs and tasks that previously had to be done by hand. Electricity became a source of power for new forms of transportation and communication (streetcar, radio). The discovery of electricity was also important because it made possible the development of the giant electronics and computer industry of the twentieth century.

People of the 1800s witnessed extensive and remarkable growth during that century. It was the century that gave rise to the development of many new and important inventions that had a significant impact on society. Just a few examples are the development of photography, the telegraph, the typewriter, the steel plow, the sewing machine, the telephone, the radio, the phonograph, the light bulb, X rays, the camera, the gas engine, the electric generator, and steam locomotive and diesel engines.

The next milestone we consider is the development of two novel forms of transportation in the early 1900s: the automobile and the airplane. Until the 1900s, transportation existed in the form of water, rail, and beast (animals such as horses as well as horse-drawn carriages). With the development of the automobile, society was once again transformed. The automobile represented a means of transportation for ordinary people. Its development meant that people no longer had to live where they worked because the auto could transport them to more distant destinations. This led to a trend away from urban living to more suburban living. People were also able to travel outside of their immediate geographic area much more frequently than was previously possible. The need for horses and all the maintenance that went with them (stables, feed, blacksmiths) became obsolete and people employed in these areas lost their jobs. Cities had to plan for the movement of vehicles by improving street patterns and developing transportation networks, parking lots, and so on.

The development of the airplane also significantly affected society and the world. The use of air transportation made it much easier for people to travel to, trade with, and communicate with people in other countries. Prior to this time, people and goods moved to other countries by water. It was a slow and tedious process, far different from that of today when people, mail, and goods are moved long distances in short periods of time.

A few decades later, another historic milestone is manifest: the computer. The first computer, built in the 1940s, was developed for military purposes. The U.S. military wanted a machine that would reduce the time and tedium required for the calculation of trajectories of artillery shells by its personnel. The computer was originally developed to meet this need. The first computer, ENIAC (electronic numerical integrator and calculator), occupied the space of a small gymnasium, weighed thirty tons, was very expensive to build, and had much less power than today's personal desktop computers.

Since the 1940s, computers have continued to grow in speed and power through the development of vacuum tubes, transistors, silicon chips, microchips, microprocessors, and so on. Today, computers and microchip technology are very much part of our lives and are integrated and used in some way in almost every sector of our economy and society. Computers have allowed people to work and think in previously unheard of ways and they save millions of person-hours in labor. As computer technology continues to improve and evolve, new products, processes, and developments are generated on a continuous basis. There is no need to explain the extent to which computers and microchip technology have affected our lives.

These, of course, are only a few of the remarkable number of innovations that were developed during the 1900s. People of the twentieth century have witnessed a previously unparalleled explosion of new developments and creations that have expanded human ability and potential to previously unknown levels. Never before have so many creations and developments occurred in so many sectors of society at the same time and at such a rapid rate. Just some of the developments of this century include laser technology, the transistor, electronics, microelectronics, high technology, microtechnology, fiber optics, robotics, computerized offices, computer networks, the information highway, satellite broadcasting, microwaves, atomic energy, nuclear energy, airplanes, jets, spaceships, fax machines, cellular phones, voice mail, guided missiles, stealth bombers, radar, nuclear submarines, computer-aided manufacturing, computer-aided design, air conditioners, camcorders, compact disc players, tape recorders, vaccines, heart transplants, antibiotics, genetic engineering, test tube babies, television, dishwashers, electric stoves and refrigerators, clothes dryers, microwave ovens; the list goes on and on. There are numerous applications of these technologies in almost every sector of society including science, agriculture, medicine, industry, business, communication, education, transportation, and entertainment. As each of these new creations was developed, people had to learn about them and adapt to them by integrating them into their lives.

How People Reacted to Change

*T*he reaction of people to many of the technological changes that occurred in history is familiar. They often reacted to change with resistance, skepticism, fear, and anxiety. For example, while the development of the printing press is perceived as one of the most revolutionary and beneficial developments created in history, many people who lived at the time of its development were skeptical, fearful, and resentful of it. They couldn't understand how a machine could produce so many books at the same time and how they could all look exactly the same. They didn't think it was necessary to disseminate information to masses of people and they thought that doing so would cause great harm. They believed that the printing press was a product of "the devil" and that its use would only lead to evil.

While we view the industrial revolution as one of the great milestones and periods of progress in the history of humankind, many people of that era were fearful of all that was happening during that time and they rebelled against many of the changes it brought to their lives. In the early 1800s, for example, members of a British trade union set out to destroy new machines being installed in factories at the time. They didn't want the machines installed because they thought the machines would put them out of work. They thought that destroying the machines would bring factory production to a halt and would reverse the introduction of industrialization into society, and thereby save their jobs. Resistance to industrialization also persisted among artisans, weavers, and craftsmen at the time. Many refused to get jobs in the factories and continued producing their goods and wares at home in the manner they always had. They were certain that their ways of production were better and would continue to be preferred by the public. As mass production became the standard and people bought goods that were mass produced and cheaper, these people were left behind.

During an economic depression that occurred in the United States in the 1830s, people were becoming increasingly alarmed at the rate and number of new inventions being developed and produced at the time. They demanded a law to end all inventing. Experiencing economic hard times, they feared the continued creation of new machines and other developments would eliminate or take away much needed jobs and their livelihood.

As cities and towns grew as a result of the industrial revolution, the spread of disease became a great threat in the cities. The need for adequate sanitation and a clean water supply became a major problem. Many people died from water-born diseases, such as cholera, carried in water contaminated with raw sewage. However, when attempts were made to try and change (improve) the conditions that bred disease, people protested against the sanitary inspectors, doctors, and members of the boards of health who passed laws to clean up the cities. They felt that the inspectors and doctors were imposing on their right to live as they pleased. For example, they saw no reason why they couldn't continue to dump their garbage and sewage on the streets as they always had and why they should have to change their ways to accommodate the "obsession with cleanliness."

Later, when the radio was invented, some people did not approve of its presence or use. They complained that using radios involved invisible radiation that would no doubt have adverse effects on people.

In the early days of the automobile, people objected to their presence on the streets. They feared the new automobiles with gasoline-powered engines were in grave danger of exploding. They thought innocent bystanders would be maimed or killed by those using the "high speed, poorly controlled vehicles." At the same time, executives at companies that manufactured horse buggies set about to present mathematical proof to government authorities that allowing the introduction of automobiles would lead to the elimination of their industry. That, they claimed, would leave the North American economy in ruins.

Many times in the past, when something new was developed, people could not believe that anything bigger and better than this new invention could ever appear. They tended to believe that man had reached his zenith in terms of standard of living and ability. They could not fathom future discoveries nor could they foresee future potential for existing or new creations. This attitude was pervasive even among educated people. For example, in 1899, Charles H. Duell, the director of the U.S. Patent Office said that everything that could be invented had been invented.

When the telephone was invented, the top technical journal of the day, *The Telegrapher,* reported that the telephone had no direct practical application. Even Elisha Gray, the telephone inventor runner-up, said in 1876 that the telephone created interest only in scientific circles and that its commercial value would be limited.

When Remington first produced the commercial typewriter in 1874, few people paid any attention to it. In fact, they couldn't sell many at that time because people saw no use for it. Similarly, when the photocopier (Xerox machine) was developed, critics of the day said that it was interesting but had no future.

When the Wright brothers first experimented with flying machines (airplanes), they were scoffed at, ridiculed, and laughed at by almost everyone including their own father. People of the time believed that man would never fly. They said that flying was only possible for angels.

And when the computer was invented, people could not foresee much future use for it either. In 1943, when Thomas Watson, chair of IBM, was asked if there was a market for computers in the future, he responded that there might be a world market for maybe *five* computers! Scientists who worked to improve the computer and who tried to develop more uses for it were subject to research cuts and funding problems for many years.

Observations about People, Change, and Progress over Time

While the overview of significant milestones in the history of humankind presented here is brief and limited, there are some observations we can make about people, change, and progress over time. First, the further back in time we go, the longer it took for major changes or progress to occur. For the first few millennia of recorded history, the number of milestones were few and far between. Although changes were significant when they occurred, they were limited in number. From the time a discovery or invention was made to the time its use spread to large masses of people, centuries or decades had gone by. Similarly, it took a significant amount of time for new developments to be improved or replaced by something better. Progress was slow and steady. Major technological changes eased into society over generations.

This scenario contrasts sharply with the one we find in the recent past and today. As we look at the milestones and discoveries of the last two hundred years, we find the number of discoveries *increases* dramatically as we get closer to the present while the amount of time between one significant discovery and another *decreases*. During the second half of this century in particular, we experienced a tremendous explosion of rapid technological innovation in almost every area of society and life. There has been continuous development and progress at a faster and faster rate. Consider the World Wide Web, for example. It was invented in 1992 and was originally used by only a handful of physicists to share their research. Within a year, pictures and sound were added. Another two to three years later, millions of people all over the world were using the World Wide Web to communicate, obtain information, and put their own content on it by creating their own Web pages and Web sites! The length of time it takes from the discovery of something new to its production, distribution in the marketplace, and integration into society and culture is the shortest it has ever been. Consequently, as we enter a new millennium, the time it takes for changes and developments to occur in our society is no longer measured in centuries or decades but rather in years, months, and weeks. Change and progress, as a result, are no longer slow and steady but rapid, ongoing, and widespread.

The significance of this change of pace on people today is profound and is the focus of our next observation. For those living in past millennia or centuries, change happened at such a slow pace that people had time to adjust as they went along. In those days, the world did not change much from the time a person was born to the time a person died. In contrast to that, a sixty-year-old person living today has witnessed more change and progress in his lifetime than a person of any generation of the past. In fact, more change and progress has been made in our society in the last fifty years than in all of previously recorded history.

While people of the past had to contend with a limited number of changes and innovations over long periods of time, people today not only have to adjust to more changes in technology within limited periods of time, but they also have to cope simultaneously with an increasing number of new innovations simultaneously produced in various areas within these shorter periods of time. Thus, the nature of change and how it occurs has itself changed over time!

Because change is now occurring more and more rapidly and because it is occurring at the same time in so many areas, people today no longer have the time needed to adjust. In fact, most can barely keep up with changes occurring in their own field of endeavor or interest. People are under constant pressure to cope with and adapt to change on an ongoing basis. When they are bombarded with having to adapt to changes in many different areas of their lives at once, they can experience circuit overload. Stress, burnout, and illness are often the result. A family doctor today, for example, not only has to keep up with the latest techniques in surgery, the newest treatments available for his patients, the latest kinds equipment used to treat patients, the newest drugs available to treat various diseases, and the most recent diagnostic tests, he also has to keep up with the constant changes being made by the many insurance companies he deals with (rules and regulations on patient treatment and billing for example), the latest computer/office automation and equipment/methods to use within his practice, the changing local hospital procedures, and so on. And there are changes occurring in all of these areas on an ongoing basis. There is no break. There is no time when the doctor can feel that he can relax. And these changes are just the ones he faces related to his professional life. There are also many changes in society and in his personal and home life to be considered as well. One can well understand how this situation can generate stress for people who work in similar environments or under similar conditions today.

Another observation we can make as we move away from the past and toward the present is that the number of discoveries and innovations made over time have increased tremendously. This happened largely because the creation of one new innovation (e.g., electricity) made possible the development of other new ones (e.g., vacuum tubes). These others in turn generate more creation and spin-offs (radio, television, radar, and computers) within those areas. This multiplying effect creates a continual profusion of new developments, improvements, and ongoing changes in many different areas over time.

As innovations are quickly brought to market, they are soon followed by the release of improved or updated models. This results in obsolescence, another problem people have to contend with in modern times. In the workplace for example, word processing software and computer hardware are continually updated. That means secretaries must keep abreast of the ongoing changes in software to remain current and office managers must reevaluate and replace computer/technological equipment on a continual basis as equipment becomes outdated. Ordinary consumers, in much the same predicament, buy the latest in electronic equipment/products only to find it out of date or surpassed by a new and improved model within a few months to a year after the purchase had been made.

Another observation we can make from our brief historical overview is that once a significant discovery, innovation, or change has been introduced into society and proved beneficial, it changed people's lives and society forever. From that point on in history, there was no turning back. There was no returning to the way things used to be. Protesting and rebelling against innovation didn't stop the change and progress. Once there were steam engines to power things, there was no going back to using human or animal strength. When cars became available to the masses, there was little further use for horses and buggies, even though they had been used for hundreds of years.

And finally, our last observation concerns the reaction people had to many of the technological developments and subsequent changes they brought over time. In the past, resistance, fear, anxiety, and skepticism were common reactions to new innovations and change even when the changes ultimately improved people's lives considerably. People of the past, like those of the present, were fearful of many of the same things: harm, losing their jobs, the uncertainty that change brought, and the inconvenience of having to adapt to new ways. It seems that throughout history people have enjoyed the progress and benefits that change brought to their lives, but they didn't like having to cope with the uncertainty and adjustments that inevitably came with it.

chapter two

Why People Fear Change

*F*ear of change is not new to our generation and time. As discussed in Chapter 1, throughout history, people responded to change in much the same way: with fear, resistance, reluctance, and uneasiness. Many people today react to change in the same manner as their ancestors did. It seems that fear of change has persisted throughout time and the ages. Why have these reactions to change endured? Why are people so afraid of change? What is it about change that makes them so uncomfortable? These are some of the questions we address in this chapter.

How Change Affects People's Lives

*I*n each area of our lives (home, job, relationships), we structure things to make our environment as comfortable and accommodating as possible to our needs and desires. This is done by building into our environment the maximum number of things we like, prefer, and are comfortable with and by avoiding or keeping to a minimum things we don't like or find uncomfortable. People make decisions about their lives on this basis. For this reason, they choose to live in certain neighborhoods, work at particular jobs, live in particular homes or apartments, and develop friendships with people they like. In structuring their lives and environment to meet their preferences, people form habits that result in the development of certain patterns of behavior. Over time, people become comfortable with these patterns of behavior in each area of their lives, and these patterns become stable and predictable routines.

Anne

Anne is a twenty-eight-year-old dental hygienist of African American descent. She is not a "morning person." Consequently, she does not like to get up early in the morning. Rather than shower in the morning, she takes a bath before going to bed at night. She also lays out her clothes for the next day and sets the table for breakfast, thereby ensuring that she can sleep until the last possible moment before having to get up and go to work.

Anne's evening routine developed as a result of her dislike of getting up early in the morning and her preference for sleeping as late as possible. For Anne, this is the best way to accommodate her needs. But then, Anne has a baby and her routine is drastically changed. She has to get up much earlier than usual in the morning as well as for feedings during the night. Although she doesn't like the change, her love for her baby is her motivation to make the needed changes in her routine.

When change comes along, it disturbs the way things are by throwing them out of balance and breaking the familiar routine. Change often results in the introduction of something new that must be integrated and assimilated into one's routine or daily pattern of behavior. Because the change is not already a part of the existing behavior or environment, it disrupts the normal flow of events and behavior and means that things will have to be done differently. People who are used to a familiar situation often feel threatened by the introduction of change. Whereas they know they like an existing situation, they are uncertain how they will like or cope with a new one. This brings a natural hesistancy, reluctance, or resistance to change. Usually, the greater the potential impact of the change, the stronger the feelings of resistance.

Josephine

Josephine, a fifty-one-year-old married woman of Italian descent, lives in New York City. Before marriage, she had worked as a secretary and continued after marriage until her first child was born. Her last child left home when Josephine was 49 and had been out of the workforce for twenty-four years. After a lengthy search, she found a job as a secretary–office manager for a Roman Catholic church parish. It was one of the few jobs she could find that did not require computer-related skills or a knowledge of office automation systems. That meant she didn't have to go back to school for any training and didn't have to deal with computers, which she feared. She was very happy to find the job and liked it very much.

After working at the church office for three years, the older priest who hired her announced that he was retiring and that the bishop had appointed a much younger priest to take over the parish. He also told her that the younger priest was being brought in to update the parish and modernize the office with a computer system that had been used successfully in other churches in the area. Josephine began to panic. "A new priest? Will I like him and be able to get along with him? Computers in the church office? What will I do? Will I be able to keep my job? Will I have to learn about computers? Will I have to go back to school? Will I be able to do it? What if I can't? Why do they want to change the way the office is run anyway? It is just fine the way it is."

Josephine is facing not just one change in this situation (getting a new boss) but several others that stem from the initial change. First, she must adjust to having a new boss, and get used to his personality and the way he wants things done. The manner in which she performs her job on a daily basis will also be changed as a result of the computer system that will be installed. She will have to learn new computing skills and be able to apply them in her work situation. She may also have to return to school for retraining as she has little knowledge of computers and is in fact afraid of them. She may lose her job altogether, with bleak prospects of finding another, if she is unwilling to learn computing skills.

Having to give up the known, the predictable, and the familiar causes people to fear change. It is much easier to see what is in the present than what is coming in the future. It is the fear of the unknown that is frightening and threatens their sense of security. People are familiar with situations of the past and present but when faced with future unknown situations, they experience anxiety and stress. They worry about what will happen and whether they will be able to cope.

People often feel that there is no need to change things when the old way is working fine. Because they are familiar with the old way, they are reluctant to let go of it to embrace something unfamiliar and new. They prefer to stick with the status quo even though the new way is proved to be more effective than the old.

When people give up the familiar for the unknown, it puts them at risk for failure. It puts them in a situation of uncertainty where they cannot predict the outcome of their actions, and hence they have to deal with the possibility of making mistakes. The fear of failure and of making mistakes are still other reasons why people fear change.

Change also requires personal effort. It takes time to accept, adjust to, and get used to something new and make it part of one's new environment or routine. Also, it takes effort to learn new ways of doing things. In contrast, it is easier to stick with the old and familiar ways.

Ray and Peter

Ray and Peter, painters of Hispanic descent in their late thirties, were partners in a small business that they operated in northern California for fifteen years. They subcontracted their painting services mainly to new house builders. Ray's wife took phone calls from contractors at their home during the day, and they used Peter's garage to store their van and painting supplies. Peter's in-laws owned a cabin on a northern remote lake, which they allowed him to use at any time. Peter loved fishing and went to his in-laws' cabin whenever he had the chance. He would always return to his job with fishing stories to tell Ray after one of his trips. One Saturday night, after Peter had gone on a fishing trip for the weekend, Ray's wife took a phone call. It was Peter's father-in-law. He told her that Peter had been killed in a boating accident earlier that day. Ray went into shock when his wife told him the news. He couldn't believe it. He had worked with this man for fifteen years and now he was gone. He couldn't sleep. He couldn't eat. He couldn't concentrate. He felt numb and walked around in a daze the next day. As he began to think about it, the implications of Peter's death started to hit him. His thoughts included, "How will I run my business? Will I have to close it down? How am I going to work without Peter?"

After the funeral, which was very hard on Ray emotionally, he reported to his job site for work but couldn't seem to "get going." He was disoriented because Peter wasn't there doing his usual routine. Peter used to do the wall preparation and now Ray realized that he had to do it. He had to think about how he would rework his routine to include both his job and Peter's but he couldn't seem to get organized. He would disappear into his van looking for equipment several times before he was able to start. Then as he was working, he kept talking about Peter to the other construction workers, many of whom hardly knew him. Then Ray would tell them some of Peter's fishing stories. As he recounted the stories, he'd laugh about the good times they had had together. Then at other times, he seemed to be overcome with emotion and stopped talking.

Having to do all of the painting work himself now, by the end of the week Ray was falling behind in his work. He realized he couldn't continue on his own and that he would have to get a new partner if he was going to keep his business. He began worrying about where he would find someone, what kind of person he would get, and whether he would be as good as Peter was. And then he worried about what he would do if he couldn't find someone qualified and interested in a partnership.

Peter's sudden death brought Ray a change in the form of a loss. But that one change generated many others. First, he had to struggle with the emotional impact of losing a friend and someone he worked with every day for fifteen years. Then he had to contend with the fact that he lost his business partner as well. His routine on the job was disrupted as a result of Peter's death. And finally, he had to deal with the problem of looking for a new partner to replace Peter, not knowing if he would find someone suitable.

Many times, change involves loss. The loss can involve a home, health, part of one's body, or relationships. It can also include loss of feelings, freedom, pride, or identity. Loss is painful because it involves an emotional and psychological attachment to a situation or person that has been built over time. When the situation, person, or thing is lost, people feel a sense of grief and have to mourn the loss, which can be painful. People need to adjust to a loss physically, emotionally, psychologically, and socially.

Jim

Jim is a forty-four-year-old married man who worked as a business executive for a large, secure "blue chip" company on the outskirts of Chicago. It was a good corporation to work for. He was hired shortly after he graduated from college and had been with the company for eighteen years. When he was hired, he was all but promised a secure job and lifetime employment. The company had experienced continuous growth for three decades, had a sound financial base, and a "no layoff" policy for its employees.

Then a recession came. The company's growth had slowed down prior to the recession, but company officers thought they would ride out the recession as they had with previous ones. They soon realized, however, that the recession they were experiencing was no ordinary one. It lasted longer than usual and was affecting many other companies around the nation. Like others, Jim's company was losing millions of dollars as the recession went on. Despite their policies of the past, massive layoffs and downsizing seemed to be the only way for the company to survive.

One day Jim's supervisor came in to tell him that the company was closing down his department and that Jim's job would be eliminated as a result. The supervisor said there was nothing he could do for Jim in that office but said the company could offer him a position in another branch office across the country. The position would be one level below Jim's current position.

Jim was devastated. Over the years, he had worked very hard for the company and had expected to work there all his life. It was such a safe and secure place. He never thought of working anywhere else. He couldn't believe what was happening to him. It just didn't seem real. It didn't seem possible. He had planned to stay in the area for the rest of his life. He had built a new home in the suburbs a few years back and recently had bought a speed boat. His family and his wife's family lived in the area. They were very happy living there. The idea of moving across the country didn't appeal to him at all. But he had two kids in high school and an $80,000 mortgage. His wife worked and had a good job, but he knew they wouldn't be able to maintain their standard of living on her salary alone. What was he to do?

He didn't like the idea of having to move but if he turned down the transfer, he knew he would have difficulty finding another job in the area. As a result of the recession, there were many other executives his age with his qualifications looking for jobs and there weren't many to be had. Some of his associates who worked with other companies were still out of work after a year. Some of Jim's thoughts were, "How will I pay the bills and the mortgage if I stay where I am? Will I have to sell my beautiful home? What will my friends and relatives think of me? I used to be a successful business executive and what am I now? An unemployed nobody?" His identity and sense of self-esteem was threatened. He felt he had worked hard to get what he had and couldn't understand why he should lose it all now. If he took the transfer, his wife would have to quit her job too.

He wondered what it would be like to work at the other branch office and what it would be like working at a lower level position. "What if I don't like the job or the supervisory person? What if I don't like the area geographically? What kind of house will I be able to afford and will I miss my family and friends? What about the kids? How will they react to the idea of changing schools and friends and moving away from relatives?" Jim felt as though his whole world was coming apart. The decision he faced was a difficult one. He felt angry about being in his position and betrayed by the company that fired him. He had given them so many years of his life.

Jim had to deal with many changes as a result of losing his job. That one change generated so many others. He had to accept the fact that he lost a job he thought he would have forever and that his family, children, and lifestyle would be affected by this event. His future security and lifestyle were threatened. He had to come to terms with the anger he felt over being caught in this situation through no fault of his own. His sense of pride was affected as well as his self-esteem. His identity was shaken. He had to deal with the loss of control he had over the future and all of the uncertainty that goes with it. He had to face the problem he had and had to make decisions without knowing what the outcome would be. He also had to deal with the stress and anxiety that the whole situation generated not only for him but for everyone in his family.

Coming to terms with change and learning to accept it can be stressful. A sense of predictability in life is a fundamental human need. People like to live in fairly predictable environments. Stress and anxiety are common during times of change because people can't predict what will happen and they don't know what to expect. They also have no way of knowing how they will like the new situation generated by the change or how they will adjust to it. People worry about what others will think of them and their ability or inability to cope. They worry about what others will think of them if they fail or make mistakes. In many situations of change, one's sense of self-esteem and self-worth is affected.

Venturing into the new and unknown also generates feelings of loss of control. Without control over things in life, people feel threatened, frightened, anxious, helpless, powerless, and overwhelmed because they do not know where the change will take them and how it will affect their lives. There is tremendous uncertainty that comes with losing something familiar, and feelings of insecurity are a result.

Reasons Why People Fear Change

The preceding discussion of how change affects people's lives gives us some insight into the reasons why people may fear or be apprehensive about change. We now isolate and identify various factors or reasons why people fear change and focus our discussion on them. While each factor is listed and examined individually for purposes of our discussion, it will become apparent that these factors are very much interrelated and interdependent. In reality, they seldom occur in isolation.

Change Threatens the Structure of Our Lives

The ability to cope with life depends on the existence of consistent, predictable, and reliable structures in our lives and environment. These include such things as our relationships, family life, job, beliefs, daily routines, and patterns of behavior associated with them. Structure is important because it provides people with a framework for their lives: a foundation or base upon which to build, organize, and live their lives. It allows them to have a dependable frame of reference so that they can make decisions and judgments about things. Structure also allows people to feel a sense of security and stability as they go about daily living.

A lack of structure in people's lives leads to disorder, disintegration, uncertainty, a loss of control over life, and the erosion of one's stability, security, and confidence. People cannot live without structure for long periods of time without suffering negative consequences mentally, emotionally, or physically. As Alvin Toffler explains in his book, *The Third Wave,*

> Individuals need life structure. A life lacking in comprehensible structure is an aimless wreck. The absence of structure breeds breakdown. Structure provides the relatively fixed points of reference we need. That is why (for example), for many people, a job is crucial psychologically over and above a paycheck. By making clear demands on their time and energy, it provides an element of structure around which the rest of their lives can be organized.[1]

When something new or different comes into our lives in the form of a change, it can disturb the way things are and thereby challenge the existing structure(s) of our lives. In many instances, we are then forced to alter structures in order to accommodate or adapt to a change. This process can result in a great deal of disruption, inconvenience, uncertainty, and emotional turmoil.

When we encounter new events, behaviors, things, or ideas, we interpret the meaning they have for us by determining where they fit into the existing structure of our lives. When a change fits easily into an existing structure, (e.g., getting a new car because the old one has become unreliable), it is not disruptive (because we already had a car and the new one improves the existing conditions associated with the use of the car). As a result, we can assimilate or adapt to such change fairly easily. When a change does not fit into the existing structure of our lives (e.g., losing a job), it becomes a disruptive force, threatening the structure of our lives (e.g., our daily routines, the lifestyle we are able to maintain), our sense of security (loss of paycheck or steady income), and our sense of control over life (How will I pay my bills? Will I have to sell my house?).

Major change can cause the structure of people's lives to collapse. When structure collapses, it produces feelings of disorientation, confusion, and anxiety. People no longer know how to interpret things or events in terms of the structure of their lives because the structure no longer exists or has been altered to a new and unfamiliar form. When structure collapses, life becomes unmanageable until structure is restored.

Change Disrupts the Purpose and Meaning of Our Lives

When a change occurs, people are affected by the actual (physical) event, which may involve a person, place, thing, or process. But the effects of a change are not limited to the occurrence of the actual event. It also includes having to deal with *the meaning* that the object of change (person, place, thing) or the event of change had in a person's life. This includes such things as the emotional attachment a person had to it, the purpose it served in a person's life as well as other psychological factors. For example, in the case of a pet dying, like most people, you would probably be sad to hear the news of the death of someone's pet dog. While you may be sympathetic to the owner of the dog for a time, your feelings would be felt only briefly and somewhat superficially. You would not likely think about the dog's death again in the future because it was not your dog that died and you had no personal attachment to it. However, when it is your dog that dies, your feelings about the death are far more profound because of *the meaning* the dog had in your life. For example, you raised the dog since he was a puppy and the dog provided years of companionship for you. You hunted with it and it protected you. It made you feel safe from intruders. The dog always greeted you warmly on your return home from work every day. You groomed the dog, fed it, and took it for daily walks. The dog was part of your daily routine and part of the structure of your life. You formed an emotional attachment to it over time. Thus your reaction to life without your dog is much more intense and serious because of the meaning it had in your life.

Our lives consist of a history of personal experiences. When change occurs, people have to be able to make sense of changes in terms of how the changes affect their lives. They do this by interpreting events of change in terms of the meaning and significance the change has made in their lives from the perspective of their personal history. Each area of our lives such as our job and relationships has a meaning we have attached to it based on our experience with it over time. When change happens in an area of our lives, the meaning we have attached to the object or event of change is also affected. Thus, change disrupts or disturbs the meaning of our lives in some way. The result is often mental and emotional upset as in the example of the pet dying.

In the event of change, people must adapt to something new and different and must assimilate something unfamiliar into the meaning and structure of their lives. When a change is consistent with a person's existing purpose and meaning in life, it is not disruptive because it leaves them intact. When a change disturbs or calls into question a source of meaning or purpose, it causes disorientation, confusion, and anxiety.

When a structure in our lives collapses, the meaning associated with the structure also collapses. We then have to struggle to regain a sense of meaning and to redefine the purpose of our lives. We need to revise, reframe, and reinterpret our perspective of things to be able to integrate or assimilate the object or event of change into the meaning and purpose of our lives in a new way. This is not an easy or pleasant task.

Change Is Disruptive

People structure their lives and environment to be as comfortable and accommodating to their needs as possible. In doing so, they form habits and establish certain routines and patterns of behavior. By following these routines and patterns of behavior over time, people get used to things being a certain way and to doing things in a particular manner.

When change comes along, it interrupts the smooth functioning and normal flow of events and behaviors, and it alters the familiar pattern, routine, and structure people are accustomed to in their lives. This causes some disorientation and inconvenience. Oftentimes, when people are faced with one change, it triggers several others, compounding the inconvenience and disruption in their lives even further. Whether a change is temporary or permanent, it means things will be different.

Change Means Uncertainty

A sense of predictability in life is a fundamental human need. We could not go about our daily lives if the physical environment were not predictable. There has to be order, a structure in place, and a system of rules so that things can go along smoothly. For example, imagine if there were no laws or rules to control traffic. The result would be chaos on the streets. Individuals would drive as they pleased, following their own rules. The consequence would mean difficulty in predicting what another driver would do, and thus people would have to be constantly vigilant to avoid mishaps.

When predictability breaks down, people become disoriented and don't know how to react because things aren't what they normally expect them to be. People need to know what they can expect in their lives on a day-to-day basis in order to feel comfortable and secure and to be able to plan their actions. They need to know that undertaking certain behaviors or actions generates certain results. If people were not able to predict the results of their actions, they would be under continuous stress and anxiety because they would never know what to expect or what would happen from one day to the next.

When change comes along, it becomes difficult for people to foretell the outcome of their actions because the usual flow of experiences in their lives is disturbed in some way by the change. The uncertainty is unsettling and makes people feel frustrated, anxious, angry, and uncomfortable. People plan for things to go a certain way in their lives, and when change occurs, those intended results may no longer be possible and therefore can no longer be anticipated. As a result, people feel angry, resentful, or disappointed.

Change Means Venturing into the Unknown

The desire for predictability and familiarity is natural among people because it gives them a sense of security in their lives. They know the situation they are in and are used to it. They know what actions their behaviors will generate because they have dealt with the situation successfully in the past. This knowledge makes them feel comfortable and confident.

When change occurs, it interrupts the flow of accustomed behavior and events in people's lives and introduces something new. This puts people in the position of having to deal with a situation or something they are not familiar with. They may have to act on or make decisions about things with no previous experience and without knowledge of the consequences of their actions. They experience new and unfamiliar territory and the result is that they feel frightened, anxious, and uncomfortable.

Many times, familiar situations may not be the best option for people or may not work well in their lives. However, the fact that the situations are familiar and predictable makes people comfortable and this becomes preferable to facing something new and unknown. Having to give up the known and predictable causes people to fear change. It is much easier to see what is in the present than to visualize what is coming in the future.

Change Breaks Continuity in Life

The need to preserve continuity in life is important as it provides people with a sense of where they came from and where they are going in life. It enables people to feel a sense of identity, purpose, meaning, security, and stability.

When familiar structures and patterns of behavior in people's lives are disrupted by change, the sense of continuity of life (or a part of life) is disturbed or broken. When continuity is disrupted, people have difficulty interpreting the meaning of events and things taking place in their lives because they are occurring outside the usual or expected order, context, and flow of things and events. The unfamiliarity causes feelings of disorientation, insecurity, and anxiousness.

Change Threatens Our Security and Stability

A sense of structure and predictability in life is needed for people to feel secure. When people are in familiar and comfortable surroundings, when they can depend on certain things, and when they can predict the outcome of their behaviors and actions, they feel a sense of control over their lives. Structure, routine, and a sense of control make people feel stable and secure.

When change happens, it breaks the structure, stability, and continuity in people's lives by throwing routines out of balance and creating conditions of uncertainty. Faced with the unknown and unpredictable, people can no longer foretell how things will be. People accustomed to a situation they like feel threatened by change because while knowing they like an existing situation, they don't know if they will like a new one. Uncertainty and fear of the unknown erodes feelings of security and makes people feel uneasy and uncomfortable.

Change Is Loss

Change often means leaving something familiar behind and dealing with something new or different. When people leave something behind that gives their lives structure and meaning, they experience it as a loss. The loss can be anything of significance either material or nonmaterial in nature. Examples are a home, job, health, part of one's body, a way of life, a relationship, an identity, freedom, and self-esteem.

When something gives meaning to people's lives, they usually form a psychological attachment to it and over time an emotional bond is built. When a loss occurs, that emotional bond is suddenly severed. The loss of something meaningful in a person's life creates a void or feeling of emptiness in its place. When an emotional bond is broken, people have to begin to detach themselves from it and deal with the void it has left. The process of detaching oneself emotionally from a situation, object, or person involves a form of mourning or grieving for the loss. During this process of mourning, people have to adjust to the idea that something they once valued is no longer there and is therefore no longer part of their lives or routine. It is an emotionally painful process.

Loss also disturbs the continuity, structure, stability, and routine of everyday life because something that was once part of life is no longer there. The future is in doubt since people do not know the direction their lives will take as a result of a loss.

Change Means Loss of Control

Having a sense of control over their lives makes people feel secure. When change occurs, the sense of predictability is gone. The future becomes uncertain and unknown and can cause people to temporarily (or sometimes permanently) lose control over their lives or some part of their lives. When people feel they have lost control, they feel powerless, helpless, anxious, frightened, and threatened because they do not know where the change will take them and how it will affect their lives. They may feel like a rudderless ship adrift at sea and can't anticipate what will happen next. A result of this loss of control is a great deal of stress, anxiety, and insecurity.

Change Means Making Mistakes

Change brings new, unfamiliar, and uncertain circumstances into people's lives. When people face novel situations, they are unsure of how to react or what course of action to take because they lack experience with this new element. With many types of change, the only way to learn how to deal with them is by trial and error, which puts people at risk of failure and mistakes. It is natural for people to dislike failure and want to avoid making mistakes since failure erodes self-esteem and lowers self confidence.

Change Threatens Our Goals and Expectations of Life

Over time, as we live, grow, and mature, we develop certain goals, assumptions, and expectations of life. For example, as we complete our formal schooling, we expect to find a job in the area of work we have chosen and trained for, and we assume that we will be able to earn a living. As time goes by, we usually also expect to find a suitable spouse, marry, and have children. We might expect to retire from work at age fifty-five and to travel in middle age. We might assume we will have our health throughout life and that our children will outlive us. We might expect to own our own company by the time we reach the age of forty or have a book published by the age of thirty. People develop individual expectations of life over time and usually work toward these goals and expectations.

When a significant change comes along, it can threaten our plans or disrupt our ability to meet them. Experiencing a major change, particularly one that is unanticipated, can put our expectations for the future in jeopardy or make them impossible to achieve.

When a person has invested a long period of time working toward a goal, identifying with a role, forming emotional attachments to people, things, or causes that are suddenly gone or taken away because of a change, it can be very difficult to accept and adjust to the loss. People find themselves in a position of having to deal and cope with a future they had not anticipated or envisioned for themselves. Their entire view of life and whole perspective of the future may have to change. The future is then in doubt since people do not know what direction their lives will take because of the loss of their expectations. This can generate a great deal of fear, apprehension, disorientation, uncertainty, insecurity, anxiety, and emotional turmoil.

Change Generates Stress and Anxiety

In predictable, stable situations, people have a sense of security and therefore are confident in their ability to cope with things in their lives. When change intervenes in their lives in some way, that sense of security is shaken or lost.

In new, unfamiliar, and unpredictable situations, people usually feel uneasy and apprehensive. They begin to worry about how things will turn out as a result of change, and they wonder if they will be able to deal with it. They become concerned about how the change will affect their lives and those around them. They are afraid of making mistakes and worry about what other people will think of them if they fail. Having to deal with all of these uncertainties produces anxiety. Change also generates stress as people are faced with assimilating something new into the framework of their lives and routines, and changing former behaviors to accommodate or adapt to change. They must struggle with painful and powerful emotions, and they have to make decisions and take actions whose outcomes they cannot predict. They may lose control of their lives or some area of their lives and are unable to do anything about it. Stress and anxiety are natural outcomes of trying to cope with and adapt to the many facets of change.

Change Means Facing and Solving Problems

Many situations of change have problems or dilemmas associated with them, and many of them are unexpected. The problems are frequently difficult with no easy solution or obvious answers. Problems people encounter in situations of change are often those they have not had to contend with before, and they do not feel comfortable with them as a result.

In trying to solve problems, people put themselves at risk for failure and for making mistakes. Since it takes courage to face problems and time and effort to solve them, people are reluctant to put themselves in situations where they know there will be problems.

Change Requires Effort

When change occurs in people's lives, circumstances in those lives are inevitably altered. Daily routines and patterns of established behavior are disrupted. Something that was once part of their lives is gone or something new must be integrated and assimilated.

Whatever the circumstances, change means things will not be the same and that usually means having to do things that haven't been done before or having to do them differently. When change enters people's lives, people are forced to react and must do so whether it is convenient or not and whether they want to or not.

The process of adapting to change takes time. It takes time and effort to integrate change into one's pattern of behavior and existing routines and to learn to do things in a new way. It takes fortitude and patience to face a loss of control, to solve problems, and to face the uncertainty of the future. It takes courage and time to confront and accept losses emotionally and to deal with the myriad emotions that accompany change. It takes time, effort, and personal resolve to rebuild and restructure life after a loss has occurred. It takes courage to put oneself at risk for failure, and it takes perseverence to deal with the stress and anxiety generated by change. Change requires time and effort that people would rather spend on more pleasurable things.

Change Means Starting Over: Restructuring and Rebuilding

When significant change occurs in people's lives, it often means something familiar and predictable will be lost. Old ways of doing things and comfortable circumstances are left behind. Familiar life structures are dissolved and existing routines and patterns of behavior are broken. The meaning that all of these had in one's life is permanently altered. Once people accept a loss emotionally, they must begin the task of rebuilding and restructuring those lives without the object, person, or circumstance of loss. They must create a new life for themselves.

Starting over and rebuilding a life that has been altered by change is seldom easy. It takes courage, effort, and time to do all that has to be done and to find new meaning in life. It involves venturing into the unknown and dealing with the uncertainty of the future. It means solving problems, suffering the pain of loss, surrendering one's security, and giving up control. These are things people would seldom choose to do if given a choice.

Change Can Be Painful

In situations of change, there is a wide range of emotions that people have to contend with, most of them unpleasant: bewilderment, shock, anger, bitterness, resentment, "why me?," helplessness, despair, anxiety, isolation, hurt, confusion, hostility, disorientation, and betrayal. These feelings make people feel uncomfortable and insecure. The more significant the change, the greater the intensity of emotion.

Change often involves loss. This loss usually has an intense emotional impact on people. Any significant loss needs to be mourned or grieved, which is painful. Significant change can also shake people up psychologically. As they turn inward for answers to the many questions that arise during times of great change, they often discover that they were living their lives (or some part of it) under illusions. Or they may find that the beliefs they had about something in life are not valid or they discover that they have not been living in the manner that they should have. Accepting these insights and realizations can be distressing.

These are the most common reasons why people fear change. Of course, not all people fear change. Some people welcome it and thrive on the challenges it brings to their lives. It is their insurance against boredom. It lends an excitement to their lives they would not be able to generate on their own. These change-adaptive people find change stimulating and invigorating. They see it as nothing more than a challenge.

And finally, change should not be perceived as all bad even though it is usually considered as such before or while it is occurring. As we noted in our discussion of progress in Chapter 1, change can be positive in the long term. However, it seems that most people need to "get over it" first before they can identify or recognize the positive aspects or benefits change can bring. For example, the changes faced by Anne and Josephine earlier in this chapter produced positive effects. Having to get up much earlier in the morning because of her baby, Anne used the extra time she had in the morning to get more of her household work done (e.g., laundry). Because she used to do these tasks at night after work, she now had more time to relax and do other things in the evening. Josephine decided to keep her job at the church and signed up for classes in computing and word processing. She also received on-the-job training from the company that installed the computing system into the church office. Although it was stressful and difficult for about a year, once she became comfortable working with the computer, she wondered what she was afraid of all of those years. She realized how much more efficient it was to have the computer system and how her job was much easier. She also realized that now that she was skilled at using computers, a whole new world of job opportunities had opened up to her and she would have many more options and choices about her work in the future. She was happy, no longer living in fear of the day things might change on her job, and she was proud of her accomplishments.

chapter three

Sources and Kinds of Change

Throughout our discussion in the last two chapters, we made reference to technological, social, and personal change. Most of the changes people have to contend with in modern times are from one of these sources. In this chapter, we examine each of these sources of change in more detail and we discuss the impact they have on our lives. It should be noted that although each source of change is examined individually, in reality, change generated by one source is often associated with or leads to change in another. For example, a change of equipment on the job (technological change) leads to the need for retraining (personal change). Later in this chapter, we also define and classify various kinds of change.

Sources of Change

Technology

Of all the kinds of change we have had to contend with in recent times, the impact of technological change has perhaps been the most profound. If we examine the history of Western industrialized nations and their cultures over the past millennium, it is clear that technological innovation has had the greatest impact on the evolution of these societies over time. Today we are completely surrounded by products of modern technology. These developments have dramatically affected the quality of our lives and the way we live and work.

During the industrial revolution, the introduction of power-driven machines reduced the need for human strength and labor. Machines took over many of the tasks formerly done by people. The introduction of computers into the workplace in recent times has had a similar effect, reducing the number of people and person-hours needed to do many tasks and revolutionizing the way people work. Computer and microchip technologies have had a dramatic and significant impact on people's lives because they are used for many purposes in almost every sector of society and life. Advances in computer technology have made possible the widespread use of personal computers by ordinary people for a variety of purposes outside the workplace including entertainment (video games), word processing, financial management, and gaining access to information and information sources.

As a result of technology, our homes now contain many labor-saving devices and conveniences unknown to our grandparents in their day. Automatic dishwashers, microwave ovens, bread-making machines, clothes dryers, air conditioning, and electronically controlled heat are things we now take for granted. These developments changed our lives by saving thousands of hours of physical labor each year and by providing a more convenient and efficient way to maintain and run a household. They also allow people more time to do things other than housework. Certainly, women would have difficulty working outside the home today without these labor-saving conveniences.

Products of technology have also affected the way people are entertained. There has been a proliferation of electronic-based equipment and devices. The availability of cable television, videocassette recorders, compact disc players, and computer/video games allows people to be entertained in their homes at their convenience.

Technology has allowed us to explore space and other planets, to travel around the globe, and to put communication satellites into orbit. Health care and human longevity have improved as a result of advancements in technology (ultrasound machines, laser surgery). Technology has generated new ways to communicate and transmit information (facsimile machines, cellular phones, cable television, the Internet) and has brought us into the world of instantaneous communication. There is little need to further explain the marvels of modern technology and how technological developments and advances have improved the quality of our lives, particulary during the last fifty years. The results are self-evident.

But while products of technology have improved people's lives and made them easier over time, in other ways they have made lives more difficult and complex. New technology is continually emerging. Existing technology is constantly changing. Thus, people today have difficulty keeping up with all the advancements and new products as well as the changing procedures and processes often associated with them. Because there are so many new and changing products, there are more choices and options to choose from, all of which make life more complex.

Not long ago, people bought new technological goods thinking they were making an investment in something that would last ten or twenty years or more. But with rapid technological change, products now become obsolete so quickly that this kind of thinking can no longer apply. When consumers buy technologically based products or equipment for personal or commercial use today, they know they will have to replace or update them within a relatively short period of time because they have become outdated or obsolete (home entertainment systems, telephones). Adjusting to rapid and constant technological change in both personal and professional lives takes time and effort. Today, with time at a premium in people's busy lives, this rapid pace can cause people a great deal of frustration and stress. They scarcely become accustomed to something new when it is replaced by something still more advanced or entirely new. People find themselves continually adjusting and readjusting (with all of the accompanying stresses and strains) in a cycle that seemingly never ends.

Technology has radically transformed the workplace because almost everything in the modern workplace is dependent on it. For example, computers, office automation systems, and telecommunications have changed the office environment and the way people work within it. Robotics on the assembly line have transformed the way people work in factories. Because of increased use of technology in the workplace, many jobs are being displaced, changed, or eliminated. For example, automatic teller machines (ATMs) reduce the number of tellers required by banks. Voice mail (telephone answering) systems reduce the need for telephone receptionists and clerks. Robots are replacing humans on the assembly line. Some jobs are becoming obsolete as a result of new technology while many existing jobs are growing much more sophisticated and requiring additional skills. For example, librarians, once accustomed to working with paper and card files, now need to use computers to work with and assist library patrons.

As technology changes in the workplace, whether they like it or not people must keep up to date with the changes in order to hold onto their jobs. Other people need to retrain for new areas of work as their jobs are eliminated or become obsolete. Yet others experience changes in the nature of the workday as a result of technological innovation. For example, technology allows a growing number of people to work at home rather than commute to an office every day because work can be transmitted through the computer and networking systems. Although people in past times may have worked hard (especially physically), with less technology and fewer labor-saving devices, when the workday was over, it was done. Workers could go home and would not have to think about work again until the next workday. They could rest or do other things at home not related to their work. There were no messages on answering machines, e-mail, and faxes waiting for them to respond to when they got home. In an increasing number of jobs today, the workday is never over because technological devices such as beepers, fax machines, and car or cell phones keep people tied to work or the office twenty-four hours a day, leaving them with little downtime or time away from work.

Technology is also transforming the economy of our country, and as a result, our work and lives are affected. For over 150 years following the industrial revolution, the American economy was dominated by manufacturing and other industrial activity. Today, many traditionally poor and third world countries are industrializing. Because of their ability to produce manufactured goods at a lower price because of lower labor costs, they are quickly overtaking the global market for many manufactured goods traditionally produced in the United States. As a result, there has been a decline in industrial manufacturing in our economy because, in the case of many manufactured goods, the United States can no longer compete with the newly industrialized countries in the global marketplace.

As the manufacturing base that once defined the American economy erodes, it is being rapidly replaced by a high-technology, information-based, service economy. These are economic areas in which the United States and a number of other advanced countries have superiority and in which they can compete globally. This new, high-tech, information-based economy, however, demands a whole range of new and different skills from its workers. This causes difficulty for those workers who were educated and trained for the industrial-based, manufacturing economy of the past and who do not have the ability or skills to adapt easily to the changes required to work in the new economy.

High technology and computers have also catapulted us into the information age. Many changes are taking place in society and the workplace because of the unprecedented information explosion we are now experiencing, made possible largely by these computers and this high technology. Information and knowledge in our society is now growing exponentially rather than linearly. In fact, in some fields, knowledge is doubling as quickly as every two or three years. Keeping up with the knowledge base in any field is difficult, if not impossible, because knowledge and information are now increasing faster than our ability to absorb and assess them. Specialization in many fields is now necessary since it is no longer possible to keep up with the massive amounts of information in a general field of study.

Information and knowledge in many fields are rapidly changing. As new knowledge emerges, it expands existing knowledge or renders it obsolete. Knowledge in many areas is becoming relative. It is only accurate and relevant until a discovery is made or a change takes place that alters it, modifies it, or renders it obsolete. Therefore, what is true today may not be true tomorrow.

When new information is discovered or new data becomes available, it affects people's lives and their work. It means products, procedures, or the environment will be different. It means people's thinking and behavior will change. For example, the discovery and public notification by scientists and medical researchers that diets high in fat are linked to heart disease, cancers, and other adverse medical conditions have changed the way people eat, think about, and prepare food. The implications generated by that one announcement are far-reaching and require change not only in people's lives but in many sectors of society and the economy. Just a few examples include the following. The food processing industry has had to make adjustments by developing a line of food products without fat or with lower amounts of fat than those they produced in the past. Pork and cattle producers have set out to breed and raise animals that are leaner than those of the past. The poultry industry has expanded because people are eating more chicken and turkey because of its lower fat content. The national food pyramid has been changed to recommend lower levels of fat consumption, and dieticians and doctors are now advising patients to reduce fat in their diets as a matter of routine.

As a result of rapidly changing technology in the workplace and the information explosion, education has become increasingly important in this new age. Every new innovation or procedure in the workplace requires that workers update existing skills and knowledge, learn new skills and information, or retrain for new jobs. There is a need to learn and upgrade skills on a continual basis as technology, information, and jobs constantly change. Although many companies and institutions of work now provide programs of training or upgrading for their employees, increasingly people have to take responsibility to keep themselves updated in their fields of work to remain competent and retain their jobs. No longer is education considered complete at the end of high school, college, or university, and education and training are no longer confined to the years spent in school. Education is now a necessary permanent ongoing process in people's lives.

Students educated in schools today need more education than people of previous generations. They need to be taught skills that will enable them to learn, adapt, and reeducate themselves throughout their lives so that they can change and adapt as needed in the future workplace as opposed to learning a specific set of skills that could quickly become inadequate or become obsolete. They need to learn skills that will allow them to become flexible, lifelong learners.

There is no longer a guarantee that the work one does after graduation is the work a person will be doing ten years later or for the rest of his or her life. People eighteen years of age today will likely change jobs or careers about seven or eight times in the course of their lives. Lifelong jobs and lifelong job security are a thing of the past. Full-time permanent jobs are becoming less and less available. As a result of the massive restructuring of the North American economy because of technological change and globalization, there is a trend toward a more dispensable workforce or the temporary employment of workers through part-time work and contract positions. In the process of downsizing, companies today are looking for ways to cut costs and increase productivity. One way they achieve this is by hiring a core group of full-time employees and hiring others on an at-need, part-time, or contractual basis so that they can remain flexible and therefore more competitive. The ability to adapt to change is needed for the growing pool of mobile workers who will work in this manner and in this environment.

In the past, middle-aged and older workers were valued for their knowledge and experience. Increasingly, however, older people are being considered more as liabilities by existing and potential employers. This is because they are perceived to be more set in their ways and thinking and are hence less adaptive to change and more difficult to educate and retrain in the workplace.

When the industrial revolution began almost 200 years ago, it created a whole new way of life and work for people who lived at that time. People felt overwhelmed by the changes it brought and their lives were dramatically affected because almost every aspect of their lives was touched by it in some way. Throughout much of the first fifty years, there was much upheaval and instability in society before things settled down and a more stable pattern of life and work was created. The high-technology, computer, and information revolution we are currently experiencing is affecting us in much the same way and is causing instability and upheaval in our society. It will take time for people to adjust. The amount of time it will take is uncertain because we do not and cannot know where technology will take us in the future. Someday we may reach a point where we have gone as far as we can go with technology, and things may stabilize. But that will only be until the next revolution comes along and thrusts us into yet another new era requiring change.

Society

The social changes we have experienced in the latter half of this century have resulted in tremendous changes in our lifestyle, values, attitudes, and culture. When change occurs in society, it forces changes within us as we adjust and adapt to those changes and integrate them into our lives. Even when people reject or disagree with changes occurring in society, they cannot entirely escape the effects of such change on their lives. Social changes accepted and tolerated by a large number of people in society permeate the culture and thereby shape the culture, norms, values, attitudes, and laws of that society. As a result, people cannot avoid the pervasive effects of widespread societal change on their individual lives.

The change in family structure is perhaps one of the most significant social changes we have experienced over the past few decades. Many things about the traditional nuclear family (working father, stay-at-home mother and children) have changed largely because so much about the institution of marriage has changed. Approximately half of all marriages in the United States today end in divorce. Divorced single parents often raise their children alone. When divorced parents remarry, new families that frequently include children from previous marriages of both spouses are created. Marriage is also no longer considered a necessary requirement for creating a family. Many unwed couples (some with children) choose to cohabit without the sanction of marriage. Some women choose to bear children on their own and raise them out of wedlock. In recent years, some gay and lesbian couples choose to live together and raise children as a family unit. Multiple marriages (serial monogamous marriages) are also more common because people live longer and many middle-aged and older people choose to remarry after the

death of a spouse. There are numerous options, choices, and alternatives to traditional family life in society today.

As a result of these changes in marriage and family structure,
society now accommodates the needs and differences among them.
For example, divorce is much easier to obtain today, and it no longer
has the stigma attached to it it once had. Children born out of wedlock are no longer looked down upon as was the case in past times.
School textbooks and curricula have been developed to include and
teach children about all kinds of families, portraying them as equal
but different.

The women's movement/feminist movement, which had its
roots earlier this century, took off in the sixties and seventies. It too
has dramatically affected society in recent times. Through this movement, women demanded rights and opportunities equal to those of
men in society, particularly those relating to work and career. For
example, they demanded the right to work outside the home, the
right to work at the job or profession of their choice, the right to be
hired on the basis of qualification and not gender, equal pay for work
of equal value, and the right to join or participate in many traditionally male clubs, institutions, and activites. This is in sharp contrast
to the past when women with children were expected to stay at home
and raise their children while their husbands went to work. In 1940,
only 10 percent of all women in the United States worked outside the
home. Today, women represent almost half of the total workforce.

Because of the women's movement, many things in our society
have changed. Girls growing up today have far more opportunities
than their mothers had and infinitely more than their grandmothers.
University campuses and fields of work traditionally dominated by
males (e.g., medicine, engineering, the military) are open to women
as are leadership roles in society and the workplace (e.g., politicians,
business executives). Public institutions can no longer deny services
or rights to women simply on the basis of gender. Employers are now
accommodating the needs of working women by providing benefits
that meet their needs such as pregnancy leave, family leave days to
care for sick children, and flexible working hours. Day care centers
have sprung up in record numbers to care for children while their
parents are at work.

Because of increased educational and career opportunities, many women are postponing marriage until their thirties, are having fewer children, and having them later in life. Men have also been affected by the women's movement as they have to adjust to their new roles and the new roles of women in society. There are also indirect changes that have occurred such as the increasing amount of convenience and prepackaged foods to meet the needs of working parents as well as the removal of male gender-specific language in books.

The sexual revolution has also transformed society. The introduction of the birth control pill led to many dramatic changes in our society within a relatively short period of time. It brought about more reproductive and sexual freedom for both men and women by alleviating fear of unwanted pregnancy and improving the sex lives of millions of couples. This led to the trend toward freer sex, sex without fear of pregnancy, the development of sexual relationships among single people outside of marriage, and to much more openness about sexuality in our culture in general. Sex is no longer a subject that is hidden or discussed in hushed tones in our society. Movies, television programs, and advertisements routinely portray sexuality in various forms, and people today openly discuss aspects of sexuality (such as condoms and masturbation) that were once considered taboo.

There have, of course, been negative changes associated with the sexual revolution. Pregnancies among unwed teenaged mothers are at an all-time high and venereal disease has become widespread. AIDS is also spreading through the population through sexual activity.

The effects of the sexual revolution on society and individual lives have been significant. For example, the effectiveness of the birth control pill is a contributing factor to more sexual freedom and in the trend toward smaller families. Because the birth control pill gave women more control over their bodies, it has enabled them to postpone having families and allowed them to have careers. Displays of sexuality in the media that were once forbidden or restricted to older viewers are now common in everyday television programming as well as in advertising and elsewhere in the media (videos). Sex education is now introduced in the elementary school curriculum to very young children whereas a few decades ago it wasn't part of the curriculum at all. Many teenage girls are having babies and keeping them even though they have not finished high school. They must then rely on social programs and public assistance that taxpayers support through their contributions. Massive public education programs have been initiated to curtail the spread of AIDS. The sexual revolution has also changed our culture by influencing our music, art, movies, the way we dress, and our relationships with others.

The environmental movement has had a significant impact on society in recent times. There is a growing awareness of the detrimental effects of pollution on our planet and the need to preserve natural habitats and endangered species for future generations. People are becoming increasingly concerned about environmental destruction (such as disappearing rainforests, depletion of the ozone layer), the safety of their food and water supply (from pesticide use, PCBs, lead), and the hazardous effects of radiation and pollution on their lives. Landfills containing millions of tons of garbage are near capacity levels in many large cities, and toxic waste haphazardly dumped in the past is causing alarm.

The environmental movement is causing changes in government and public policy. For example, because of public pressure, the government has imposed pollution-control standards on industries and on the manufacturing specifications for auto exhaust. Refrigerants in air conditioners and refrigerators are being phased out because of the damage done to the atmosphere by CFCs (chlorofluorocarbons). Toxic waste is being disposed of in a much safer manner than was the case in the past. Land is being set aside for national parks or wildlife preserves. The environmental movement has also caused people to change their behaviors regarding the way they treat the environment. Ordinary people are becoming involved in recycling their garbage (glass, tin, newspapers, plastic) to reduce the amount of waste sent to landfills, and they are using more environmentally friendly consumer products. Manufacturers are producing more environmentally safe products (cleaning solutions) and paper is being recycled to reduce the need to cut down more trees. Many environmental groups (Greenpeace for one) are becoming powerful in affecting public opinion and government policy about the environment.

The rise in crime and violence has also changed the way we live by causing our lives to become more restricted. People no longer leave doors and windows unlocked and do not walk around outside after dark. Security systems are becoming more prevalent in homes and automobiles around the nation. Security is also more common in places such as schools, hospitals, and the workplace. Retailers have had to use an increasing number of security measures over the years to stop shoplifting and employee theft.

The social changes we have discussed thus far represent only some of the more major ones we have witnessed and experienced during the past few decades. There are many more changes not discussed here. The point is that these and other changes in society have had a significant impact on the way people live both individually and collectively. As society continues to be a source of change and as it continues to evolve in the future, people will need to adjust and adapt to those changes as their lives become affected over time.

Personal Lives

People's individual lives are a third major source of change. Personal changes are those events such as marriage or promotion that affect an individual at a given time in his or her life and that are independent of those occurring in other people's lives. Whereas people in general experience many of the same personal changes over the course of their lives, these events affect individuals at different times, in different ways, and to different degrees. Today, people's personal lives are increasingly influenced by technological or societal change. As change occurs in these areas, it forces changes within individuals themselves by affecting their jobs, health, relationships, family life, standard of living, and so on.

Everyone faces changes of various kinds in day-to-day life. They may be brought about by choice, by imposition, by forces beyond one's control, or by the natural aging process. We now examine some of the most significant changes people face in their personal lives and review the impact of those changes on their lives. The changes we examine are considered major or significant because of the tremendous or far-reaching impact they have on people's lives. Each of them, though representing a single event, ultimately involves a multitude of changes precipitated by that event. Thus, these change events usually have a comprehensive impact on people that affect them physically, emotionally, psychologically, and socially.

Marriage

Despite the fact that getting married is a happy and joyous occasion, it requires many changes and adjustments on the part of the bride and groom. Although these changes and adjustments may ordinarily be seen as difficult to make, they are usually easier to deal with by newlyweds because of the joy and happiness they feel as they fall in love, are engaged, and become newly married.

Psychologically, when a person (a woman in this case) gets married, her identity changes. Her perception of herself undergoes a tremendous reorientation from that of a single person to a married one. She must leave a life of being single, autonomous, independent, and responsible for herself to enter one where she becomes a member of a partnership or team, with responsibility toward the partnership. She must also separate emotionally from her family and the security associated with it and establish a new family of her own in the marriage relationship. When she marries, she also becomes part of a new family—that of her spouse and in-laws.

For couples newly married or about to be married, many decisions need to be made as to how to set up a household of their own. As an engaged or married couple, they must decide such things as where they will live (close to his job or close to hers) or whether they will rent an apartment, buy a home, or rent and save to buy a home. They need to decide what to buy to set up the new household (furniture, appliances). They need to decide what to do with the property that each of them brings to the marriage (sell the truck, keep the boat). They need to decide who will be responsible for various chores in the home (laundry, cooking, cleaning). They need to work out and establish daily routines (mealtimes, shower times, bedtime). They need to consider how finances will be managed (how bank accounts will be set up and who will pay the bills) and so on.

Although the decision of whether or not to have children is usually decided before marriage, it too is an important consideration early in the marriage. If a couple wants to have children, they need to decide how many they would like and when to have them (immediately, in a few years). Issues of sex, birth control, and intimacy must be dealt with. The degree of independence each person will have in the relationship needs to be established, and each spouse will have to get used to the friends and colleagues of the partner.

In each of the preceding areas where decisions have to be made, spouses often come into the partnership with different backgrounds and views. Spouses will also have differences in their daily habits that require each of them to adjust. (She wants the heat in the house set higher than he does. He likes to watch the news on television while eating dinner and she wants the television off during mealtimes.) Lifestyle views, political views, religious views, values, and life goals are all areas where discussion and compromise have to be addressed and made. In second marriages, involving ex-spouses, and ex-in-laws, arrangements concerning children and stepchildren may have to be worked out as well (custody, visitation rights).

Moving/Relocating

Moving from one house or apartment to another or one geographic area to another can be disorienting and requires many changes and decisions to be made. Moving uproots people and disrupts the predictable elements and routines of everyday life, causing some emotional strain. It takes them away from a familiar (and perhaps stable) environment and brings them into a new and unfamiliar one. People's sense of security is often disturbed by the newness of their surroundings.

The process of moving involves many tasks that in themselves can prove stressful. Examples of such tasks are selling an existing house, building or finding and buying a new one, packing up all one's belongings, getting rid of excess belongings, arranging for appropriate transportation of the belongings to a new location (and hoping nothing is damaged in the meantime), unpacking and organizing belongings at a new location, and possibly redecorating, painting, or making repairs to the new dwelling.

Once the physical move has been completed, there are other tasks to be done. People need to find out where the shopping areas are. They may need to enroll children in a new school or locate a new church. They need to find a new doctor, dentist, hair stylist, and dry cleaners. All of this can be time consuming. And because much of it is done on a trial-and-error basis with little knowledge of the area, it can also be frustrating. The stressful effects of a move can be compounded even further when a person is expected to begin working at a new job (which itself requires many changes and adjustments) at the same time the move takes place.

Moving means disassembling daily life in one location and reassembling it all over again somewhere else. Moves within the same geographic area (city, metropolitan area, county) are usually least disruptive because many of the existing contacts such as doctors and friendships people have can be retained. Moving greater distances is more difficult because the farther away one moves, the less familiar the environment is likely to be. Moving out of the country is probably most difficult of all. This is because in addition to everything else that results from a move, people must also get used to a different culture, perhaps a new language or climatic conditions, new currency, new laws, new social institutions, and new ways of conducting their affairs and everyday lives.

Moving also destroys networks of established friendships. It means saying good-bye to old friends and colleagues and eventually establishing new ones. People moving away from family and relatives can find it emotionally difficult to be far away from them. Moving breaks the sense of continuity in one's life.

Birth

The birth of a child is a joyous occasion, but like other major changes, it too requires a great deal of adjustment, particularly if the birth is the first one in the family. First, there is the physical and emotional stress of pregnancy and the birth. Then the mother and father must adjust to a new identity, that of being a "mother" or a "father." They must psychologically adjust to and acknowledge that they will be totally responsible for another human being for many years to come. They need to recognize that the responsibility of having an infant or young child will cause significant changes in the structure of their lives (no more weekend ski trips, fewer dinners out). The daily routine of feeding and caring for a child will likely rearrange their daily patterns of behavior. Parents will have to get used to new and unfamiliar behaviors (crying, changing diapers, waking up earlier on weekend mornings). And they will have to adapt to the behaviors of a new person who will have a personality of his or her own. The relationship between spouses will likely be altered and if both parents work, child care will need to be arranged.

Job Loss

Losing a job for whatever reason is a stressful event because it affects so many areas of a person's life. It is a situation particularly difficult for a person to accept and adjust to if the job was lost through no fault of the person involved (e.g., part of companywide layoff). Psychologically, part of a person's identity and self-esteem is tied to the work he or she does or the title he or she has in their job. The loss of a job can mean a shaken identity, and it can take a toll on a person's pride and sense of self-worth. When a person loses a job held for a long time (twenty or thirty years), losing the job can seem like losing a whole part of one's life. In the case of people with families to support, there can be feelings of inadequacy and a feeling that the family has been let down as a result of the job loss. Feelings of failure and despair are common among people losing a job.

Leaving a job means leaving a familiar and predictable setting and daily routine as well as friendships with colleagues and coworkers that have been cultivated over time. Leaving a job means entering a period of uncertainty and giving up control over one's life for a while. People suffer stress simply because they do not know if they will get another job, when they will find one, whether it will be similar to the one they had, whether it will have the same rate of pay, whether it will be in the same city or town, and so on. Psychologically, people also worry about what others will think of them if they don't find a job or if they take a job that is in any way inferior to the one they lost.

With the loss of a regular paycheck and financial support gone, people must decide how to provide for themselves or their families until they find another job. They may have to decide, for example, if they will use accumulated savings, live on the pay of one spouse instead of two, or resort to social assistance. For the first time, they may have to join others in an unemployment line to find a new job. In times of job loss, rarely can people maintain their normal standard of living, and adjustments in spending patterns and habits have to be made as a result. Sometimes, a house may have to be sold or the family moved to another location. If one spouse is still working, there may be more stress and pressure on that person to carry the load. Losing a job also means losing benefits such as health insurance and dental coverage associated with it.

There is also a question of what people can do with the spare time they may have until they find another job. Those not used to staying home or having little to do all day can find it difficult to make the adjustment. One person's job loss often means change and adjustments for every member of the family. It is not uncommon for people who have lost a job to feel as if their whole world is coming apart, particularly if they were the sole breadwinner.

When a person does find a new job, there is the challenge to perform in a new and unfamiliar setting, new coworkers to meet, a new boss, and new expectations. These can initially cause anxiousness and insecurity.

Onset of Major Injury or Illness

The onset of an injury or illness can be stressful to individuals, particularly those with dependents. A person must psychologically come to terms with the impact of an injury or illness in terms of the physical limitations it causes (being housebound, having a leg amputated), a possible reduction in the quality of life, and the physical pain that accompanies it. Major illness precipitates anxiety because people worry about whether they will recover (if ever), when they will recover, and how their lifestyle will be affected in the meantime. In some cases, people have to accept and face the possibility or certainty of death. It is the waiting, the uncertainty, and the loss of control over one's life that is difficult to adjust to.

Good health can be a person's greatest asset because it allows one to work and earn a living. Illness and injury often mean not being able to work, and that means self-generated financial support is limited or gone. This leads to concern about where financial support will come from for the duration of the illness or for the long term. In some cases, the spouse of an injured or ill person may become the sole supporter of a family whereas, in other cases, a spouse who does not work outside the home may have to return to the workplace. The structure of one's life can be altered significantly or may collapse completely. Lifestyles and standards of living may need to change because of reduced finances or the physical limitations brought about by the illness. Psychologically, people may also have to adjust to being physically, emotionally, and financially dependent on others, or they may need to adjust to the isolation that is often created in their lives as a result of the onset of major illness. They may have to contend with feelings of guilt and a loss of pride in that they feel they have become a burden to others or that others in the family are forced to do with less as a result of their illness. If there is recovery, people need to face any new limitations in life caused by the illness or injury. An example is having to go into another line of work as a result of an injury.

Divorce

Whether amicable or not, divorce involves many painful feelings and experiences. Feelings of anger, hurt, abandonment, bitterness, betrayal, and hostility toward the spouse are common. Self-esteem and self-worth are frequently affected in cases of divorce. In letting go of a once viable relationship, there are also feelings of loss. People can feel that all the years spent with a spouse are a loss because of the failure of the relationship to thrive. The sense of continuity in one's life is broken. If one person in the relationship is not in favor of a divorce (leaving for another man or woman, disclosure of homosexuality), the emotional impact on the other can be especially difficult. The person who is left often feels unlovable and unworthy and can easily succumb to depression. Being alone again and in a situation of having to start all over can be overwhelming. Divorce that occurs after a long period of marriage can be especially difficult. For example, when a husband leaves his wife of thirty years, the wife may feel as if thirty years of her life are gone in one sweep.

The process of divorcing touches almost every area of people's lives. All possessions must be divided (house, cars, cottage, pension plan). If there are children, custody must be decided and visitation rights arranged. Relationships with the child's biological relatives (grandparents) for the noncustodial spouse can be strained.

The loss of a spouse through divorce means the loss of a companion, a confidant, a caregiver, and a lover. Getting divorced means having to get used to a new identity. A person must adapt to the idea of being unpartnered after years of being coupled. Friendships with people who were friends of both spouses can become awkward. Friends of divorced couples may not want to show a preference for or take the side of either spouse, and it becomes difficult when arrangements are made for social gatherings. This makes some divorcées feel isolated or like social outcasts. When the process of divorce is settled, each spouse must essentially start over again to build and restructure life on his or her own (look for place to live, open new bank accounts, look for job, begin dating again).

The spouse who has custody of the children (usually the mother) assumes a greater parenting role and more responsibility as a result of a divorce. This can be stressful. In the case of men (or women) who don't have custody of children, they may have to make child support payments and therefore end up supporting two households (their own and the children of their former spouse). If the custodial spouse had not been working outside the home, she may have to get a job to support herself, which may be difficult if she has been out of the workforce for years. The economic necessity of returning to work means less time to spend with children. In other cases, where a couple had a lifestyle dependent on two incomes, there may be a reduction in the standard of living and fewer luxuries because one source of income is eliminated.

While divorced parents have to deal with their own feelings and emotions about a divorce and life afterward, they must also contend with their children who similarly have to make emotional adjustments. Children may begin to behave differently (often in a negative fashion) and may have feelings of guilt and loss as a result of the divorce. In addition, reentering the dating scene after years of being married can be frightening, confusing, and unsettling to many people and can seem awkward for those who have their children living with them.

Death of a Loved One

Death is perhaps the greatest of all changes to have to accept and contend with, particularly if the death was premature, sudden, or unexpected. When we lose someone close to us through death, we lose part of ourselves. The closer the relationship was to the deceased, the greater the pain. People with deep emotional attachments and long (particularly lifelong) relationships to a person have to come to terms with the fact that the person is no longer there and never will be again. In the case of a spouse, parent, or child, the death is particularly painful because so much of the person's life was experienced with someone who is no longer there to share the memories, joys, and sorrows of the past. Through the ending of a relationship by death, there is a disruption in the meaning of one's life and a disruption in the sense of continuity in one's life. People are overwhelmed with a sense of loss and emptiness at the time of a death, and for a time afterward, life can seem meaningless without the deceased. As a person faces and accepts the death of a loved one and attempts to carry on with life, there are tremendous adjustments to be made, psychological and otherwise. In the case of the death of a spouse, so many things in the survivor's environment (the deceased's favorite chair, a photograph of the deceased on the wall, clothing, car, and so on) are reminders of the person who is gone. Activities that spouses used to do together (eating dinner, watching television, gardening, and vacationing) the remaining spouse must now do alone. The surviving person must get used to a new identity, that of a single person or widow(er), after years of being part of a couple. Eventually, a social life that does not include the spouse must be rebuilt.

There is much paperwork to be done upon the death of a spouse. The process involves rendering the deceased person a nonentity. It is a painful process as is parting with the person's possessions (clothing, trophies, sporting gear, car).

The death of a spouse usually forces the survivor to make several major life changes within a short period of time, all while a person is psychologically and emotionally overwhelmed by a sense of loss and emptiness. Some examples of decisions that must be made include: Should the house be sold? Will I be able to afford to live in it?

If not, where will I live? Will I need to move out of the area? Can existing finances provide for me for the rest of my life? Should I go back to work or should I get a job? And finally, there is the task of rebuilding a life structure without the loved one and finding new meaning in life once again.

Experiencing a Disaster

Experiencing the effects of a disaster (fire, hurricane, earthquake, flood) can be devastating. Usually it involves the loss or destruction of a home and everything in it, which often means the loss of everything a person owns. In cases where there may be no insurance coverage or only partial coverage, it can mean financial hardship for years to come or financial ruin. People can feel totally overwhelmed by the occurrence of a disaster because everything they had and everything they had worked for throughout their life is gone. When a disaster occurs, people do not have time to prepare for or adjust to the impact of the devastation, which many times they witness themselves. Thus, they have to come to terms with the losses they experience after the fact. Psychologically, it is a difficult adjustment to make. People have many questions and there are few answers. "Why me?" and "What did I do to deserve this?" are typical sentiments during these times. There can also be feelings of guilt associated with experiencing a disaster (e.g., If only I had changed the batteries in the smoke detector).

At the time a disaster is occurring, there is disbelief. A person cannot believe what is happening. Immediately afterward, there is tremendous disorientation and confusion. People don't know where to begin. They need to make arrangements for accommodations immediately. Then they need to make arrangements to rebuild for the long term. The tedious and stressful process of rebuilding and replacing things then must begin. Losing possessions that have sentimental value (wedding pictures, baby's first pair of shoes) is difficult to come to terms with because they can never be replaced. Experiencing disaster means coming to terms with many losses and living with a great deal of disruption, inconvenience, instability, stress, and disorientation until things are settled and rebuilt.

Retirement

Retirement requires a substantial number of psychological and emotional adjustments. It is a time of redefining life and one's identity. When a person retires, he leaves the daily routine and stability of a job as well as many friends and colleagues he will no longer see on a regular basis. There is a loss of everyday rituals and patterns of behavior. A large part of a person's identity is related to his profession or job title. A great deal of gratification and self-esteem comes from the work one does. When one no longer goes to work, these can be shaken or lost. Adjusting to life without work can be difficult because of the many ramifications it has for a person's life. It is particulary difficult for workaholics whose whole lives have been focused on their work.

A person about to retire must decide what he is going to do with his life once he has retired. Will he work on a hobby, will he travel, will he get a part-time job "to keep busy"? Will he do volunteer work? He must decide how he is going to live on a fixed income and how finances will be handled so that money does not run out prematurely. He has to decide whether keeping a home is possible. He has to make provisions for situations of ill health, should they arise. He has to get used to having time on his hands and decide what he is going to do with his spare time. He has to get used to a new daily routine and a new environment. Being at home all day not only requires adjustment on the part of the retiree but also on the part of the spouse or companion who may not be used to having another person around during that time.

Retirement also brings a person face to face with difficult emotions. There is often a feeling of emptiness or guilt because one is no longer contributing to society. A person may miss the sense of being needed that work provides. A person must also face the fact that the end of life is coming and the question "What is there left that I want to do?" inevitably arises.

While this listing of significant changes people face in their personal lives represents only some of the major ones, the examples illustrate the complexity of these changes and the degree of adjustment that must be made in people's lives when they are faced with significant personal change. There are, of course, many other personal changes that people face that have not been discussed here. While they may not be as significant as those listed, other examples include a son or daughter leaving home (empty nest syndrome), beginning a new job, having a miscarriage, graduating from school and getting one's first job, receiving a promotion, and caring for a ill person or aging parent. Other examples of personal changes can be found in Figure 3.1.

Getting a divorce
Becoming disabled
Having a baby
Changing careers
Becoming chronically ill
Losing a skill/ability (e.g.,
  sight)
Retirement
Losing/gaining custody of
  children
Looking after an aging parent
Buying first home
Engaged to be married
Graduating from school
Experiencing a house fire
Major financial loss/gain
Being raped
New significant relationship
Having a miscarriage
Loss of religious faith
Becoming a grandparent
Your parent divorces/remarries
Moving residence (new house,
  new neighborhood)
Son or daughter leaving home
  or getting married
Family member becoming
  seriously ill
Returning to the workforce
  after being away for years
Becoming pregnant in middle
  age
Spouse diagnosed with
  serious/major illness

Getting married
Loss of fertility
Losing a job
Starting a new job
Being seriously injured
Death of a spouse/child/
  parent
Death of a relative/friend
Receiving a promotion
Going to fight in a war
Having major surgery
First pregnancy
Starting a new business
Finding the first job
Being in a serious car accident
Being robbed/mugged
Laid off from work
Being shot at/wounded
Having an abortion
Changing faith or religion
Adopting a child
Having cosmetic surgery
Major changes on the job
  (relocation, retraining)
Major change in living
  conditions of the family
Having a spouse or child
  diagnosed with mental illness
Being diagnosed with
  serious/major illness (e.g.,
  cancer)
Losing part of one's body to
  disease or injury (e.g.,
  mastectomy)

Figure 3.1.   Examples of significant personal changes.

Kinds of Change

*H*aving identified sources of change in people's lives, we now identify and define various kinds of changes.

Permanent/Structural Change

Permanent or structural change is change that cannot be reversed.
This kind of change is comparable to the milestones in human history
discussed earlier. It is change that, once made, forever changes the
future. For example, once movable type and the printing press were
discovered, print media flourished, and there was no going back to a
nonprint world from that point in time. Another example is women
gaining equal rights in society. Once this occurred, women's lives were
collectively changed forever. The birth of a child is also considered a
permanent or structural change because it permanently changes one's
life and identity. When a person becomes a mother or father, the fact
that he or she is a parent can never change. Having a child also means
that a person will have to raise and care for that child for many years
to come. With permanent/structural changes, people need to make a
permanent adjustment to some kind of change for the long term.

Temporary/Cyclical Change

Temporary or cyclical change is short-term change. It has a beginning and an ending and is in effect for a finite amount of time. A high
unemployment rate or high interest rates are cyclical changes because
eventually they will come down. Losing a job is considered temporary
since within a period of time that has limits, a person can find another
one. With temporary change, people need only to be able to cope and
adjust to changing circumstances until things return to a normal state.

Voluntary Change

Voluntary change is change that one chooses to make. It is
change that a person can undertake at his or her own pace, which

gives a sense of control and direction. When a change is voluntary, it is usually much easier to make the necessary adjustment because the person is more prepared and committed to making the change. For example, a person may choose to take a course to learn how to use new computer software because she knows it will improve her prospects of getting a job or a promotion.

Involuntary Change

Involuntary change is change that is imposed upon a person without choice and is beyond a person's control. It is change that must be complied with or else negative consequences could result. Because a person is not expecting the change or not in favor of it, it is more difficult to make. For example, a company executive is transferred without his consent to an office across the country. If he does not take the transfer, he loses his job. Another example is a new tax introduced by the government that people are forced to pay, regardless of circumstances, or they otherwise face being fined or jailed.

Anticipated Change

An anticipated change is a change that a person knows is coming or can predict will occur. These changes are foreseeable or inevitable. Because people are aware that a change will take place, they can begin to make preparations to adjust to it psychologically ahead of time. Established life events such as retirement or graduation are examples of anticipated change. A person knows in advance they will occur and thus can prepare for them—for example, by buying a condominium in Florida (retirement) or looking for a job (graduation).

Unexpected Change

Unexpected change is change that cannot be anticipated in advance. Examples are a car accident, a robbery, a death. This change is difficult to deal with because there is no control over the situation and no time or opportunity to prepare or adjust psychologically beforehand. People must adjust to the changes and subsequent consequences after it has occurred or after the fact.

It is clear from our discussion in this chapter that there are many sources and kinds of change that people have to contend with in modern times. When change occurs, regardless of the source or kind, it forces changes within us as we adjust, adapt, and integrate it into our lives. The way in which this happens is the focus of the next chapter.

chapter four

The Process of Adapting to Change

Before we discuss how people adapt to change, we should first consider the meaning of the term "change." To change means to pass from one state or form to another, to make or become different, to be partially or wholly transformed. The words "pass," "become," and "transform" all imply a process. A process is a series of actions, a procedure, or a method and as such has a beginning, an end, and some steps in between.

Almost every kind of change we face involves making a transition from one state or set of circumstances to another. When people are affected by change, they undergo a series of actions, a method, or a procedure. This is done in order to pass from one state or form to another with the result of becoming different or partially or wholly transformed. Thus change and adapting to change is a process.

When we think of change, particularly personal change, we often think of it in terms of a specific event such as getting married or being injured. Of course, when such an event occurs, a change does take place. For example, a woman is not married on Friday and on Saturday she is. Or a man is healthy Monday morning and is injured that afternoon. When we consider these change events in terms of how they affect people, however, the change events are merely outward or external markers of change. In reality, people don't change or adapt to change at the precise moment that the change event occurs. For example, a person does not adjust to marriage on the day of the wedding when the vows are exchanged. Rather, she adjusts to the changes—in identity, lifestyle, responsibility, and so on—that marriage represents over a period of time that might begin with the engagement and end with her first wedding anniversary. A change (event), therefore, is an external trigger or signal that sets into motion a process of transformation that occurs within people as they cope with, adjust to, and adapt to that change event.

In this chapter, we discuss and examine the process people undergo in order to adapt to significant change in their lives, and we examine various conditions and factors that facilitate or hinder the change adaptation process.

Change Is a Process

Living with change means living with the process of coping and adaptation. Coping means to encounter, to contend with, or to deal with successfully. Adapting means to modify, to make more suitable, or to alter for new use. Adapting to change is a process. It is not a one-time event or occurrence. Because it is a process, it involves a series of identifiable stages and sequential steps that people experience in response to a change or change event. The process of adapting to change takes time. It is a transition that is gradually made and cannot be done overnight. The amount of time needed to adapt to a change is directly proportional to the significance of the change event being experienced. Any major change requires a lengthy period of adjustment.

How do people become different through change? How do they become partially or wholly transformed? How do they make the transition from one set of circumstances to another? The process of adapting to change is a process of changing oneself in some way and involves both external and internal forces. When a change occurs on an external level, it triggers and forces changes to occur internally. In order to adapt to an external event, people need to make changes within themselves—attitudinally, emotionally, intellectually, behaviorally, and psychologically—changes that will prepare them for and allow them to adapt successfully to the external event.

Adapting to change is a process of restructuring one's view of oneself, of life, and of the world. It is a process of understanding and accepting something new and unfamiliar in one's life and letting go of something old and familiar. To include something new or different requires adjustment and reorganization of one's life. It means learning new behaviors and ways of thinking and giving up old ones. Change needs to be integrated into one's existing routines and patterns of behavior. To be considered complete and successful, it must be integrated physically, behaviorally, attitudinally, emotionally, and intellectually into one's life in a comprehensive manner. Change transforms people's lives in some way and people's lives evolve by experiencing change.

The Process of Adapting to Significant Change

When a person is faced with a major change in his life, he is also faced with the process of adapting to that change. Whereas one can assimilate and adjust to minor changes in one's life more easily, adapting to a major or significant change requires more time, effort, and focus. Change involves making the transition from one state or set of circumstances to another. At the time a person is confronted with making a change or adapting to change, it usually means that something, an existing state or set of circumstances in his life, will come to an end and then be replaced by something new and different. We said that change is a process and as such, it has a beginning and an ending. The process of adapting to change is a seven-step process through which two major tasks are accomplished. The first task is understanding, facing, and accepting the breakdown or ending of some state or circumstances in one's life, and the second is the acceptance and integration of new circumstances into one's life. We now discuss the nature of the two tasks involved in adapting to change, and then we review the seven-step process through which these tasks are accomplished.

Task 1—Coming to Terms with Breakdown/Endings

The process of adapting to change begins with the task of facing, accepting, and dealing with the dissolution, end, loss, or breakdown of something old, familiar, or currently in existence. The ending can be anything of significance to a person including a way of life, a familiar condition or situation, a method of doing things, a relationship, or an identity. The ending can also represent the loss of something significant such as a job, loved one, material possessions, part of one's body, status, spirituality, and so on. (*Note:* While the loss, breakdown, ending, or the new conditions referred to here will be discussed in general rather than specific terms throughout this chapter, the reader can choose to interpret the type of ending, loss, or new condition in accordance with his or her own life and circumstances.)

Before a person can be expected to adapt to a new or unfamiliar situation, it is necessary for that person to focus on the specific situation that will change and to identify and recognize what will be lost or what will end as a result of the change. Once that has been done, the process of accepting the loss or ending must begin. This is done by beginning to separate and detach oneself from the old or familiar and by saying good-bye to that situation. During the breakdown phase of a significant change, people undergo a period of "mourning" the end or loss of something much as they would mourn the loss of a loved one through death. The process of adapting to a major or significant change, particularly one associated with loss, involves many of the same elements and responses that are part of the process of bereavement. A person cannot make the transition or adjust to something new until they have recognized and accepted physically, emotionally, and intellectually that the old and familiar way, situation, process, or whatever is gone, lost, ended, dissolved, or broken down cannot be retrieved in its existing state. The old familiar situation and the feelings and emotions associated with it must be dealt with and brought to a conclusion so that a person can eventually make the transition to a new situation. As William Bridges, a consultant on human development, states in his book, *Transitions*, "Endings must be dealt with if we are to move on to whatever comes next in our lives. The new growth cannot take root on ground still covered with the old and endings are the clearing process."[1]

Saying good-bye and giving up something familiar that has meaning in one's life is difficult for most people. People can usually accept the end or loss of something on an intellectual level because the facts and evidence are there to indicate that a change has occurred or must be made. However, what is surprising to most people is the degree of difficulty they experience when they attempt to accept the end or loss on an emotional level.

There are many feelings, sentiments, and emotions associated with a situation that is ending, particularly if it is something that has a great deal of meaning to an individual or has been an important part of his life. Also, the longer it has been important to him, the more difficult it is to let go of the situation emotionally. In times of change, people often feel as if they are giving up part of themselves and their lives. For a time, there is a feeling of emptiness, created by the void that the loss or ending produces in people's lives. The emotions associated with a loss or ending are usually uncomfortable and often painful, which can make it difficult to come to terms with letting go. These emotions can be even more intense when a change is unwanted or not of one's choosing. For most people, accepting the end or loss of a situation emotionally is the most difficult part of the process of adapting to change, but until a person has internalized and emotionally accepted the ending, the process of adapting to change cannot be complete. One cannot deal with a new situation if one has not resolved the conditions of the old and of the past.

Task 2—Rebuilding, Restructuring, and Beginning Again

The second task in the process of adapting to significant change is understanding, accepting, and dealing with something new or unfamiliar (condition, way of life, relationship, identity, and so on) and restructuring and rebuilding one's life to reflect the new reality that results from the change.

Once a person has faced the ending of an old way, has expressed the emotions associated with it, and has come to terms with it, he is ready to deal with the new situation or the beginning of something new. He needs to identify what is required to make the change or adjust to the new condition and can then take the appropriate steps to do so. He can modify or alter existing conditions or create new conditions in his life in order to integrate the new and accommodate the change. In doing so, he is, in effect, reconstructing his life or part of his life to reflect the new reality brought about by the change. The purpose of the reconstruction phase is to rebuild one's life to include the new reality. At the end of the rebuilding phase, a person has resumed a "normal" life that includes the new change.

Seven Steps in the Process of Adapting to Significant Change

The two tasks people face in the process of adapting to significant change are accomplished through a series of seven steps. Each of these seven steps is now examined.

Step 1—Disbelief

When a person first becomes aware that a significant change will affect him, the initial reaction is usually one of (some) disbelief. (I can't believe this is happening.) The fact that the change has occurred or is about to occur doesn't seem real. It seems more like a dream or nightmare. When a person attempts to deal with the news of a change for the first time, she or he can feel numb, stunned, or shocked and can become disoriented or overwhelmed for a time. Because of the sense of unreality one can feel at this time, there are often feelings of denial as well. (This can't really be happening. It really can't be true.)

Step 2—Intellectual Acknowledgment

Faced with evidence or facts concerning a change, a person can no longer continue to disbelieve or deny the reality of it. Thus, after a period of disbelief, disorientation, or shock, the reality of the change begins to sink in. A person then begins to accept the change but does so only on an intellectual level. As the reality continues to manifest itself, the person begins to realize and assess the impact or implications the change could have on him and his life. This intellectualizing quickly leads to step 3.

Step 3—Emotional Reaction

Acknowledgment of the reality of the change and an assessment of the implications it might have on one's life are followed by a period of emotional reaction that is often intense. The emotions expressed by an individual at this time are many and varied. They include anger, resentment, hurt, worry, pain, helplessness, confusion, doubt, bitterness, and anxiety. Emotions can also be positive in the event of a positive change. They can include happiness, joy, relief, and elation. Emotions are not only felt at this time but are also openly expressed (crying, yelling, and screaming). Accompanying the intense emotional agitation can come questions such as, "Why me?" "Why now?" "What did I do to deserve this?" "It's not fair. It's not right." At this time, people can become anxious about their ability to handle or cope with the change. (How will I get through this? What will I do? Where do I begin?) Their emotions are intense and they do not feel normal. They feel very uncomfortable, and at this point some people become afraid that they're going to "fall apart" or "have a nervous breakdown," or they are afraid they "won't be able to handle it" or "won't be able to take it." In the case of a positive change, even though a person has chosen the change or is generally happy about it, this is the time when they may develop doubts, however fleeting, about whether or not they have made the right choice and whether or not they will be able to meet the challenge the change will bring.

Step 4—Limbo

Once a person has accepted a change intellectually and has expressed the intense emotions associated with it, for a time he then enters a state of what can be described as limbo. The state of limbo represents a time-out period when a person withdraws and reflects on what is actually happening. It is a period of time when a person does not act on the change but instead thinks about it in terms of what has happened and what will happen. People feel uncomfortable in the state of limbo because although they have come to terms with the reality of the change, they haven't yet let go of the past condition and haven't thought about making the transition to the new situation. They commonly feel lost, alone, disoriented, insecure, empty, and "neither here nor there." Emotions are often unstable and people vacillate between positive and negative emotions. For example, a person might feel anxious about the change (negative) but at the same time feel relief because a negative situation they anticipated is finally over with (positive).

There is reminiscing and ruminating about the past and about how things used to be. There is longing for the old situation and wishing things could have worked out differently or things could go back to the way they used to be. There is talk about how much the old way was liked, how well one did in the old situation, how much one will miss the old things, and so on. There may be idealization of the past even when the past may, in fact, not have been all that good.

Step 5—Transition

Having accepted the reality of the change and having spent some time in limbo thinking about it, a person in step 5 begins to make the adjustments required by the change situation (even though he may not like or agree with it). The person has acknowledged and accepted that the old way or situation has ended (or is coming to an end), and he finds ways to begin to detach and separate himself from it. Rather than dwelling on the past and the negatives associated with the change situation, he begins to look for any potential gains and benefits that might come from the new situation. Although he has not yet let go of the past completely, he begins to think in terms of how he will cope with the new situation. He becomes more focused on making a new beginning, formulating plans, and setting goals pertaining to the new beginning. He makes a genuine effort to reorient his thinking and beliefs in order to adjust to the new. At times during this process, however, he will revert back to thinking about the past, may become emotional about it, and may have doubts and some negative thoughts about the change. The transitional process is often a two-steps-forward, one-step-backward process.

Step 6—Emotional Acceptance

Having left behind the old situation intellectually and having made progress toward integrating the new situation into her life, a person then reaches a point when she finally accepts change on an emotional level. For most people, emotional acceptance is the most difficult step in the process of adapting to change because it is difficult and painful to break emotional bonds with things we value. People can usually understand or accept the need for a change from an intellectual perspective, but they have a great deal of difficulty accepting it emotionally. Fully accepting change emotionally, especially when a person may not like or agree with the change, takes time, usually a great deal of time. For that reason, it is one of the last steps in the process of adapting to change. Emotional acceptance comes gradually over time, sometimes in waves at first. Emotional acceptance of change is needed before the change adaptation process can be considered successful and complete.

Step 7—Integration

During the last step of the process, a person has accepted the change both intellectually and emotionally even though he may not like or agree with it. He has also been successful in letting go of the loss or ending, has made a new beginning, and has restructured or rebuilt his life to include the change. He puts into practice new goals and directions that have been established during the transition phase or as a result of the change. He works with the new situation and begins to feel more comfortable with it as time goes on. He has accepted the new and has come to terms with how it will be handled. While he can still be unsure about how things will turn out at times, he has confidence in his ability to handle it. He begins to think of himself and his life in a new way. The change becomes fully integrated into his life and part of his new "normal" life as a result.

Factors Relating to the Adaptation Process

Several important points should be considered in relation to the steps involved in the process of adapting to change, including factors that make adapting to change easier or more difficult.

How Steps Are Experienced

Although the seven steps have been individually defined and delineated in the process of adapting to change, in reality, they are seldom experienced as separate, individual steps with a clear beginning and ending. Rather, what happens most often is that one step of the process blends into the next one and the preceding one fades away. Sometimes steps overlap and people experience two of them at the same time. In other cases, people may not experience the steps exactly in the order they are given. Thus, there is variation in how people experience the process on the whole.

The Amount of Time Spent on Each Step Varies

Each person goes through the process of adapting to change at his or her own pace. Because individuals differ in the amount of time they need to spend on each individual step, they differ in the amount of time they need to make the overall transition. Variation exists because no two people respond to change in exactly the same manner, even when the changes they face are exactly the same.

Adapting to change takes time and a person cannot be pushed prematurely into the next step of the process before he is ready. The process of adapting to change should not be rushed but neither should it be left to drag on for extended periods. It can be useful to monitor one's progress through the steps over time since doing so can serve as an indicator of the progress being made and can reveal areas where one might be getting bogged down.

It Is Necessary to Experience All the Steps

A person cannot skip a step in the process of adapting to change. People must experience all the steps even if only for a brief period of time. A person cannot suddenly end something one day and start something new the next without working through the steps involved in between and without taking the time needed to make the adjustment. It is understandable that people want to look for shortcuts out of difficult, painful, and time-consuming situations, but shortcuts rarely work.

One of the worst ways of implementing change is to put a person in a position where she is immediately faced with implementing a new change without a period of adjustment or without enough time to work through the change adaptation process. For example, an employer plunks down a new program manual on an employee's desk with a statement such as, "We just got this new manual from the head office. It is the new program they want us to follow. We expect your work to conform to this new method effective Monday." In this situation, the employee is disoriented and overwhelmed as she is left to struggle with the program, trying to learn it through trial and error in a short period of time. Most likely, she will be stressed by her efforts to cope, and she will likely be seething with anger and resentment because she was put in the position of having to do so. She might resent her boss or employer and develop a negative attitude toward them and the program.

When change occurs or something new is introduced, people need time to get used to the idea that something new is coming. They need to determine how it will affect their jobs. They need time to integrate it into the existing routine. They need time to read about it, practice it, adjust their ways, and so on. In short, they need time to work through their feelings about the new program. An employer who does not take these factors into consideration when implementing change can expect to have less than positive results.

Anxiety and Difficulties Are Part of the Change Process

The process of adapting to change is seldom a smooth one. Expect to make mistakes along the way. Anxiety, difficulties, and uncertainty are part of the process. Things will often go wrong before they go right. Expect this to happen and do not become upset when it does. Adapting to change is often a two-steps-forward, one-step-backward process. You should not become critical of yourself in any step of the process when you make mistakes, temporarily regress, or are taking a little longer than expected to deal with it. As long as there is overall progress in the right direction, success will eventually come. However, if progress is not being made, a person needs to go back to the beginning of the process and review it to determine what has gone wrong, what he has missed, or where he has become bogged down. Then another attempt can be made to deal with it. If difficulties persist, some outside intervention or assistance may be in order, such as talking to a psychologist, social worker, or other counselor (see Chapter 9) who can assist in identifying the problem or the stumbing block and getting a person back on track.

Change Must Be Accepted Emotionally

In the process of adapting to change, the change must be accepted emotionally as well as intellectually in order for the adaptation process to be successful. This important point warrants further explanation. As we said previously, it is much easier to accept a change intellectually than it is to accept it attitudinally or emotionally. For example, Tony is a middle-aged factory worker and he can understand why the company that employs him is installing a new piece of technological (robotic) equipment. The piece of equipment operates on a much more accurate level than a human could. It does not require coffee breaks, vacation time, benefits, and so on. It will save the company money in the long run. But because the installation of the equipment affects Tony's job (in that he has to be retrained to work with the machine and needs to integrate new skills into his working routine), he is not thrilled about it emotionally. He likes doing the job the old way. He feels the old way is better. He is good at his job and most of his work has been accurately done in the past. Also, Tony doesn't see why he should have to go back to a classroom at his age and learn about robotics. He thinks that the company should give him another job he can do manually and hire a younger person who can learn more easily or someone already familiar with this technology to take over his job.

Tony, like anyone else faced with a similar situation, needs to come to terms with his negative feelings about the situation and needs to resolve them on an emotional or attitudinal level. People in this position can feel anger, bitterness, resentment, and hatred. They can develop destructive negative attitudes, develop a chip on the shoulder, harbor grudges, and withdraw from full participation. If Tony does not resolve his negative feelings about the change, he may go through the motions of making the change because if he doesn't, he will lose his job. He will appear to make the changes outwardly but inwardly, he will be reluctant, resistant, angry, and unhappy. In his anger and unhappiness, he might resolve to do only what is necessary to get by on the job, keeping his effort and involvement to a minimum (because of what "they" did to him). He might just "put in time" until retirement or even try to sabotage the system to prove the change is not a good idea or the new way doesn't work. He might also try to influence other coworkers to be negative about the change and cause them to rebel in a similar fashion.

Change often has an emotional impact people don't expect to have to deal with. People often try to manage situations of change intellectually and equate intellectual acceptance with emotional acceptance. But emotions operate independently of thought processes. You cannot intellectualize emotions. In order to resolve emotions, they need to be expressed and dealt with by each individual in his or her own way. *People frequently underestimate the impact of emotions during times of significant change, and they underestimate the amount of time it takes to resolve them.*

While so much in our world has changed technologically and socially over time, human nature and people's emotional needs have not. We still have the same needs (e.g., for security, stability, order, and control in our lives) and the same emotions (e.g., fear, grief, anxiety, and pain) that our ancestors had a thousand years ago. Despite all the advances in technology and all the discoveries, innovation, and progress we have made to improve our lives, we have not yet found a modern way to get rid of or get over emotional pain. We still have to feel the pain before we can heal, much as our ancestors did in the past.

When faced with potentially negative emotional situations, people have a natural tendency to avoid them, resist them, or ignore them or to divert their attention away so they won't have to think about them or face the pain and discomfort associated with them. They think that if they ignore their emotions and continue on with their lives as usual, the negative emotions will eventually go away. However, this does not usually happen. That is why it is critically important to face emotions, accept them for what they are, experience them, and express them. When people find ways to distract themselves from negative emotions or to cover them up, they are sending their unresolved emotions underground where they will fester at an unconscious level and cause problems (unhappiness, depression) in the future. Suppressed emotions eventually come out, even years after a significant incident. They can surface later at the next personal crisis or can lead to further problems such as alcohol or drug abuse. Suppressed emotions can appear in any number of unpredictable ways and cause a great deal of underlying stress in a person's life. Only by working through the anger and pain can people come to terms with the loss, get over it with time, and heal themselves so that they are ready to accept and deal with something new.

One of the simplest ways to release emotional pain and tension is by crying. Crying is nature's way of helping us to adapt to emotional stress. It is part of the process of our evolution. We were given tears and the ability to cry to help cleanse us from distress and to keep us emotionally healthy. Thus, crying has a purifying effect.

Crying is not easily accepted in our culture where it is often interpreted as a sign of weakness and where those who don't cry are viewed as stoic. This is not the case in a great number of other cultures around the world where men and women alike are encouraged to cry when there is a need (as in times of grief, pain, or sorrow).

Crying to release emotions is very healthy, despite what our culture says. So when there is a need to cry to release emotional pain, do it. People who feel best mentally and emotionally are those who cry easily and who don't worry about the fact that they are doing so.

Another form of denying or suppressing emotions occurs when people purposely become so busy or involved with unrelated things after a major change that they don't have time to think about the ending or the loss they've suffered. This is another way of trying to avoid dealing with emotions in an effort to avoid pain. While it is good to keep busy to some degree so one is not focused entirely on the loss or ending, there needs to be time to think about and deal with one's feelings about a loss as well. A healthy balance needs to be struck so that there is appropriate time for both.

Another problem dealing with losses and endings emotionally in modern times is that people don't seem to have time to deal with or resolve their emotions in a manner that is healthy. They don't have time to mourn losses or to let go of situations so they just keep on going as they usually do in their daily lives. Because of this lack of time, they put their emotions on the back burner or "shelve them" in the unconscious mind to deal with later or to forget about them. The problem is that today a lack of time always seems to be a problem. And so, when the next significant change occurs, a person doesn't have time to deal with that either. Over a period of time when a person has accumulated a series of undealt-with emotions associated with the changes she has undergone, she one day finds herself with three or four situations of unresolved emotions on the back burner. Then one more change or stressful event comes along and becomes the straw that broke the camel's back, so to speak. The person can no longer handle any further change and, in reaction to the overload, has an emotional or mental breakdown or crisis, becomes depressed, physically ill, burned out, stressed out, or experiences any other number of negative reactions including turning to drugs and heavy alcohol use. The person is then faced with resolving all of the shelved emotions and feelings at once, making it more difficult and painful to deal with than if she had dealt with them individually as they occurred. Situations such as these can take years to resolve.

Some Changes Are Easier to Adapt to Than Others

Changes that people perceive to have benefits or potentially positive outcomes associated with them motivate people intrinsically and are, therefore, easier to make. The same can be said of changes that are chosen or desirable. Anticipated or predictable changes are easier to adjust to because people can plan for them and adjust to them on their own terms and in their own way. Changes over which a person has control and those that can be made gradually are easier for many of the same reasons. There is time to think about them, plan for them, and adjust to them on one's own terms and in one's own way. Changes that fit easily into the structure and meaning of one's life, those that fit into one's existing pattern of behavior or daily routine, and changes that are in keeping with one's philosophy of life and beliefs are also easier to deal with. When change occurs in the form of a loss that can be replaced, it is not as difficult to cope with. Changes that are equivalent extensions of something already familiar (replacements or improvements) are usually not hard to make (new car, new furniture).

On the contrary, changes people perceive as undesirable, changes that are imposed, not freely chosen, and not anticipated are more difficult to adapt to. Changes that are hard to adapt to also include those that are beyond one's control, are sudden or unpredictable, appear to have little or no personal benefit (or positive out-come) associated with them, do not fit into one's existing life struc-ture or one's philosophy of life, or require significant changes in one's behavior and routines. Changes that involve the loss of an emo-tional attachment are among the most difficult.

The Length of Time Needed to Adapt to Change Varies

It is difficult to say how long it will take for a particular person to adapt to a particular change. Each individual comes to the situa-tion with different amounts of experience and a different set of cop-ing skills. They have different personalities and perceive the significance of change events differently. The circumstances sur-rounding the event may also affect the amount of time needed. The same change event can be experienced by different people in totally different ways. For example, if a person frequently changes jobs, then losing a job is "no big deal" to him. However, if a person has worked at the same company for twenty years or all of his life and loses his job, it is much more devastating to him. If a person who has lived in the same house for all of her life moves out of it and into another area, the transition is much more difficult emotionally than, for example, a person in the military who routinely makes a move every three years.

As a general rule of thumb, significant or major changes take anywhere from six months to two years to adjust to. Occasionally, it may take a little longer. The more significant the change is to an indi-vidual person, the more time is needed to adjust. For the most sig-nificant changes (e.g., death, divorce), the overall process from beginning to end takes about two years.

Each Person's Capacity to Deal with Change Is Different

While there are many similarities about the way people experi-ence and adapt to change in their lives, change affects different peo-ple in different ways. No two people experience or react to a change event in exactly the same way. People adjust to change at different rates and with differing degrees of ease or difficulty. The factors insti-gating the change event, the circumstances surrounding a change event, a person's character traits and personality, a person's perception of the change, and his past experience in dealing with change all contribute to the way in which that person reacts to and copes with change. Each person's capacity to deal with change is different from the next.

Some People Are More Change Adaptive Than Others

People who adapt most easily and successfully to change are those who have the desire and will to do so and a positive attitude toward it (see information on developing a positive attitude in Chapter 5). In fact, a desire to change and a positive attitude toward it are two of the most important predictive factors of a person's ability to successfully adapt to change. Adapting to change is also easier for people who tend to be flexible and open-minded in their thinking.

People who adapt easily to change do not see change as something to fear or dread. Rather they see it as a challenge or as something that needs to be done. Change-adaptive people find change stimulating, invigorating, and exciting. For them, change represents opportunities for growth and innovation. They welcome change and thrive on it.

Younger people tend to adapt more easily to change because they have grown up in a more rapidly changing environment and world and are more accustomed to the rapid pace of change that currently exists. Young people also tend to be more flexible in their thinking and more amenable to change because they have not yet developed the rigid routines and set patterns of behavior in their lives more commonly associated with older people.

The Role of Motivation

Motivation (the incitement or inducement into action or the movement of the will) is an important factor in the change-adaptation process. Motivation often provides the initiative and furnishes the reason and the desire to change or adapt to change. When motivation is present, the likelihood of success is much greater. Among some of the more common conditions that motivate people regarding change are the following:

✦ *Fear of losing something.* A person risks losing something important if changes are not made. For example, a person risks losing a job if skills are not updated or risks losing a marriage relationship if alcohol abuse continues.

✦ *Gaining advantages or benefits.* By making changes, a person is in a position to gain advantages or benefits. For example, a person obtains a graduate degree in his field to increase his level of pay and to become eligible for promotion, neither of which would be possible without the degree.

✦ *Remaining current or keeping up with the times.* Change often needs to be made if a person wants to keep up with modern life and technology. For example, learning to use a computer opens up a whole new world of opportunity and possibilities to a person who hasn't used one before.

✦ *Improving conditions.* If an old situation or existing condition is no longer suitable or an old way of doing things is not working, people need to make changes to improve the situation. Examples are buying a bigger house because a family is growing in size or getting a divorce because a relationship is no longer working.

✦ *Boredom or a desire for something new or different.* When people get bored or tired of the same thing, they may want a change or something new. Examples are changing one's hairstyle or buying a new car.

✦ *Feeling distressed.* When people are feeling distressed in a particular situation, they need to make a change to relieve the distress. For example, a person diagnosed with colitis knows she has to change her lifestyle (to significantly reduce stress) in order to alleviate the condition and avoid further deterioration in health.

✦ *Responding to major life events.* People need to adjust and make changes in order to respond to and accommodate major changes in their lives. For example, a retired couple might sell their large home and buy a condominium in its place to reduce living expenses and the amount of yardwork and housework that needs to be done in their senior years.

✦ *Obsolescence.* When old ways or products become obsolete, people replace them with new ones that are improved or more convenient to use. For example, word processors have replaced traditional typewriters, compact discs have replaced vinyl records.

Factors that Can Hinder Adaptation to Change

There are also factors that hinder the process of adapting to change, making it more difficult. Among the greatest factors that deter people from change are:

- ✦ *Fear of change.* People who fear change tend to avoid making changes because they fear the uncertainty and unknown conditions that changes might bring to their lives. People who are sufficiently afraid will endure the greatest of tensions and frustrations to maintain the status quo and to keep from having to make a change even though the change might be of significant benefit to them.
- ✦ *Negative attitude toward change.* If people are unwilling to accept or adjust to a change (even though they may recognize it is necessary), the negative attitude they have toward it makes it unlikely that they will adapt to change successfully, if at all.
- ✦ *Lack of motivation.* When there is no reason to change or when people do not perceive a need for change or associate a purpose with it, it is unlikely they will be motivated to make a change.

Change Often Occurs in Cycles

As with many other things in life, change tends to occur in cycles. Most people experience periods of great personal change, periods of moderate change, and times of little or no change over the course of their lives. This can be reassuring to those who are experiencing a cycle of great personal change and fear it will go on forever and never end.

When asked, older people often recall a period of great personal change in their lives (and subsequent stress). Frequently, it is a specific period of time such as a three-year, five-year, or seven-year period that they remember as being very difficult but that they successfully lived through. For some people, it may have occurred during childhood or adolescence. For others, it may have happened during their thirties, middle age, or even late in life.

Older people can often be a source of comfort and reassurance to those younger than themselves in that they can view a period of great change from the perspective of a person who has lived through many changes over many decades.

Sometimes There Is a Period of "Living Hell"

For many significant changes, particularly those that involve a personal crisis, people often endure a period they usually describe as a time of "living in hell" before the crisis is resolved. It can be reassuring to recognize the existence of this phenomenon and to know that others who have had similar experiences made it through the period successfully.

Only You Can Adapt to Change Yourself

And finally, you are the only person who can adapt to change yourself. No one else can do it for you. Other people can make it easier or more difficult to do but ultimately the work has to be done by you. Knowing and recognizing that hundreds, thousands, or perhaps millions of people have gone through similar changes and have gone on to have happy and productive lives can be of some consolation during times of change and personal crisis.

The process of adapting to change is not always easy because it is complex and cannot be done quickly or overnight. It requires time. It is the requirement of time that puts it at odds with the fast-paced and instantaneous lifestyle we live. We seem to have less and less time in which to do more and more things. Taking the time to adapt to change does not naturally fit into this kind of existence. Nonetheless, we must find a way to do it, or otherwise we may suffer some of the negative consequences that are discussed in the next three chapters.

part two

Companions to Change

chapter five

Shattered Illusions, Mistaken Beliefs, and Personal Growth

Over time, people develop certain patterns of thinking and behavior and visualize how they want the future to be. As they live life and work toward achieving their goals, they assume that their beliefs and behaviors are valid and that life will go on as they envisioned and planned with perhaps certain ups and downs to be expected along the way. People seldom question their beliefs and views of life and rarely imagine or think about a future different from the one they envision for themselves.

When people face major change, particularly in the form of a personal crisis or trauma, their lives (or some aspect of their lives) become altered or different in some way. It is usually at these times, when circumstances force them to do so, that people are compelled to examine their lives, goals, beliefs, and behaviors. As they do this, it can become apparent to them that the future they had envisioned and planned for themselves may be in jeopardy or is no longer possible. They may suddenly realize that they have been living life (or some aspect of it) under an illusion. They may recognize that beliefs they had long held about life are not valid. Because the change or crisis they experience can demonstrate the invalidity of their views, their perspective of things and view of the world can be drastically altered. With many circumstances of change, vulnerability comes to the forefront of people's lives as they realize that things they thought could only happen to other people can also happen to them.

Major change shocks people into facing and thinking about things in life they never had to seriously think about or deal with before, particularly things they took for granted. It forces them to confront important issues, examine their beliefs, and think about themselves, their lives, and the world from a new or different perspective. In this chapter, we review the process of coming to terms with such issues as we examine how people's thinking and psychological makeup are affected by major change and how difficult and painful experiences people have during times of change can result in tremendous personal growth and insight into the meaning of their lives.

Shattered Illusions

Adults of all ages today, like those of generations past, experience feelings of disorientation, disappointment, and anxiety during times of major change or crisis in their lives, especially when change is unexpected. However, people of the baby boom generation (those born after World War II, between 1946 and 1963) and those born afterward seem to experience negative emotions much more profoundly. Perhaps the most significant reason for this can be attributed to the differences in the views and expectations of life held by people born after World War II as opposed to those born during earlier times.

Before World War II and the arrival of the baby boom generation, there were great disparities between social classes in society, namely the rich and the poor. The average person was not well off materially and financially and therefore the average person's expectations of life were not great. Life was hard with many difficulties and restrictions that made it almost impossible for ordinary people to achieve many of the things taken for granted by middle-class people today (e.g., owning a home/cars, taking vacations, going to college). In generations past, there were fewer choices in life. If you were a

man, you went to school for as long as you could, got a job (not necessarily one you liked), got married, raised children, and hoped you
lived long enough to retire and see your grandchildren. If you were a
woman, you went to school for as long as you could, got a job (typically for a short while, if at all), got married, had children, and set
about raising them while your husband worked. Women worked
hard in those days with few or none of the conveniences and ameni-
ties available today.

Many women of past generations died in childbirth or at a
young age and left behind a husband with young children. Children
had little time to play. They had responsibilities and chores to tend to
and many quit school long before graduation to get a job to help support the family. Children were often left to fend for themselves at an
early age. Disease killed many children as well as adults. People who
lived in those times realized they were on their own and responsible
for themselves. If they lost a job, couldn't find work, or had problems, they turned to their families and friends for support. The government did not have the range of social benefits available today.
People living in past times were concerned with and focused on providing themselves and their families with the necessities of life. They
worried about surviving from day to day, putting food on the table,
being able to afford shelter and clothing for their family and perhaps
a gift for their child's birthday. A vacation, cars, owning a home in
the suburbs, having an interesting job or career, and sending children
to college were things they only dreamed about. Those were not for
average people.

All of that changed for people born after World War II. Because
of the booming economy, rapid technological innovation, and growing affluence in the country, the baby boom children and those born
after them no longer had to struggle for the necessities of life as did
generations of people before them. The necessities were already provided for them by their parents (or in some cases, social programs).

The rise of the middle class and the existence of various social
movements (such as the women's movement) that emerged after
World War II brought about fewer responsibilities and greater opportunities and choices in life for children (especially girls) growing up
at that time. Children no longer had to quit school to help support
their families. They did not have to be tied down to burdensome

daily chores. They were free to pursue and achieve other things in their lives. Parents of baby boom children recognized that it was possible that their children could have a much better life than they had (financially, materially, educationally), and they sacrificed and worked hard to provide their children with things that would bring them a better (easier) life. Parents saved money to send their children to college, and they told their children to study hard because having a college degree would enable them to get a good paying job that would allow them to afford many things of the "good life."

While the baby boomers were growing up in the sixties and seventies, society was changing significantly, mainly as a result of the newfound affluence of the middle class. Culture began to be shaped and influenced more by the philosophy of "the good life" and achieving the "American dream." With their basic needs in life met, the baby boom children began to pursue goals beyond those of the basics of life such as self-fulfillment, happiness, pleasure, and a comfortable lifestyle. Having an exciting career, owning a beautiful home in the suburbs, having two cars, a good marriage, vacations, being able to send children to college were no longer things this generation dreamed about. With an increasing number of children growing up in homes where these things were already reality, living this lifestyle and having these things became the norm for this generation. They became what most children and young adults of this generation expected they would get in life.

The baby boom generation was also the first one to grow up in an age of mass communication, which came about as a result of the development and proliferation of technology and mass media. Television and other media began to transmit ideas and influence culture unlike anything there had been before that time. The media messages reflected the philosophy of the growing affluent times by focusing on freedom and the dreams that people were trying to achieve and telling young people how to achieve them and be happy. Themes centered on the delivery of pleasure, happiness, status, prosperity, instant gratification, and the idea of being able to "have it all." These themes reflected a lifestyle unknown to the average person of any earlier generation.

But as common as these themes were (and still are) in the environment of young people growing up during these times, they were quite unrealistic. However, many young people did not consider them as such and it was difficult for them to do so. Being surrounded by images of fantasy, idealism, and perfection that were repeated day after day and year after year in their environment (movies, television shows, magazines, music, videos, and so on), they began to think of them as the norm. In fact, they were so inundated and surrounded by messages about achieving the good life from so many sources that they began to expect to get these things for themselves, believing that they were deserving of them and that it was possible to do so, regardless of their personal circumstances. For many of them, things that were once considered privileges in society became rights and entitlements.

The baby boom children grew up at a time and in an environment where all their basic needs were provided for and they took them for granted. They were the first generation to grow up in a highly idealistic, contrived, and unrealistic cultural environment of fantasy and perfectionism. It was inevitable that people of this generation would develop a different philosophy of life and different views and expectations of life than those of their parents and grandparents. While their parents were grateful to be able to achieve basic needs in life, that was not enough for the baby boom children. With their basic needs met, they pursued a life of self-fulfillment, pleasure, happiness, and success, often with excessive and idealistic expectations far beyond what was humanly possible to attain. With their expectations of life set so high, it was inevitable that they would be in for a great letdown and disappointment when things in their lives didn't materialize in the manner they had envisioned or expected they would. Their inflated expectations thus set them up for disappointment and disillusionment and made it more difficult for them to have to face anything less than what they had come to expect in life, or what they had come to believe they were entitled to.

In contrast, their parents and those born in generations before them didn't have inflated, unrealistic expectations of life. They were not exposed to the same media messages of fantasy, perfection, and idealism when they were young. They were much more grounded in the harsh realities of life trying to survive from one day to the next. Facing disease for which there were no treatments or cures, going off to fight in wars or suffering the ill effects of war (such as being bombarded, having goods rationed, being in concentration camps), suffering through hard economic times and joblessness (the depression), facing the early death of children and other family members and friends, contending with the loss of crops (due to drought, pestilence), being hungry and not having enough to eat, not being able to finish school, and not being able to attend college for lack of funds were just some of the circumstances they had to regularly face. They had to work hard to get whatever they had and to survive from day to day.

They did not expect things or feel entitled to things. What they expected was to be able to provide themselves with the basics if they were fortunate. Anything they achieved beyond the basics of life was a plus—a bonus. They started at the bottom with little or nothing and therefore anything they got or earned was appreciated and celebrated. This was unlike the post–World War II children who started with so much in life materially that when they could not achieve what they expected or when they lost what they had, it brought great unhappiness, loss of self-esteem, disillusionment, depression, and disappointment. Starting out life with so much and with expectations set so high, they had nowhere to go but down, and it was a long fall to the bottom where their parents and grandparents began. It is this perspective of life and these expectations of what they should have or are entitled to in life that are at the root of many illusions baby boomers and people born after them have about life today. More examples are discussed throughout this chapter.

Coincidentally, when we consider the differences in expectations of life between those born before World War II and those born afterward, it is interesting to note that the incidence of severe depression among people in modern developed countries such as ours has increased ten times since World War II. Young people today therefore are ten times more likely than their grandparents to suffer severe depression and according to research will experience it earlier in their lives than their ancestors.

Shedding illusions about the world and life in general can be a painful process. With age and maturity, most people learn about the reality of life and the hardships that are an inevitable part of it. For others, the reality sets in when they face a major life change or crisis. It is difficult to let go of the expectations of how we want our lives and the world to be. The world cannot be how we individually want it to be, no matter how long we wish it were so. We cannot pretend that things are different than they actually are. Our views about reality have to change. We need to stop thinking about the way things are "supposed to be, should be, or ought to be," and we need to learn to be more accepting of how things are in actuality. Facing major change or having a personal crisis has a way of shattering our illusions about the way things are supposed to be, allowing us to see, feel, and ultimately accept the reality of a situation, perhaps for the first time in our lives. As Ann Kaiser Stearns summarizes in her book, *Living Through Personal Crisis:*

> *One of the hardest things to do is release our unrealistic expectations concerning what we feel life* ought *to be. . . . Life is what it is. We are all vulnerable and needful people. In human life, fairness has nothing to do with illness, death, divorce, accidents, shattered dreams and with a host of other losses. The world cannot be what we want it to be.*
>
> *We find that as we release our unrealistic expectations of life, the space is created for realistic self-renewal. In other words, we begin to recreate ourselves, our goals, our relations with others, our approach to living. Because our expectations of ourselves and others gradually become more realistic, we become less easily disillusioned and more easily satisfied. Life is so much a matter, we realize, of walking in gardens and learning to recognize that a garden is where one is.*[1]

Mistaken Beliefs

Most people take the beliefs they have about life and themselves for granted, seldom thinking about them for any length of time. But mistaken beliefs are often part of the illusions people develop about life and as such, can set them up for disappointment and disillusionment.

What do we mean by beliefs when we speak of them? By beliefs, we mean the truths people individually hold about life, themselves, and the world, ideas that people hold to be valid without question. Although people often think of religion when they think of beliefs and although many beliefs can be religious in origin, for purposes of our discussion here, we will not consider the role of religion or religious beliefs.

People live their lives according to their beliefs and as such, use beliefs to make judgments about everything in life. How one chooses to behave, think, work, and play are all reflective of one's beliefs. Beliefs are usually deeply ingrained. People accept their beliefs because they are what they know and they become comfortable with them over time. Through their beliefs, people also have a way to understand themselves and things in the world. Because each person has a different upbringing, has different experiences growing up, and is influenced in different ways by culture and society, people have different belief systems by which they live.

When we think of beliefs, we often think of them in terms of whether they are right or wrong. What we usually don't consider is whether they are valid, rational, provable, or factually based. Just because something is a belief doesn't make it a truth or a fact. Facts are certainties but beliefs are not. Many of our beliefs are emotionally based and subjective and therefore reflective of individual judgment and opinion. When we make judgments or form conclusions about things based on beliefs that are not facts, they may be flawed. As a result, many of our beliefs about life, ourselves, and the world are often mistaken or faulty because they are not factually correct or reflective of reality.

People's beliefs and perceptions of life come from several sources. Our culture and society influence our beliefs. Beliefs people have about themselves, others, and the world also result from what they are taught in childhood, from the experiences they have growing up, and from experiences they have as adults. We now review examples of how people develop faulty beliefs in each of these areas.

The culture we live in and are raised in influences our beliefs and behaviors throughout life. What is customary in a culture usually dictates much of what the people in that culture believe and how they should live within that culture. For example, in North American society, we believe in freedom of speech and equal opportunity for all. In our culture, individual families live in separate houses or apartments, women get married in long white gowns, and people retire at about age sixty-five.

In other countries and cultures, people do things that are not customary in our culture. In some countries, people have siestas every afternoon or families live in communal settings with several generations living under the same roof. In other cultures, women are prohibited from driving an automobile while in still others the father of a bride is expected to pay a dowry to her groom's family before they can marry.

It is not difficult to understand how culture has a great influence on the way people live and what they believe. For centuries, people have modeled many of their beliefs and behaviors on those of the culture they grew up in, and they continue to do so today. Culturally based beliefs are beliefs that reflect the standards of behavior or the way things are done in a particular society. They are based on how things are supposed to be in a culture. For example, in North American culture, if you are a woman, you are supposed to receive a diamond ring when you become engaged. If you are going to a fancy restaurant, you are supposed to dress in more formal attire. If you are a student, you are supposed to find a job after you graduate. If you do someone a favor, they are supposed to do one for you in return.

Our culture today has become highly influenced by the media. What we see and hear in the media on a daily basis has a significant effect on our thoughts and behaviors. While the media is supposed to reflect our culture, the way things are portrayed in the media is often idealized and unrealistic. Much of what is shown on television, in videos, movies, and magazines is fantasy that is contrived and planned in great detail to evoke a particular audience response (such as to sell products, increase ratings, influence behavior). The images are seldom realistic. They are artistic representations. While many of these representations do not portray what is real or normal, when people see the same themes or messages repeated often enough, these messages can easily be assimilated and become part of people's system of beliefs. People then end up developing certain expectations and making judgments about their lives and behaviors using these idealized representations as standards. For example, in the media, women who are most desirable to men are often portrayed as beautiful, big-breasted, small-waisted, long-legged, and sexy. Women, particularly young women growing up in our culture, use this standard against which to measure their own degree of desirability or attractiveness to men. If they are not beautiful, don't have big breasts, aren't small-waisted, and so on, they may feel inferior and thus believe that they are less desirable to men as a result.

When standards of our culture are portrayed in the media, they are most often standards of cultural perfection, standards that reflect what things would be like if everything were perfect in our culture. When people's beliefs and expectations of life are based on how things are supposed to be according to these standards of perfection, their beliefs are faulty and their expectations misguided because the standards upon which they are based are unrealistic. The truth is nothing is perfect in our culture and nothing is perfect in reality.

Similarly, these faulty beliefs and expectations in life, based as they are on how things are supposed to be, can lead to disappointment and disillusionment if things don't work out the way they are supposed to in people's lives. For example, when you get married, you are supposed to remain married for life. But we know that, in reality, things don't always work out that way.

People who base their beliefs on how things should be or are supposed to be need to ask themselves such questions as: Who is it that determines how things are supposed to be? Is the way things are portrayed in the media the right way of doing things, or the way things are supposed to be? Is the way things are done in our culture the right way? Who says so? How does one know things should be a certain way? Is there some great power out there or book of rules that explains how things are supposed to be? Is there someone somewhere who has been appointed to make sure that things are done according to how they are supposed to be done in this world? Who says that things in your life are supposed to go a certain way? Where are the guarantees that if you do certain things, you are entitled to something or deserve something? Where is it written that if you do this (get a college degree), you will get that (a high paying job)? Basing one's beliefs on how things are supposed to be or should be leads to the development of faulty beliefs and ultimately to disappointment and disillusionment because, in real life, things don't always turn out the way they are supposed to. As psychologist Penelope Russianoff illustrates in her book *When Am I Going To Be Happy?*:

> *Our culture . . . lures us into emotional booby traps by baiting us with false expectations. Somewhere out there is the rosy notion that if I follow certain rules, if I behave in a certain way, I am entitled to certain prizes: "They owe me. I did all the right things. So I deserve the good life (usually seen by my*

female patients as a superhusband, two adorable kids and a grassy colonial in Connecticut)." "I've done everything he wants. I deserve better. I played by all the rules, I'm entitled to more out of life. All I want is what other women have." I run into these expectations all the time. I get the feeling that many of my patients have swallowed a television commercial as their vision of the good life. It is supposed to be theirs. They deserve it.

If I had my way, I would banish the words, "deserve, owed and entitled to" from the English language. All they do is set us up for disappointment, resentment and rejection. Thinking we have something coming or that we are owed, is a surefire prescription for disappointment.[2]

Things we were taught in childhood and childhood experiences can also be sources of mistaken beliefs. Of course, parents seldom intentionally teach their children to have beliefs that are faulty. Nonetheless, children acquire them from their parents for several reasons. Among them, parents may have mistaken beliefs themselves that they have never recognized or resolved and therefore inadvertently passed them on to their children. They may also have problems dealing with some aspect of life, and children follow their example or take on their beliefs because they know no other way. Whatever the reason, people are not perfect and neither are parents. As a result, children do grow up with some faulty beliefs that stem from their upbringing. Some examples of these faulty beliefs are as follows.

You always get what you deserve in the end. This is what Sarah's parents had taught her as a child. Sarah was considered a model wife and a kind, considerate, loving, and caring person. After several years of trying to get pregnant, she conceived and had her first child. He was born with deformities. Thinking back to how she had been brought up, Sarah felt devastated by the birth and overwhelmed with guilt. Why? Because she believed she must have done something wrong in her life to deserve a baby with deformities. Since her pregnancy had gone well and she had been careful about what she ate and did during that time, she couldn't understand how it could have happened. She ruminated and searched her mind for reasons why it happened, thinking that if she searched long enough, she would find the reason why she got what she deserved. Of course, Sarah didn't deserve a baby with deformities and she is mistaken in thinking so. Sarah didn't have this baby because she deserved it for something bad she did in her life. She had the baby because now and then a small percentage of women give birth to babies with deformities even under the best of care. Unfortunately, in this case it happened to her. Deformities do not occur because someone deserves it, yet Sarah believed that was the case because that is what she had been taught as a child and still believed as an adult.

A second example: *Always play to win: Winning is what counts.* Dan's father had told him this repeatedly as a child to encourage Dan to do well, get ahead, and be the best at what he chose to do. As an adult, Dan worked hard and became "a winner" on all counts. He had a prestigious executive job with a company, a beautiful home in the suburbs, a nice car, a loving wife, and so on. Then his company, caught up in bad economic times, had a massive layoff. Dan was one of 6,000 employees across the country to lose his job. Because of his upbringing, Dan felt that if he wasn't winning at any given time, he was a total failure. He became depressed and his self-esteem plummeted. He began to drink heavily because he couldn't deal with it. He couldn't face himself, his father, or his friends because he believed that he was now a loser. Of course, the reality was that he was not a loser. The job loss had nothing to do with his performance. He was just a person who had been caught up in bad economic times by circumstances beyond his control. He lost his job because of a recession, not because he was a loser. In fact, he still had all of the skills and abilities he had prior to the job loss. So how could he be a loser? Dan believed he was a loser because of what he had been taught by his father as a child.

Negative experiences children have growing up can lead to the development of faulty beliefs. Children growing up in abusive homes with alcoholic parents, for example, can develop faulty beliefs about life and themselves as a result. For example, Christine was told repeatedly by her alcoholic father during her childhood that she was no good and was never going to amount to anything. It is no surprise that Christine grew up believing she was inferior to others. In reality, however, she wasn't inferior at all. She was a talented athlete with many skills and abilities. But because of her father's repeated messages, she believed she was inferior and could not rid herself of these feelings, even when she won several sports championships and awards.

And finally, significant experiences people have as adults influence their beliefs. Valerie was a twenty-eight-year-old schoolteacher. Her parents were immigrants. Having arrived in the country with little but the clothes on their back, they lived with relatives for a while and worked hard to save for a down payment on a small grocery store. Within a few years, Valerie's parents were able to take out a mortgage on a store and they lived in the apartment upstairs. Valerie and her younger brother grew up there, working and helping out in the store when they were old enough. Valerie's parents worked hard, twelve hours a day for almost twenty-five years. Her parents saved every penny they made so that they could pay off the mortgage on the store, which they did within fifteen years. Throughout her life, Valerie's parents stressed the virtues of working hard and the importance of saving money. They never ate in restaurants (too expensive), never went on vacation (a waste of money), never had nice furniture or clothing (not necessary). They saved their money and put it in the bank. Valerie adopted her parents' thriftiness and values about money and saving. After she finished college, she got a job teaching and saved all the money she made.

When Valerie's mother turned fifty, she was diagnosed with cancer and died within a year. Valerie was devastated by her mother's premature death because they had had a close relationship and she had great admiration for her mother. She couldn't understand why her mother had to die so young since she had always thought her mother would be around forever. She began to realize how fragile life was. As time passed, she became angry that her mother had worked so hard and never been able to enjoy life. Her mother had never gone anywhere or done anything except work and save. Valerie felt her mother had deserved more. She was angry that her mother had died with a pile of money in the bank, money that could do her no good now that she was dead. Valerie wondered why her mother hadn't spent some of her money to enjoy things and make life easier for herself. But of course, she didn't expect her mother to die so young. So now it was too late, too late for her mother but not for Valerie.

At that point, Valerie's beliefs about life and money changed dramatically. She recognized how fragile life was and that it could be taken at any time. She vowed she wasn't going to save every penny she earned. She was going to start living while she had the means and the health. She was going to start traveling during her summer vacations, she was going to buy steak or lobster once in a while, and she was going to get rid of her old clunker of a car to buy a new one. She decided she could afford to do it and still have some savings for the future. And so the beliefs that Valerie had held without question since her childhood were challenged as a result of her mother's death and changed forever as a result.

As we can see from these examples, whether faulty beliefs come from one's culture, childhood upbringing, experiences people have growing up, or experiences people have as adults, they can cause considerable distress and make people lead less than satisfactory lives. Regardless of what one's beliefs are or where they came from, if they have a negative impact on a person's life in any way, they need to be identified, examined, and changed. Unfortunately, it often takes a major change or crisis to prompt people to do so. Experiences people have as a result of major change often force them to examine their lives and question the beliefs they have had all their lives. What many come to realize in times of crisis or difficulty is that their long-held beliefs are not valid. Once again, illusions can be shattered.

Learning to recognize faulty and self-defeating beliefs, under-standing how they can undermine one's life, and learning new patterns of thought can greatly improve a person's quality of life. Beliefs, even deep lifelong beliefs, are changeable and are most easily changed at a time in a person's life when circumstances demonstrate that they are not valid and are no longer useful, as often happens in times of major change or personal crisis. It is at these times that people are most receptive to and most motivated to changing their beliefs because they have evidence of the distress their beliefs are causing in their lives. Beliefs can change when people recognize that their beliefs are only beliefs, not necessarily facts or truths. A change event often acts as a catalyst to help open people's eyes and allow them to see things more realistically. Gaining insight into one's mistaken beliefs and recognizing them as such can be a tremendous relief.

In order to change beliefs, people must recognize why they are faulty or mistaken. For example, they need to discard beliefs that reflect how they wish things were, beliefs based on illusions and fantasy, or those based on the way things are supposed to be. People need to unlearn the inaccurate ways of thinking about life and themselves. They need to objectively examine their beliefs and the statements they make to themselves to determine whether the beliefs or statements are realistic, factual, and rational in nature. To facilitate the process, people need to check the accuracy of their beliefs and look for evidence of validity. They need to look to see if there are facts to support their beliefs, and they need to challenge their beliefs, attack them, and dispute them by calling them into question. In the book *A New Guide to Rational Living,* Albert Ellis and Robert Harper address the issue of dealing with and disputing faulty beliefs. There are also many other self-help psychology books available that can be used to help individuals identify and change faulty thinking and beliefs such as David Burns's book *Feeling Good: The New Mood Therapy* and Martin Seligman's *Learned Optimism.*

While some people eventually realize that their beliefs are faulty and can work to correct them on their own, others need to get counseling from a psychologist, social worker, or other person who is trained to look for and identify faulty beliefs as well as the the root cause of inappropriate thinking. Trained professionals are able to be objective in looking for faulty beliefs and pointing them out to their clients. What is not obvious to a person with faulty beliefs is often obvious to another person who can be objective.

Self-Esteem

When people experience major change, their self-esteem (how people feel about themselves, how they value themselves) is almost always affected even when the changes are positive in nature. Change involves coping and adaptation and it frequently involves loss. When people have to adjust and adapt to new situations or circumstances without knowing what to expect, it is natural to experience feelings of anxiety, apprehension, and doubt about their ability to deal with it. At times such as these, people frequently ask themselves questions like, "How will I cope?" and "Will I be able to do it?" Self-esteem is often challenged or shaken by having to deal with change.

If a person's self-esteem is solidly based, adapting to and coping with change may only present a temporary challenge to a person's self-esteem or a temporary weakening of self-confidence, all of which return over time. If a person's self-esteem is not solidly based, however, experiencing major change can result in considerable loss of self-esteem, which may be difficult to recover.

When a person's self-esteem is strong, it is not solely dependent on external factors such as one's title and position or accomplishments, the approval of others, one's material possessions, or one's appearance. Rather, it is based mainly on internal factors such as self-respect, self-acceptance, integrity, and personal growth.

If a person's self-esteem is dependent on external factors, when those external things are altered or lost (as they often are during periods of change), there is a corresponding loss of self-esteem. For example, when a person's self-esteem is dependent on his position, profession, accomplishments, status, and achievements, he needs to continually accomplish, achieve, and maintain his status in order to sustain his self-esteem. This being the case, a person who loses his job or position or who can no longer achieve may feel like a nobody without his job or title.

Similarly, if one's self-esteem depends on the love and approval of others, it is difficult to maintain over time. People who feel good because they are loved by others may no longer feel that way when others leave them (as in death or divorce) or no longer approve of them (as in breaking up or severing of a relationship or friendship). People who spend their lives doing things to gain the approval of others and who worry constantly about what others think of them cannot be themselves and cannot have a solid base of self-esteem because their self-esteem is dependent on what others think of them and how others evaluate them. When the others are no longer there to love or approve of them, they can experience a tremendous loss of self-esteem.

If one's self-esteem depends on the aquisition or ownership of material things (such as money, clothes, jewelry) or the type and kind of possessions one has (such as expensive car, home), when these are lost or altered during times of change (e.g., financial adversity, disaster), a person's self-esteem is negatively affected.

If one's self-esteem is dependent on one's appearance, that self-esteem is lost when a person loses her good looks (through an accident or disease) or when the aging process sets in. The more people identify with what they do, who they are married to, what they have, and who they know instead of who they are and what they understand, the more open they are to losing self-esteem when these are changed, lost, or are gone.

Coping with change often forces us to examine our self-esteem. When self-esteem is eroded during periods of change, one needs to look for the underlying cause. People need to ask themselves if their self-esteem is only shaken, suffering temporarily because of the circumstances, or if their self-esteem is crumbling because it was built on a poor foundation, faulty beliefs, or illusions. If the latter is the case, the root cause needs to be identified and examined so that an attempt can be made to reorient and rebuild on a more appropriate and solid base. When self-esteem is based on internal factors, regardless of what losses or changes occur externally, a person always has that which is within himself to sustain and help him through any experience.

Self-esteem can also be positively affected by change. When people meet the challenges that face them during times of change, crisis, or uncertainty, and survive the experience, they feel better about themselves as a result. Their self-confidence increases and their belief in themselves and their ability to handle future situations of change or difficulty is greatly strengthened. They believe that if they have survived a difficult ordeal, they can survive anything.

Perfection

For some people, self-esteem is dependent on achieving perfection in whatever they do. Perfectionists continually evaluate themselves and compare themselves to ideal standards. These standards are often far above and beyond what is humanly possible to achieve. Perfectionists mistakenly believe that if they cannot do things perfectly at all times, they are no good or failures. Perfectionists have faulty beliefs because they believe that total failure lies ahead if things are not done perfectly. During times of change, things are often unpredictable and out of one's control. Such circumstances make it more difficult to do things perfectly and thereby cause perfectionists tremendous frustration and disappointment and ultimately erode their sense of self-esteem.

While most perfectionists will acknowledge that no one is perfect, they still somehow mistakenly believe that they themselves can achieve perfection in spite of this fact. They do not recognize that perfection is an illusion. In his book *Feeling Good: The New Mood Therapy*, psychiatrist David Burns explains:

> *Perfection is man's ultimate illusion. It simply doesn't exist in the universe. There is no perfection. It's really the world's greatest con game; it promises riches and delivers misery. The harder you strive for perfection, the worse your disappointment will become because it's only an abstraction, a concept that doesn't fit reality. Everything can be improved if you look at it closely and critically enough—every person, idea, every piece of art, every experience, everything. So if you are a perfectionist, you are guaranteed to be a loser in whatever you do.*[3]

Many perfectionists strive for perfection because they do not want to be average. They want to be much better than average. They want to be superior, better than everyone else. Perfectionists mistakenly believe that being perfect will bring them a great sense of well-being, satisfaction, and love. But those who continually expect perfection leave themselves open to many disappointments and letdowns. Rather than experience well-being and happiness, they experience distress, frustration, and dissatisfaction with themselves, their careers, their children, marriage, and personal lives because things are never good enough, things are never perfect. In reality, there is no evidence to suggest that perfectionists are any more successful than nonperfectionists at what they do.

Another faulty belief often held by perfectionists is that they have to be the best at what they do. Perfectionists believe that if they are not the best at what they do, they are somehow inferior. In reality, only one person can be the best in a field or endeavor. If someone wants to be that person, she is putting herself under tremendous pressure and stress because the odds are so much against her. She is competing with hundreds, perhaps millions of people. To carry this idea even further, perfectionists want to be the best at everything they do. But how realistic is it to think that a person can be a perfect mother, perfect employee, perfect wife, perfect lover, perfect cook, perfect housekeeper, and so on? These are totally impossible standards to meet. A person who is not perfect is not inferior. No one is perfect. Everybody has faults and weaknesses and everybody makes mistakes. That is reality.

Since mistaken beliefs, faulty thinking, and illusions are at the root of perfectionistic thinking and behavior, perfectionists need to examine their beliefs about their need for perfectionism. They need to learn why they have become perfectionists. They need to realize that perfectionism is more of a negative trait in many ways than a quality. Most of all, perfectionists need to give themselves permission to be imperfect. It is not reasonable or realistic to expect anyone, including oneself, to be perfect. Perfectionists need to recognize that they are like everyone else; they are fallible. They make mistakes. They are imperfect beings. They need to learn to forgive themselves for their mistakes and need to learn to accept themselves for what they are, strengths, weaknesses, and all. When perfectionists acknowledge their weaknesses instead of making excuses for them or trying to cover them up, they remove a tremendous burden on themselves and experience a new sense of freedom. Likewise, learning to settle for 80 or 90 percent perfection reduces the pressure enormously while still maintaining a very good standard. Perfectionists need to try to be just average for a while. Average performance is perfectly acceptable performance and will generate a tremendous release of pressure, allowing more time and energy to focus on other things in life. And, needless to say, relieving oneself of standards of perfection, particularly during times of change, is clearly one of the easiest ways to simplify life and alleviate stress and pressure.

Developing a Positive Attitude

People's attitudes toward life are greatly affected by the beliefs they hold. Developing a positive attitude about life is important and can make a tremendous difference in how one experiences it. People with a positive and optimistic outlook on life tend to live longer, have better health, and age well over time. They also tend to cope better with change.

While a positive attitude can be beneficial to people all their lives, in times of change, a positive attitude can be an important coping tool. Change involves coping with and adapting to new or different circumstances. People naturally feel some anxiety and stress in these situations because adapting to change means dealing with the unknown, unfamiliar, and unpredictable. Having a positive attitude and optimistic outlook can help alleviate the stress and anxiety that arise in these situations and can help people get through difficult times more easily.

When we speak about positive thinking or a positive attitude, we do not mean the kind of Pollyanna, mindless positive thinking that has been promoted in many forms in the past. Simply thinking everything will be fine or mouthing the words, "Everything will be OK," when in reality it is not, is not positive thinking. Neither is wishing that everything will be fine or pretending that everything is OK. Idealistic pie-in-the-sky thinking, wishful thinking, and mindless optimism are not positive thinking. They are self-deluding because they imply that things will work out simply if you tell yourself that they will. People engaging in this kind of thinking are not coping realistically with a situation. While a person can be hopeful that something will turn out in his favor, a person simply does not have the power to make things turn out a certain way by wishing alone. One cannot make things over which one has no control turn out in a particular way. So what do we mean then by positive thinking? What does having a positive attitude consist of?

Positive thinking is accurate thinking and realistic thinking. Having a positive attitude means trying to make the best of every situation in life as it happens. Positive thinkers consistently look for the positive aspects or the good that can come from a negative situation even if the good is the fact that things can't get any worse. Positive thinkers may not like the way a situation turned out and they may have preferred that there was a different outcome, but they recognize they can handle things as they are and they make an effort to do so. They do not dwell on and become consumed by the negative aspects.

Because positive thinkers are realistic thinkers, they know that things aren't going to go well all of the time and they don't expect them to. They recognize that problems and struggles of one kind or another are part of life and will always be there. Rather than worrying about problems or pretending they don't exist, they take responsibility for them and deal with them as best they can. They don't pretend that a negative thing isn't happening and they don't delude themselves into thinking it will somehow disappear if they ignore it long enough.

When positive thinkers recognize that a situation is out of their control, they let it go. They recognize that worrying about things that are out of their control does no good whatever. Positive thinkers see failures as opportunities for change and growth. They ask themselves what they can learn from their mistakes or the negative situations or changes they must cope with. Using humor as a tool to help them cope with stressful situations as well as many of life's adversities is also characteristic of positive thinkers. Being able to think positively during times of change is definitely advantageous.

The following is an example of a situation viewed from the perspective of a negative and a positive thinker:

NEGATIVE THINKER: Oh, my husband left me. Now what do I do? I think I'm going to cry myself to death. How will I be able to cope? I'm a failure as a wife. If he doesn't want me, no one else will ever want me. . . . If only I had done this. . . . If only I had done that. . . . I'm so depressed. My future is hopeless. I'll never be happy again. I can't stand this. I can't handle this.

POSITIVE THINKER: Oh, my husband left me. Now what do I do? How will I cope? I feel so bad about it and I'm crying a lot, but I guess it's only natural that I'm going to be upset and disoriented for a while until I get used to it. After all, a person doesn't get over ten years of marriage in a week. But I'm not the first woman whose husband has left her. It has happened to many other women. If all the other women made it through the process, so can I. I am just as capable as the others. For now, I'm going to force myself not to think about all the implications of being on my own at once because that makes me feel too overwhelmed. Instead, I'm going to take things one day at a time so that I can deal with it. I've handled some difficult situations before and if I take this one step at a time and one day at a time, I can do it again.

Self-Talk

When people encounter various situations, including those involving change, they mentally evaluate the situation and instruct themselves how to feel about it, using a silent inner voice. How a person thinks about, interprets, and talks to himself about how to react to a particular situation is self-talk. People can talk to themselves positively about an event or negatively about it. Self-talk can have a profound effect on how people feel, how they handle events in their daily lives, and how they react to and cope with change.

In general, it can be said that people feel the way they think. If they think positive thoughts, they feel positive emotions (happiness, optimism). If they think negative thoughts, they feel negative emotions (anxiety, depression, stress). There is a direct relationship between how people think and how they feel.

Similarly, if people view or interpret events in a positive light, they will have positive thoughts about them, which in turn will generate positive emotions and feelings. If they view or interpret events negatively, they will have negative thoughts and subsequently negative moods and feelings. The role of self-talk in this process is important because it is not the occurrence of an event or change that causes people to feel a certain way about it (e.g., stressed, anxious). Rather it is *what people tell themselves about the event or change (or the way they interpret it) that determines how they will feel and react to it.*

It is important to recognize that although we cannot always control the things that happen to us in life, *we can control our thoughts about them and can thereby affect how we feel about them.* One of the most important discoveries made in the field of psychology over the last two or three decades is that *people can choose the way they think* and inappropriate thinking can be changed.

Because much of what one says to oneself can directly affect one's thoughts, emotional state, and behavior, positive self-talk can be one of the greatest coping techniques a person can use when faced with situations of change and uncertainty. Positive and appropriate self-talk is a powerful tool that can also be used effectively for many purposes in ordinary daily life. Some examples include the following:

1 *To calm oneself down when one is upset.*
   Example: Two-year-old baby Jessica has just pulled the tablecloth off the table where her birthday cake was situated, pulling the cake down onto the floor with it. Guests are arriving for her birthday celebration within a few minutes.

HER MOTHER'S REACTION: "Oh no! Look at that mess. The birthday cake is ruined and the floor is a mess." Then she uses positive self-talk: "Well, there is nothing I can do about it now. There is no time to run out and buy another cake. Guests will be here in a few minutes so I better clean this mess up right now. In the meantime, I am going to remain calm and and am going to try and think of what I can use as a substitute for the guests to eat. I have some cookies in the cupboard, canned fruit in the pantry, and some ice cream in the freezer so I guess I will serve fruit and ice cream with cookies instead of the cake. I'm sure the guests will understand and things will work out fine once I explain to them what happened."

2   *To control negative thoughts.*
    Example: Karen is worrying about why her husband, who is rarely late, hasn't come home from work on time and hasn't called: "I wonder what's happened to my husband. He usually calls when he's going to be late. I wonder if something has happened to him."

    POSITIVE SELF-TALK: "He's probably tied up in traffic or is somewhere where he doesn't have access to a phone. Maybe he just forgot to call me this time. Well, I will look for something to do while I'm waiting for him so that I don't worry about it too much. I know worrying isn't going to do any good."

    POTENTIAL NEGATIVE THOUGHTS: "I wonder what has happened to him. He must have been in an accident. Maybe he's lying in a hospital bed somewhere. Maybe he's been robbed or mugged. He's always on time and he always calls if he's going to be late. Something terrible must have happened! . . ."

3   *To reduce fear and anxiety.*
    Example: Laura is driving home from out of town and finds herself in the middle of a rainstorm. It is raining so hard she can hardly see.

    POSITIVE SELF-TALK: "I can't see much out of the windshield because it's raining so hard, but I better not panic. I'm going to drive slowly. I've driven in heavy rain before and I can do it again. I'll keep on going and if it gets to the point where I just can't handle it anymore, I will pull off to the side of the road and wait until the rain slows down before I continue. In the meantime, I'm going to stay calm and keep driving until the heavy rain passes."

4   *To increase or boost self-confidence whenever there is a need.*
Example: Michael is about to make a speech in front of a crowded auditorium.

REACTION AND POSITIVE SELF-TALK: "There's a lot of people out there and I'm feeling a bit nervous but I'm going to remain calm because then I'll be able to deliver my speech better. I've spoken in front of groups of people before and I can do it again. I made notes and practiced and prepared as best I can. There really isn't anything else I can do to prepare except to remain calm so my delivery will be good. If I draw a blank, I'll check my notes. If I make a mistake, I'll just correct myself and keep going. Nobody's perfect so if I make a mistake, I make a mistake. So what! The world won't come to an end."

5   *To prepare oneself to deal with an uncomfortable situation.*
Example: Matthew prepares himself to have a broken bone set on one of his hands in the outpatient department of a hospital.

REACTION AND POSITIVE SELF-TALK: "I hate hospitals and going to doctors and I don't like getting needles, but this is a necessary medical procedure and there's no way of avoiding it unless I want to jeopardize my health for the future. Since I don't want to do that, I have to cope with getting this done and over with so I might as well think of how I'm going to do that. When the doctor inserts the needle, I'm going to look the other way and sing my favorite song to myself. In fact, I'll ask the doctor if I can wear my walkman headphones on my ears. Then I can listen to my favorite tape the whole time he is doing the procedure. I'll concentrate on the music and pretend that I am lying on a sunny beach in the Caribbean. When he's putting in the stitches, I won't watch that either. I'll keep thinking of ways to divert my attention and thoughts away from my hand until he is done with it. I'll keep telling myself that I can stand it because the procedure will last only a short while and then it will be over. I'll bet that before I know it, he'll be done and I'll be on my way."

6 *To provide a means of examining expectations when something is not working out in the manner that was expected.*
Example: Harry, a newly retired person, is beginning to feel depressed.

REACTION AND POSITIVE SELF-TALK: "I wonder why I'm feeling so blue. I looked forward to retiring for years. I could hardly wait to get out of that place and look at me now. I'm moping around here feeling miserable. I thought I would be so happy once I retired but it looks like it is not turning out that way. Why am I feeling like this? Why aren't things turning out as expected? Was I under an illusion about what retirement would be like? As I think about it, I do miss my friends and colleagues at work. I enjoyed talking to my coworkers every day. Socializing with them was a positive part of my job. Now I don't see them anymore and that might be part of the problem. Maybe I should call some of them up so we can get together sometime or maybe I should join a club where I can socialize with others my age. I wanted to do nothing when I retired, just have a nice long rest, but maybe that's not the thing to do. Maybe I'm resting too much and that is contributing to my feeling blue. Maybe I should find a new hobby or find a project to occupy my time and see if that makes me feel any better. . . ."

7 *To control stress.*
Example: Barbara's boss is being pressed for time by a client who ordered a report and would like to have it a day or two earlier than planned. Her boss has asked Barbara to have her share of the work done by the end of the day.

REACTION AND POSITIVE SELF-TALK: "The first thing I am going to do is not panic or get nervous because then I won't be able to type or think. Secondly, I am going to look for ways to eliminate any disturbances around me for the rest of the day.

I'll forward my telephone calls, put a "do not disturb" sign on my door, and I'll take a shorter lunch. That will set things up so that I can get maximum productivity for the day. All I can do then is take things one step at a time. I'm going to try not to worry and I'm going to do what is humanly possible and what is reasonable. I can't do any more than that. I think I can probably finish the work by the end of the day but if I don't finish, I don't finish. I'll explain to my boss that I did my best. He knows I'm a hard worker and that if it had been possible to finish it today, I would have done it."

8   *To maintain a positive mood and outlook on life.*
By using positive self-talk on an ongoing basis throughout the day, every day, a person can improve his overall mood and develop a much more positive outlook on life over time. A positive outlook means more happiness, less stress (particularly during times of change), and a more fulfilling life.

Analyzing one's self-talk is a way to identify negative and self-defeating thoughts that can lead to faulty beliefs, negative emotions, unhealthy behaviors, and the inability to cope with things. By identifying and examining negative and distorted thinking and by correcting what goes on in your thoughts (i.e., replacing negative thoughts with more appropriate, accurate, logical, and positive self-talk), you can change negative behaviors and emotions. (*Note:* In his book, *Feeling Good: The New Mood Therapy*, listed in the Recommended Readings list, David Burns outlines ten different patterns of distorted or negative thinking that people are guilty of when they engage in negative self-talk. Readers who are interested in pursuing this topic further should obtain a copy of this book to learn more about it.)

While psychologists often analyze people's self-talk to help them see how their negative thoughts can be self-defeating, you can train yourself to do this on your own. The next time you find yourself talking negatively to yourself, analyze your thought patterns and self-talk. Use the following method as a guide, if you like.

First, step back from the situation and try to objectively look at the event that triggered the thought. Ask yourself what happened? (I made a mistake.)

Second, ask yourself what you are telling yourself about the event or situation. How are you interpreting it? (I'm so stupid! How could I have done it?)

Third, once you look at what you're telling yourself about the event (step 2), determine if what you are telling yourself is accurate and true. Look for inaccuracies in your thinking. Check for mistaken beliefs, illogical statements, generalizations, irrational thoughts, one-sided thinking, and self-blaming statements and identify negative messages. Argue with yourself as a strategy to correct your inaccurate thoughts. (Well, actually I'm not stupid. I am an intelligent person and I do many useful and productive things over the course of a day. Today, I just made a mistake, that's all! Because I made a mistake, as everyone does, it does not mean I am stupid.)

And last, having reviewed your thought patterns for errors in thinking, determine what you can tell yourself about the event and substitute more appropriate, logical, positive, and accurate thoughts in their place. (Everyone makes mistakes from time to time and I made one this time. I'm going to learn from this mistake so that I don't make it again in the future.)

In your first attempts at reforming your self-talk, you may want to do it formally by putting these steps in written form. For example, take a sheet of paper, place it in front of you horizontally, and divide it into four columns across the page. In the first column, write down the event or describe the situation that occurred. In the second column, write down what you are telling yourself about it. In the third column, write the errors you find in your thinking (your analysis). And finally, in the last column, write down a more positive, accurate, and appropriate statement you could make about the situation.

To become proficient at positive self-talk takes practice. Do not become discouraged if you struggle with it at first. With time, it becomes easier and easier. In the future, whenever you find yourself facing a disturbing or stressful situation, you can repeat the process of analyzing your thoughts and using positive self-talk. Having an inner dialogue or conversation with oneself and turning negative self-talk into positive self-talk can contribute immensely to improving a person's mental and emotional outlook and all-around quality of life. There are many other examples of ways in which self-talk can be used positively in other parts of this chapter and book. Readers who are interested in learning more about positive self-talk can consult David Burns's book *Feeling Good: The New Mood Therapy*, in which he provides a much more thorough and extensive discussion of this subject matter.

Happiness

The pursuit of happiness is a major goal and motivating force in life. The decisions people make about almost everything in their lives revolve around what will bring happiness.

During times of change, our happiness is almost always affected. We can become happier as a result of a change or less happy because of it. Since one's happiness is usually affected during times of change, experiencing change often motivates people to think about happiness and the nature of happiness—that is, what happiness is and whether they will be able to achieve it.

While most people make achieving happiness one of the most important goals in life, many do not fully understand what happiness is or how it is achieved because they have faulty beliefs or are under false illusions about it. Consequently, people can spend a lifetime searching for happiness in places and in things where it doesn't exist. There are many myths, illusions, and mistaken beliefs about what happiness is. In the book *Stress, Sanity and Survival*, psychologists Woolfolk and Richardson provide us with some insights:

> *Happiness cannot be achieved when it is pursued directly as a goal in living. Efforts to capture happiness, nail it down or make it a secure possession always either spoil it or miss it completely. Happiness in any form is a transitory experience, not some final state at which we arrive. Much of what is pleasurable about happy moments is their spontaneous and unexpected character. . . . Happiness is never sought and achieved directly. It is always the byproduct of other activities. The expression "the pursuit of happiness" is a contradiction in terms. Pursuing happiness leads to worry over how happy we are and hence, to stress and self-preoccupation. Self-preoccupied people are rarely happy. Happiness usually results from an ability to stop focusing on yourself and become absorbed in other activities . . . activities from which you derive intrinsic satisfaction.*[4]

For some people, happiness would be theirs "if only" circumstances in their lives were different. For example, if only I had married so and so . . . If only I could go to . . . If only I had that job . . . If only I looked like her . . . If only my husband would . . . If only my boss would . . . If only I had . . . , I would be happy.

Others feel that happiness will come to them when their problems go away. But people who keep waiting for the day that their problems will go away so that they can be happy are wasting precious time. The day when problems end and happiness reigns permanently over their lives will never come. While people spend years waiting for this or that to happen so that they can be happy, life passes them by. Suddenly, their lives are coming to an end, and they realize they've been miserable for most of it because they've spent much of their time dwelling on past hurts and grievances, in pursuit of illusive dreams, or looking for happiness in the wrong places.

Everyone has problems that have to be faced and dealt with in life. People can choose to solve their problems as they arise, take their knocks when they come, and move on with life as soon as they can afterward. Or they can spend the rest of their lives, or a good part of them, being a victim, wallowing in self-pity, blaming things in the past or others for their problems, and waiting for someone to save them from their misery, in which case many years that cannot be relived or recovered will be lost. People need to realize that whether they are happy or miserable (depressed, bitter, angry), *their lives are going to go by.* When time has passed, it is gone. It cannot be retrieved. We don't get another opportunity to relive it. That is reality. That being the case, wouldn't it be preferable to be happy for the time we have?

People can be happy when they realize that in the end, *they must rely on themselves to create their own happiness.* Happiness is not something out there waiting to be discovered. Rather, it is to be found within us. Each individual has the power to find and create happiness in his or her life, in his or her own way. While there are times in life when one clearly cannot be happy and when one is entitled to a period of negative emotion (e.g., death of a loved one, serious illness), it is possible to be happy most of the time if one chooses to be.

Regardless of their circumstances, people can work within those circumstances to find and create happiness for themselves. Developing a positive attitude, getting rid of faulty beliefs and illusions about life (such as those promoted in the media), and recognizing the reality of human limitations can do a great deal to help.

People also need to recognize that once found, happiness is not theirs forever. It is not an ultimate state nor a permanent one. People who think they have to be happy all the time put tremendous stress on themselves. Instead of enjoying life, they are focused on what could be wrong with it. After all, something has to be wrong if they are not happy all of the time. They continually look for ways to try and fix it. Under stress to be happy all the time, they become self-critical and continually disappointed because although it is possible to be happy much of the time, it is impossible to be happy all of the time.

And finally, people and things cannot be the main source of one's happiness because, as so often happens in times of change, people and things can be taken away or lost at any time. If happiness depends on external things, it will disappear when they do.

Happy people seem to have certain traits in common. Happy people have a positive attitude and a positive outlook on life. They don't expect that great things will come to them. They don't have unrealistic expectations of life. They don't think they deserve things or are entitled to things. They consistently look for the positive or good that can come from situations. They do not dwell on or become preoccupied with the negative aspects of life.

Happy people have a good sense of self-esteem. They accept themselves just as they are. They acknowledge and accept their weaknesses but they prefer to focus on their strengths. They accept their failings and learn to live with them. They do not long for the time when they will look better, be different, or have something they don't have now. They do the best with what they have at any given point in time. They don't worry about what other people think about them. They live for themselves and not to get the approval and praise of others. As they are accepting of themselves, they are also accepting and tolerant of others. They can see things from other people's perspectives and don't expect others to conform to their thinking and way of doing things.

Happy people live one day at a time. They realize that life is short and they want to make the best of each day. They don't worry about what happened yesterday or what might happen tomorrow.

They live in the present and get as much as they can from each day. They love spontaneity. They don't let anger, bitterness, and hurt from the past rule their lives.

Happy people have a sense of humor about life. They can laugh at things as a way to reduce their anxieties and stress. And they can laugh at themselves as a way of coping with their weaknesses and mistakes.

Happy people have achievements and accomplishments, but *they get as much satisfaction out of the process of achieving as they do from the final result.* They engage in activities that provide intrinsic satisfaction (personal growth and development). And while they have achievements and accomplishments, they leave room for other things in their lives like family, friends, and time to relax.

Happy people are not overly preoccupied with themselves and their happiness. They find other people, causes, and things to care about and focus their energies on them. Doing things for others and making others happy are great sources of fulfillment for them.

Happy people realize that they cannot be happy all of the time because they recognize that is an unrealistic and impossible goal. They do not focus their lives on avoiding pain, sorrow, and reality. Nor do they engage in activities to trick themselves into artificially feeling good (drugs, alcohol), thereby allowing themselves to escape from life's pain. They do not run from their problems or make excuses for them. Rather, they face problems and deal with them so that they can get on with their lives. When life deals them a blow, they are sad, they cry, they grieve, and they mourn. But it does not go on forever. When the time for grieving is over, they get on with life and make the best of it *as it is.* Happy people experience anger, fear, sorrow, and hardships like everyone else, but they don't let it become the focus of their lives or let it dominate them. They experience these negative emotions for a limited period of time and then they let them go.

Personal Growth

*E*xperiencing major change, particularly in the form of a crisis or trauma, often marks a turning point in a person's life. At these times, people are compelled to think about their lives and the direction it is taking. Dealing with the effects and aftermath of change helps people to clarify their priorities, and it can give them tremendous psychological insight into themselves and into the meaning of life. This is insight that would not have been gained had the change not occurred. The opportunity to reflect on life can be a positive outcome of experiencing change. By reinventing our thinking and reshaping and redirecting our lives in the aftermath of change, life can become much more meaningful in the years that follow.

While much of what is discovered and learned in the period following change is unique to the individual, there are many lessons about life that significant numbers of people discover as a result of their experiences and introspection. Some of these follow.

Live in the Present. Enjoy Life One Day at a Time

The need to live in the present and to enjoy life one day at a time is an important lesson. So many people (particularly overachievers and workaholics) live their lives focused on the future. In doing so, they feel they are creating and ensuring a happy, prosperous, and secure time for themselves in the years to come. But at the same time, they are also (unconsciously) ignoring life in the present.

Future-oriented people ignore life in the present because they feel it is irrelevant to what they perceive they are creating for themselves in the future. They don't live in the present because the present is only a stepping-stone to a future goal or objective. It is only a means to an end. Future-oriented people often achieve a great deal, but they do not really enjoy the process of achieving because they are so focused on attaining the end result.

Future-oriented people live for the future because they believe that it will be better than the present. They hope and believe that if they work hard enough at it, someday they will have all their problems resolved and things will be just right (or, at least, so much better) for them.

Unfortunately, as many people discover during times of change, life does not always work out according to one's vision or plans for the future. People who have worked for and focused their lives on the happy future they anticipated for themselves do so only to find out that the future will not be there for them in the way they envisioned it would be, because of a change. For example, a person may lose a spouse or child (who was an integral part of their future plans) or a person may become stricken with disease, losing his health and rendering him unable to work or complete his life in the manner he had planned. Or people can experience any one of a number of life-limiting adversities before the future they anticipated for themselves arrives.

For these people, the reality of what happened to their future as a result of change comes as a great shock. And learning to accept the change and implications of the change is a difficult and painful experience. The position that many future-oriented people find themselves in when faced with major change, personal crisis, or trauma is well described by Woolfolk and Richardson in their book *Stress, Sanity and Survival:*

> *Some simple truths about the human condition escaped these sincere hardworking individuals. They believed that through their efforts they could guarantee a successful and happy future. Therefore they aimed their lives toward the future, struggling and sacrificing to reach that better day we all dream of. They seemed to repress the knowledge that their plans could be smashed at any time by accident or misfortune. It seemed to them very likely that they could reach the future—that life would deal them no unexpected blows. They did not realize the extent of our human limitations. They did not acknowledge how precarious and uncertain life really is and how limited is our ability to anticipate and control future events. They failed to see clearly that they could not avoid the pain, the tragedy that, in some form, are inevitably part of every human life.*
>
> *The greatest tragedy of these lives, however, was that believing the future was under their control—they put off many kinds of satisfaction and joy in living until a later time that never arrived. They failed to savor life as it was lived, to smell the flowers as they walked along. They turned down opportunities to engage in many intrinsically satisfying and pleasurable activities because they were not instrumental in achieving future goals. They consequently did not develop their abilities, interpersonal relationships and personal philosophies so as to have enabled them to better understand the inevitable hardships of life. Instead, they concentrated on trying to achieve happiness in the future. Of course, the future never quite works out the way we think it will.*[5]

And so, a lesson is learned. We need to live in the present and we need to enjoy today and what we have today because we do not know what we will have tomorrow and what the future holds. Each day of our lives is precious. Once it has passed, we can never live it again. Thus we need to make the most of each day as it unfolds because the future is uncertain and likely to be different than the one we have in mind for ourselves.

People focused on achieving goals for the future forget to enjoy the present or the time they spend getting to their goals. But the process of getting to those goals is where most of our time in life is spent. So little of our time is actually spent in the final moments of realizing or completing our goals. They are but fleeting moments in a lifetime. If we don't make the time we spend getting there count or we don't enjoy it, we are dismissing huge chunks of time in our lives. That is why the process has to count as much as reaching the final goal.

Of course, all this does not mean that the future should be ignored or that we should not prepare for the future. That creates the opposite problem, which can be just as bad. People need to prepare for and save for the future but in a flexible way and with an appropriate amount of focus. The future should not be the sole focus of our lives nor the main target of our energies. There is a balance to be achieved and we can reach that balance by working for the future while enjoying the present.

Stop to Smell the Roses

People who have experienced major change or personal crisis often emerge from their experiences with a recognition of the need to stop and smell the roses along the path of life. They discover that one of the ways to experience the richness of living is to learn to enjoy the simple pleasures of daily life. People who adopt the philosophy of living one day at a time and living each day to its fullest recognize the importance of savoring life's simple pleasures every day. Experiencing these daily pleasures can contribute tremendously to a person's sense of happiness and well-being on a day-to-day basis. What are some of these simple pleasures?

Watching the morning sunrise, smelling freshly brewed coffee in the morning, enjoying a cup of tea while relaxing, watching the clouds in the sky take on different forms, listening to rain falling on the roof, walking along a deserted beach or coastline, growing plants and flowers in your own garden, going to pick strawberries in season, taking a ride through the countryside to look at the color of the leaves in the fall, eating and enjoying good food (a simple pleasure that can be had three times a day), eating dinner together with the family, observing holidays and individual family traditions and rituals (family reunions, summer picnics), celebrating birthdays, anniversaries, births, marriages, and other joyous occasions, watching your daughter take her first step, watching your son hit a home run in Little League, looking at old family photo albums, and generally appreciating the colors, smells, textures, and sounds that nature has bestowed on us—all these are simple pleasures.

We Are Vulnerable

Change has a way of revealing to us how vulnerable we are in life. Until our vulnerability is exposed through enduring a major change, we somehow feel that we are immune to misfortune or that we can escape it. Experiencing a major crisis often thrusts vulnerability to the forefront of our lives where we are forced to face it. When we experience an adversity, we suddenly realize "Yes, it can happen to me and it has." We can no longer deny or think that misfortune will pass us by. On the contrary, for a period of time directly in the aftermath, people often overreact by thinking another adversity is just ahead, just around the corner. Once a bad thing has happened to us, we know it can happen again at any time. When the illusion of invincibility has been shattered, we often change our views about things and almost always develop a more realistic view of life and ourselves.

Bill was a twenty-four-year-old graduate student. His best friend, Nick, was killed in a car accident. Nick had been intoxicated at the time and not only caused his own death but also killed two innocent people in a head-on collision. Bill was devastated by his friend's death, particularly when he knew it could have been prevented or avoided (by not drinking and driving). Nick was a lifelong friend and Bill could hardly bring himself to face Nick's parents and his sister at the funeral. He had known them all his life. They were such good people and now they had to deal with such a senseless tragedy. Bill was a witness to the grief, the pain and sorrow that Nick's death brought to his family and friends and he couldn't even begin to think about how it must have been for the families of the innocent victims. It took Bill a long time to get over Nick's death.

Bill's father had always told him (as had Nick's) not to drink and drive. But Bill just never believed that anything like this would happen to him or anyone he knew. Because alcohol was the cause of the tragedy, he vowed he would never touch it again.

Taking Things for Granted

Very much related to living in the present and recognizing vulnerability is a lesson concerning taking things for granted. When people live their lives on automatic pilot, when things are going along fairly well, they tend to take things in their lives for granted. We (unconsciously) make certain assumptions about people, things, and events in our lives. For example, we assume that our spouse and children will be with us as we age, that our parents will be around until they reach old age, that we will have our health and be able to earn a living, that we will be able to travel when we want to, that we will be able to maintain a certain standard of living, and so on.

When a major change comes along, especially one that involves loss, it becomes clear to us how fragile life really can be. It makes us realize that the things we have and the things that have been given to us can be taken away at any time, sometimes in an instant: money, possessions, job, relationships, people, and everyday commodities of life. As a result, many people experiencing loss learn that they can no longer take life, things, people, or relationships for granted. Thus, people grow to appreciate the things they have while they have them because they know that they can be gone in an instant.

Allan and Maria's house was badly damaged by a hurricane. For several months, they lived in a tent city constructed by a disaster relief agency of the government. Allan and Maria were distraught by the damage and losses the hurricane had caused in their lives. They were equally distressed by the way they had to live in the tent city in the months that followed the disaster. They had to eat mainly prepackaged food because refrigeration and cooking facilities were extremely limited. They had to eat off paper plates. When they were finally able to cook food, it was on a one-element hot plate that was shared with others. Bottled water was available for drinking. Water for any other purpose (such as washing dishes) was available from a communal tap some distance from the tent. They had to shower in makeshift public showers and they had to use communal toilet facilities. They slept in tents with temporary bedding provided by the relief agency. There was no heating or air conditioning. Most of their possessions had been lost or damaged in the hurricane so they had to make do with what little they had left or what they could buy. They had little privacy as many other families were living in similar conditions only yards away from them.

Allan and Maria managed to survive the ordeal and, after several months, were able to move back into their home where major repairs were almost complete. The day they were able to return to their home, Maria was ecstatic. She recalls some of her thoughts from that day: "I walked into the house realizing that we were finally going to be alone. We were going to have privacy and there would be no noisy neighbors, no cars, and no dogs waking us up at all hours of the night. I was so thrilled. Then I turned the light on and I remembered thinking, Wow! electricity. I can use the stove—all four burners. I can finally cook a decent meal in a reasonable amount of time. Then I opened the refrigerator and couldn't believe we were finally going to be able to have cold soda and crisp salad greens again. I turned on the tap and there it was, a continous source of safe water— all I wanted. I was so excited. Then I headed upstairs to the bathtub and decided to have a bath. I had dreamed about sitting in a nice hot bathtub for months. I could go on and on. I just can't express to you how happy I was to have all these things back in my life again. They were things I always took for granted. Now that I know what life can be like without them, I appreciate them so much more. Having lost so much and been through so much after the hurricane, simply having things back to normal brought me such happiness. Whoever would have thought that I would get excited about electricity and tap water. But after all we've been through, I look at life now with a different pair of eyes."

Life: This Is It

When faced with a major change, people will often review the impact it has on their lives. Many discover that until the change occurred and shook them up, they had taken many things for granted, including life itself. They knew there was an hourglass of life but they never paid any attention to it. With a major crisis or change, people often begin to look at the hourglass of life and see the grains of sand falling for the first time. They see that the time left is getting shorter and shorter and they realize, "Hey, this is it. This is my life. It is not a dress rehearsal or a practice run for anything. What am I getting out of it and what do I want to do for the future?"

Evaluating what they've done with their lives and thinking about how they want to live it in the future in light of the recent experience with change is a natural outcome. On reflection, priorities are reorganized and those deemed no longer valid or useful in life are eliminated. New plans, ideas, and philosophies replace the old. Life has more meaning and takes on a greater sense of purpose and focus.

Learning What Is Important in Life

Major change and personal crisis can give us great insight into the meaning of life. As such, they can help us to redefine our values, the purpose of our lives, and our future goals as individuals. In the process of pondering these things and in experiencing the change event, we often discover what is important to us in our lives, and it is frequently different from what we thought was important in the past.

While people discover the importance of many things in life during times of crisis, one of the most common findings is how meaningless life can seem when it has been built on material or external things. People who have focused their lives on careers, status, acquiring power, and accumulating wealth or possessions recognize how insignificant these are when, for example, they have to face the loss of a loved one or the possibility of death themselves.

No matter how high up the corporate ladder a person climbs, no matter how big or luxurious a person's home or car is, no matter how much political power a person has achieved, being struck with a personal adversity (such as getting cancer) can bring everything tumbling down in an instant. At such moments, people realize that none of these things mean anything or really matter because they are essentially alone in having to face their loss and experience their grief. The following story illustrates this point well. Jack, an executive with a Fortune 500 company, made the following comments after recovering from a serious heart attack.

"When I was in the hospital, struggling for life and on life support, my company couldn't do a thing for me. Neither could my fancy home or car. I would have traded them for my life in an instant if I could. What I wanted most was the support of my wife and kids and they were there for me day and night until I came through. Now I know I'm a lucky man, not only because I survived, but because I had my family there for me when I felt so alone and helpless. I could easily have lost their love and support working sixty and seventy hour weeks and neglecting them in the meantime. I've never been to any of my son's Little League baseball games and I barely made it to my daughter's graduation. But that's behind me now. I'm so glad I have my family and from now on, I'm going to be there for them.

While I was lying in the hospital recovering from my heart attack, I was thinking, Here I am with a heart attack and what is the company doing for me after all the years and time and effort I put in? They sent me a card and some flowers. Well, that was nice but what if I had died? They would have replaced me with someone else and life at the office would go on. Who would really care? I'd be just another former employee. I probably had this heart attack from the overwork and the stress of the job and where did it get me? Now I'm suffering, not the company. What am I killing myself for? Why am I doing this? When I'm dead and gone, I want to be remembered as a loving father and husband, not as the guy who got the company 200 new accounts. . . . I must have been blind all these years to not realize it. Why couldn't I see it before? My wife tried to tell me many times that I needed to spend more time with the family, but it was no use. I just didn't get it until now. Why did I have to have a heart attack to find out what was important in my life? And why did I have to be fifty-five years old before I found out?"

Psychological Rebirth

Sometimes a person has to deal with a change that is so great, so profound, or of such magnitide that it psychologically transforms them. In these cases, the change is so significant that it represents a turning point in a person's life or an intense psychological crisis that shakes the very foundation of his or her life.

In many of these circumstances, the experiences of change that trigger the transformation are precipitated by circumstances beyond a person's control. They also frequently involve some kind of loss: physical, personal, emotional, material, spiritual, or the destruction of something meaningful from a person's past. There is a great deal of emotional turmoil (and sometimes physical pain) associated with these kinds of changes. People feel at odds with themselves trying to understand or comprehend what has happened as well as why it has happened. The event challenges all their inner psychological work- ings as they experience intense emotional and psychological battles and struggles within themselves. People often describe this period of time as living hell.

In the midst of a profound experience of change, people are too emotionally wrought and too busy contending with the effects of the change and subsequent issues that must be dealt with to think about the significance of the event on their lives. But when it is over, there is time to reflect. At that point, while there is still the pain of accept- ing what happened, some answers or insights begin to emerge and evolve. A light begins to flicker in the distance. A person then begins to see things in an entirely new way.

When the pain finally lifts and they emerge from the depths of hell, it feels like heaven. In fact, simply returning to what was once a normal state of affairs feels wonderful. In the aftermath of such change, many people discover new meaning and happiness in their lives—not over the circumstances they have suffered through, but because of what they have learned about life and themselves in the process.

People find that once they have experienced tremendous loss and pain, they are able to experience the pleasure of being alive. The pain they have suffered sensitizes them to joy and happiness. A per- son who has never known the depths of pain and sadness can never fully experience the heights of joy and happiness. And so, as strange as it may seem, out of life's greatest pain can come some of life's most powerful lessons and messages.

With time, sometimes as long as two years, a person emerges from the change experience as a psychologically different person because he knows that from what he has experienced and learned, his life can never again be the same. He has undergone a revolution in his consciousness. He has experienced a psychological rebirth.

The period of rebirth is characterized by the rebuilding, reconstructing, and regeneration of one's life on a new and more meaningful level. There is a greater and different understanding of the meaning of life that affects a person's entire being. With time, people find ways and means to integrate their new selves back into society and begin to live life in a new and more meaningful way.

It is not unusual for people experiencing this psychological death and rebirth to feel isolated from the world and alone for a period of time. That is because while they are experiencing something truly profound, those around them are not. Their coworkers, friends, and even family members can be very sympathetic, but they cannot truly understand what is happening inside of them. Other people can't understand simply because they have not had the same experience or have not been affected in the same way as that of the individual himself. As it becomes obvious to the individual that others can't relate to his new feelings about things, he becomes reluctant to discuss them with others.

Thus, we conclude this chapter on shattered illusions, mistaken beliefs, and personal growth. The purpose of reviewing the issues addressed in this chapter was to make the reader aware of some of the things that can happen to people psychologically when they encounter major change in their lives and to provide some explanation as to why they occur. Unfortunately, space does not allow for the provision of a more in-depth discussion on each of the topics addressed in this chapter. Fortunately, there are many books, articles, and other resources written on these individual topics (self-esteem, happiness) that provide much more depth and detail for interested readers to explore further on their own.

chapter six

Stress and Change

Coping with change is a major cause of stress. It is not surprising that the rise in stress in our society coincides with the accelerated rate of change in modern times. Since change requires adjustment and reorganization of some area of one's life, it inevitably leads to some stress, as do the uncertainty, unpredictability, anxiety, loss of control, and other feelings associated with situations of change. Today, change has become a major source of stress in people's lives.

In times of significant change, people usually experience the most stress. Therefore, it is important for people experiencing change, particularly personal change, to recognize that there is a relationship between change and stress. There is a need to understand this relationship as well as a need to understand the nature of stress, how stress affects the human mind and body, and how stress can be dealt with to keep the negative effects to a minimum. In this chapter, we examine these areas.

What Is Stress?

*T*he study of stress as a phenomenon is relatively new. It has only been studied objectively by scientists for the last fifty years or so. During that time, researchers have made significant progress in understanding stress and how it affects the human mind and body.

Stress is a reaction that occurs when people perceive that they are in danger or are being threatened in some way. The perception of a threat activates a series of physical and emotional changes within the body. People experience these feelings and physical changes as stress. How does stress occur? The explanation begins with an examination of the effects of evolution in the distant past.

In the days of the caveman and primitive life, human beings needed to respond immediately and automatically to a threat when they faced any danger. This was needed for them to protect themselves from the dangers of their environment and to be able to survive as a species. Through the process of evolution, the human body was equipped with the mechanisms necessary to keep it alert to danger through a system called the autonomic nervous system. As a caveman perceived a threat in his environment (e.g., a dangerous animal approaching), his body, sensing the danger, reacted immediately and automatically to the threat by activating the nervous system, which in turn prepared his body to respond to the danger. The caveman responded in one of two ways. He decided either to attack and fight the predator (fight) or run away from the danger or predator (flight). This phenomenon is known as the fight-or-flight response. When the autonomic nervous system was activated to prepare the caveman for the fight-or-flight response, a series of predictable physical changes occurred within his body to prepare him for the action he would face (running away or fighting) in dealing with the danger.

When the brain perceives a danger signal (or stressor), it activates hormones that begin circulating within the body. These hormones send messages to various parts of the body, instructing them to prepare for action (to fight or flee). Some examples of the physical changes that take place follow. Breathing becomes more rapid and hands and feet perspire. Blood pressure is elevated and the heart rate increases. Muscles become tense and there is less saliva in the mouth.

Hydrochloric acid is released in the stomach and there are changes in the nervous system and brain wave patterns. In addition to these physical changes in the body, emotions such as fear, anxiety, and anger are also aroused.

In today's world, the fight-or-flight reaction is still necessary to protect us from physical harm. For example, in attempting to cross the street, the sound of a horn honking alerts us to the danger of an oncoming car and we react instantly to remove ourselves from the danger. The response of the body to a perceived danger or threat is automatic. Modern man is equipped with the same mechanism to alert him to danger and protect him from harm today as the caveman was in prehistoric times. But while the threat of physical harm to people has been substantially reduced today because we no longer live in the wild and fear threats from animals and so on, the built-in protective automatic response mechanism to alert us to danger remains.

Interestingly, when scientists began studying the phenomenon of stress, they discovered that physical threats or dangers were not the only type of threat that the human body responds to. They found that when a person perceives a nonphysical threat, the body becomes aroused and goes into the fight-or-flight mode in the same way it would if the threat or danger perceived was physical. Thus, scientists concluded that a threat perceived by the body did not need to be a physical one to activate the autonomic nervous system. It could be intellectual, social, emotional, or behavioral in nature. The source or kind of threat or danger perceived by a person made no difference because the body reacts to the threat in the same way.

For example, Melanie is driving to the airport and gets stuck in traffic. She looks at her watch continually and eventually realizes that her flight will leave in twenty minutes. It appears likely that she will not be able to reach the airport on time to make her flight. While Melanie is not physically threatened, the fight-or-flight response kicks in because she perceives that she is in trouble. She feels stress because she knows she will likely miss her plane, which means she will miss an important out-of-town meeting which in turn will put her at a disadvantage, upset her boss, threaten her job in the future, and so on. While her perception of the threat is not a physical one and does not require Melanie to fight or flee, she is nonetheless experiencing the same range of physical and emotional changes the caveman did when facing a physical threat long ago. *Regardless of the source or nature of the threat or stressor, when a person perceives a situation as threatening, the human body is aroused and reacts to the stressor in the same way.*

Stress Begins in the Mind

As a result of the discovery that the body will react in the same way regardless of the kind of stressor, researchers discovered something important about the nature of stress. They found that *stress begins in the mind* because a situation must be *perceived as stressful* before the autonomic nervous system is aroused, triggering the subsequent series of physical bodily changes that accompany the fight-or-flight response. The body does not react to a situation until the *perception* of a threat is there. And that perception, whether based on physical, emotional, intellectual, or social discomfort or on unpleasantness begins in the mind.

Since it is the perception of an event and not the event itself that arouses the autonomic nervous system (or creates stress), stress is related to *how we perceive and interpret circumstances or events* in our own individual minds. Because different people perceive things in different ways, *stress is unique to the individual.* For example, Marcia and Robin are told by their boss that each of them will have to drive to a nearby big city one day a week as part of their new job responsibilities. Marcia hates driving and gets very nervous driving in big cities. She immediately begins to feel stress just anticipating having to make the drive. On every day that she does make the drive, she doesn't sleep well the night before. Upon awakening, she can't eat much for breakfast and she is very anxious and nervous from the time she leaves her garage to the time she arrives at her destination.

Robin, on the other hand, loves to drive and thinks driving to a big city is exciting and challenging. She looks forward to the drive and to escaping the office routine once a week. She doesn't lose any sleep the night before and doesn't experience any nervousness at all in relation to the trip. Robin does not experience stress because she does not perceive any discomfort or threat in this situation. Marcia is experiencing a great deal of stress because she does.

While everyone experiences stress, each person experiences it under different circumstances and in different ways. People who continually perceive threatening circumstances or discomfort around them on an ongoing basis experience a lot of stress whereas people who don't often perceive threatening circumstances experience little stress. An individual's perception of things, events, and circumstances, therefore, has a great deal to do with the amount of stress he or she will experience.

Stress Can Be Controlled

If stress is created by a person's perception and interpretation of a situation or event, then people can learn to control stress by *changing how they perceive and interpret events and circumstances. Perception is a learned behavior.* People can learn to cope with stress by learning how to recognize and change inappropriate thought processes and by learning how to perceive potentially stressful situations as non-threatening. For those who have difficulty recognizing and understanding how the way they think about and perceive things causes them stress, psychologists, social workers, and other trained counselors can help to identify negative or inappropriate thought processes that may be causing stress.

Why should people experiencing change (or anyone else for that matter) be concerned with stress and its effects? The answer is because stress is not only unpleasant, it is dangerous. And because it is dangerous, people have to protect themselves against the ill effects of stress. Before one can do that, one needs to become aware of how it causes harm.

Stress Leads to Illness

In study after study, stress has been increasingly linked with illness and disease. Researchers now report that as much as 75 to 80 percent of all illness today can be traced back to the ill effects of stress. How does stress cause illness?

As we discussed previously, whenever a danger or threat of some sort is perceived by a person, the fight-or-flight response is automatically triggered. This sets into motion a complex series of physical changes in body chemistry to prepare the body to react to the perceived danger. Again, these changes in chemistry take place whether the threat perceived is physical, emotional, or otherwise.

Upon perception of a threat, the brain sends messages throughout the body that prepare it for fight-or-flight. Over thirty different hormones set into motion various changes in the body. Some of these include increased muscle tension and contractions, elevated blood pressure, decrease in saliva, increased heart rate, increased sodium retention, increased air supply, increased perspiration, change in respiratory rate, the shutdown of the digestive tract, increased secretions of hydrochloric acid and serum cholesterol, thickening of blood, and alterations in brain waves.

In the days of primitive man, each of these changes served a specific and useful function. For example, increased perspiration made it more difficult for a predator to grab and hold on to the caveman because it made the body slippery, thus allowing him a better chance of escape. Perspiration also cooled the body to stop it from overheating. Pupils became dilated, providing better peripheral vision and better vision in a dark (night) environment. The digestive tract shut down so that blood could be diverted to muscles, lungs, and the heart for added strength. When these body functions are altered for only brief periods of time to prepare the body to deal with a threat as intended by nature, they serve a purpose and the body returns to its normal state shortly afterward. If, however, the changes in body chemistry and function remain in an altered state for long periods of time (which they do when a person is experiencing stress), they no longer serve their intended purpose. Rather, the chemicals and by-products begin to weaken or damage the body, causing disease. By nature, the human body was not meant to be sustained in this chemically altered state for long periods of time. The longer the body remains chemically altered as a result of experiencing stress, the more opportunity there is for damage to be (inadvertently) done. That is why stress is dangerous. It maintains the body in an unnatural physically and chemically altered state for periods of time much longer than intended by nature, thereby causing the body to be weakened or damaged as a result. Chronic stress inevitably leads to illness and disease. People in a chronic state of stress are usually people with poor health. And many people who are under stress for long periods of time often develop a state of health where they are neither really sick nor well but somewhere in between.

An example of how stress can cause or contribute to an illness such as heart disease can be illustrated by examining ways that stress brings about changes in the cardiovascular system. Stress causes an elevation in heart rate, an increase in blood pressure and volume, increases in serum cholesterol, and an increase in fluid retention. These make the heart work harder to function and cause a decrease in oxygen supply to the heart. All these are recognized risk factors in the development of coronary disease. Add these to other known factors that may already exist in an individual (high-fat diet, lack of exercise, smoking) and the results could prove dangerous, even fatal.

Examples of other illnesses or diseases that can be caused by stress or linked to it include hypertension, stroke, migraine headaches, tension headaches, allergies, asthma, acute dermatitis, colitis, diabetes, backaches, TMJ syndrome, rheumatoid arthritis, and even cancer. Recent research also suggests that long-term exposure to stress can cause permanent memory impairment when the brain's memory center is damaged from being exposed to too much stress.

Stress also adversely affects the immune system. People under stress have an abundance of hormones in their bloodstream for prolonged periods of time. This excess of hormones impairs the body's ability to function normally by weakening the immune system. People with weakened immune systems are more suseptible to catching diseases and becoming ill (colds, flu). When exposed to infectious agents, they are also more likely to be sick for longer periods of time and have more severe bouts of illness than those with healthy immune systems. When stress increases, immunity decreases. When people learn to control stress, they are in effect learning to keep disease at bay. New fields of science, called neuroimmunology and psychoneuroimmunology, have been developed to study the effects of stress on the immune system. The focus of researchers in these fields is to examine the chemical basis of communication between the mind and the nervous, endocrine, and immune systems.

Disease that results from stress (or other mental distress) and the physical alterations it makes within the body is called psychosomatic disease. Contrary to popular belief, the term "psychosomatic" does not mean that an illness is all in your head. It is physical disease (e.g., colitis) that has resulted from mental distress (stress). Psychosomatic disease is not imaginary. It is real disease. It can be diagnosed by its physical symptoms. Another term now being used to replace the term "psychosomatic" is the term "psychophysiological" disease, meaning disease that results from the effects of psychological processes on the physical body.

Stress Often Precedes Illness

People experiencing change, particularly major change, must be acutely aware of the relationship between stress and illness. Exposure to a number of stressful changes within a limited amount of time increases susceptibility to physical illness. Physical illness often follows periods of stressful life changes because they require continuous coping and adaptation and, as a result, tend to precipitate stress. This is true for both positive changes (marriage) and negative ones (job loss) because both types of change require tremendous adjustment.

Maintaining good health is essential to maintaining a happy and productive life. In fact, good health can be a person's greatest asset. Without health, a person can be limited, perhaps severely limited, in what he can do. Poor health can lead to job loss, financial loss, loss of ability to raise a family, inability to travel, chronic pain, limited social life, and limited freedom and physical movement.

Two well-known researchers who have documented that stressful life experiences can bring about disease are Doctors Holmes and Rahe of the University of Washington Medical School. They devised an inventory (social readjustment rating scale)[1] of forty-three life change events that have been a proved predictor of the onset of physical illness. (See Figure 6.1.) Many follow-up studies by numerous other researchers have demonstrated over and over again the validity of this scale in its ability to predict the onset of disease or disability.

In order to use this scale, determine which of the events listed you have experienced within the previous year and note the number of points assigned to the events. Then add all the points together to obtain a total score of life change units (LCUs). This score represents a measurement of significant change you have experienced and to

Rank	Life Event	LCU Value
1.	Death of Spouse	100
2.	Divorce	73
3.	Marital Separation	65
4.	Jail Term	63
5.	Death of close family member	63
6.	Personal injury or illness	53
7.	Marriage	50
8.	Fired from job	47
9.	Marital reconciliation	45
10.	Retirement	45
11.	Change in health of family member	44
12.	Pregnancy	40
13.	Sex difficulties	39
14.	Gain of new family member	39
15.	Business readjustment	39
16.	Change in financial state	38
17.	Death of close friend	37
18.	Change to different line of work	36
19.	Change in number of arguments with spouse	36
20.	Large mortgage	31
21.	Foreclosure of mortgage or loan	30
22.	Change in responsibilities at work	29
23.	Son or daughter leaving home	29
24.	Trouble with in-laws	29
25.	Outstanding personal achievement	28
26.	Wife begins or stops work	26
27.	Begin or end school	26
28.	Change in living conditions	25
29.	Revision of personal habits	24
30.	Trouble with boss	23
31.	Change in work hours or conditions	20
32.	Change in residence	20
33.	Change in schools	20
34.	Change in recreation	19
35.	Change in church activities	19
36.	Change in social activities	18
37.	Small mortgage or loan	17
38.	Change in sleeping habits	16
39.	Change in number of family get-togethers	15
40.	Change in eating habits	15
41.	Vacation	13
42.	Christmas	12
43.	Minor violations of the law	11

Source: Social Readjustment Rating Scale, reprinted from *Journal of Psychosomatic Research*, 11, 213–218, 1967. Copyright 1967, Pergamon Press, Inc. Modified slightly to reflect the current economy. Reprinted with permission from Elsevier Science.

Figure 6.1. Social Readjustment Rating Scale.

which you had to adjust during the previous twelve months. If your total score is 150–199, you have a 37 percent chance of developing illness or disease in the following year or two. A score of 200–299 gives a 51 percent chance, and a score of over 300 a 79 percent chance.

Two observations have been noted with regard to this scale. First, people who learn to successfully manage stress are not as susceptible to the ill effects of stress as determined by this scale. Second, the desirability of the change (whether positive or negative) affects the outcome.

Stress Leads to Other Problems

Stress can not only lead to poor health and all the subsequent adversities associated with it, but stress also leads to decreased productivity and increased absenteeism in the workplace. It can lead to strife and tension in the home, contributing to instability, marital breakdown, and child and spouse abuse. Stress can lead to alcohol and substance abuse and all the negative consequences they can generate in the home, family, and workplace. People are also more prone to having accidents during times of stress. The list of negative effects people can suffer from stress is lengthy. Stress costs billions of dollars annually in terms of health care, lost productivity, and personal unhappiness.

The Effects of Stress Can Be Cumulative

The negative results of stress (illness, marital breakdown) do not stem only from experiencing major life events. Researchers have also found that stress caused by the hassles of everyday living can build up over time and eventually have the same negative effects on a person as a major stressful event. Thus, the physical and mental effects of stress can be cumulative over time. Many people who live with constant stress or those who have stressful jobs and are keeping just one step ahead of things might survive the effects of stress without serious negative effects for a long period of time. But as soon as an already stressful life is confronted with a serious crisis or multiple major problems, the mind or body reaches the limit of what it can handle or tolerate. Serious illness or chronic illness (physical or mental) can set in and people can feel as if their entire lives are falling apart. It may then take years to recover. So while some people with high stress lives and careers often feel that they can avoid or get away with experiencing the negative effects of stress forever, at some point it usually catches up.

Controlling Stress Is Essential

Stress is part of life and it cannot be avoided. How people handle stress affects their health, happiness, and future years. The relationship between change, stress, and illness is such that it must be taken very seriously. The key to surviving stress is to be able to control it. The ability to control stress is essential to maintaining good mental and physical health, particularly during periods of great change. People who learn stress management skills can reduce or minimize the negative effects of stress by learning to recognize their stressors and their onset. When they are faced with stress, they make an effort to intervene and stop the stress process from escalating. As a result, the body returns to its normal state shortly afterward. People who do not know how to manage stress remain in a state of stress for much longer periods. It takes a much longer time for their bodies to return to their natural biochemical state. As a result, they are likely to experience more of the ill effects of stress. People who ignore stress and never learn to deal with it find themselves caught in a vicious cycle from which there is no escape.

Several factors influence a person's ability to cope with stress. They include a person's philosophy of life (whether negative or positive in orientation), a person's level of self-confidence, the level of personal control a person feels she has over situations, a person's understanding of how stress affects the body and how it causes physical disease and disability, the amount of social support a person has in her life, and a person's willingness to work hard at learning a range of stress-management skills.

As a result of a great deal of research done over the last few decades, there are many methods that have been identified and devised to help people deal with stress. A growing number of experts and researchers in the field of mental health and stress management recommend that people learn to cope with stress using a variety of methods that can be used in different kinds of stressful situations.

It should be noted that not all stress is bad. People have to experience some stress in order to keep motivated to do things; otherwise life would be dull. Without any stress, people would sit around all day and not do much of anything. Some stress serves a useful purpose. The stress discussed in this chapter, however, is excess stress: stress that is not necessary and that serves no useful purpose.

Stress Management

Managing stress means changing one's lifestyle and habits. There are three general ways to effectively manage stress. The first is developing a preventive approach to stress through lifestyle management. That means structuring one's environment and altering routines and habits in a manner that would prevent stress from occurring to the greatest degree possible. The second approach involves learning relaxation techniques that can be used to relax and destress the mind and body. The third method involves learning to view and perceive circumstances and life events in a nonstressful way. These ways to effectively manage stress are briefly reviewed and discussed next.

Lifestyle Management

Lifestyle management focuses on keeping stress at bay by managing one's daily lifestyle (things over which one has control) in a manner that minimizes the potential stresses of daily life.

Diet

Eating a well-balanced diet every day is necessary for good health, but it can also help to lessen the effects of stress by buffering the body against its adverse effects. Stress negatively affects nutritional chemistry in the body. Under stress, the body uses up nutrients faster and less efficiently than it normally would. Prolonged periods of stress or chronic stress results in mineral loss and depletes the body of vitamins, especially vitamins B and C. When the body is under stress, calcium absorption is reduced (an important note for women, especially those prone to osteoporosis). Too much salt can result in a rise in blood pressure (an adverse effect for a person who already has high blood pressure and is under stress). Some foods contain substances that can actually induce a stresslike response in the body. These include caffeine-laden foods such as coffee, tea, colas, and chocolate. Nicotine found in cigarettes has a similar effect. A bad diet and eating poorly does not cause stress, but it can certainly aggravate the problem and therefore is a factor to consider in the management of stress.

A well-balanced diet includes a variety of foods from six different groups to be consumed on a daily basis, as recommended in the food pyramid developed by the U.S. Department of Agriculture. It includes 6–11 servings of grain products (bread, cereal, rice, pasta), 3–5 servings of vegetables, 2–4 servings of fruit, 2–3 servings of milk products (cheese, yogurt), 2–3 servings of meat and alternatives (dry beans, eggs, nuts). Fats, oils, and sweets are to be eaten sparingly. A healthy diet consists of an appropriate balance of protein, carbohydrates, vitamins and minerals, fats, fiber, and water. The body needs fuel to keep in good physical shape.

As well as eating nutritious food, some consideration needs to be given to the manner in which foods are eaten. Adapting sensible eating patterns such as chewing food thoroughly, eating slowly, eating in a relaxed mode, and sitting to eat are examples.

Exercise

People need regular exercise not only for good general health but also to reduce stress. Like good nutrition, physical fitness does not prevent stress. However, a strong physical body can be a significant buffer in reducing the negative effects of stress. People tolerate stress better when they exercise regularly.

The beneficial physical effects of exercise on general health are numerous (e.g., exercise improves the functioning of lungs and the circulatory system and decreases serum cholesterol). Physical fitness and exercise can be beneficial in alleviating stressful feelings (frustration, anger) and in burning up harmful stress by-products in the body. Exercise can also reduce muscle tension that often accompanies stress. Another benefit of exercise is that it allows a person to redirect his thoughts away from problems and stressful situations while exercising. Endorphins, chemical substances resembling morphine, are released by the body during exercise. These endorphins cause a decrease in feelings of depression and anxiety. They can reduce feelings of pain and produce feelings of well-being. Regular exercise, thus, is needed not only for good health but also to reduce stress.

Sleep

Having enough sleep and sleeping well does a great deal to improve the body's resistance to stress. Well-rested people are better able to cope with stress because the body goes into a stress-relieving state when people sleep. In fact, sleep takes the body away from the fight-or-flight response and allows the body to rejuvenate. For example, during sleep, the overall pace of body processes slow down (heart rate and blood pressure go down). People need more sleep than they normally would during periods of stress. To be of benefit, the sleep needs to be restful and sufficient to be of benefit. Adhering to a regular sleep schedule, forgetting about solving problems once in bed, and keeping extra office work out of the bedroom can all do much to improve the quality of sleep.

Rest and Relaxation

Taking regularly scheduled breaks from work and having periods of relaxation are therapeutic to people experiencing stress. When people under stress are able to take a break from their work and problems, they can often come back to them relaxed, rested, and rejuvenated and can cope better with the problems and stress as a result.

In work situations, taking a five-minute stretch break or taking time for a refreshment or snack can serve this function. By doing something different for a few minutes, the mind can rest and stamina is restored.

Getting some relaxation by doing something different during nonwork hours is also beneficial. Getting away for a weekend, taking a drive in the country, going hiking for a day, or going for a long walk in the park can be helpful. Taking traditional vacations can also relieve the effects of stress on everyday life, provided the vacation time is not overly scheduled with too many activities. After a vacation, people return rested and relaxed and better able to cope with problems.

Hobbies also provide outlets for relaxation. With the mind focused on the activities involved in hobbies, it cannot be focusing on problems and worries.

Many people with workaholic personalities feel that taking a rest or break is a waste of time. They think of all the things they can do if they work straight through the day, if they do not take a vacation, or if they take a short one. Rests are not a waste of time. They are needed by the mind and body to rejuvenate themselves and they help to reduce stress that often accompanies the lives of workaholic people. The ability to relax is an integral part of overall health and stress management. Contrary to what some people believe, learning to relax does not make people unproductive, less successful, lazy, or bored. Rather, it contributes to good overall health.

And finally, people need to pamper themselves, within their means, on a frequent basis (daily or weekly). Looking forward to something special each day or week makes it easier to get through because one knows a reward is coming in the near future. A hot bath at the end of the day, being able to read for twenty or thirty minutes after the kids are in bed, or going out for a relaxing dinner without the children once a week can be beneficial.

Getting Organized

Being organized is an important part of stress management. Disorganization contributes significantly to the creation of many day-to-day stresses and, with some effort, it can easily be corrected. People who are disorganized in any area of their lives cannot operate efficiently in that area and become vulnerable to the effects of stress as a result. A disorganized person is a person not in control. A person not in control can never really feel on top of things and therefore can never really relax. They are constantly on alert (for what they forgot, what they were supposed to do, where they are supposed to be). They often feel frustrated and have a sense of impending disaster.

Organization in all areas of one's life is important. Being organized means structuring one's environment so that it is as problem free as possible. That means being organized on the job, at home, with finances, with social life, and in any other applicable area. By organizing the environment, a person is in control of things in that environment and therefore in a position to better prevent the occurrence of feelings of frustration that lead to stress.

Planning is the key to being well organized. For every ten to fifteen minutes that are used to plan, people can save an hour's worth of work. A few minutes taken every night to plan what needs to be done the next day can save much time and effort and prevent much unnecessary stress. Thinking out what needs to be done and writing a to-do list can be helpful in accomplishing this task. Things to ponder and questions to ask might include, What do I need to bring to work tomorrow? What will I wear? What will the children wear? What will they have in their lunch boxes? What will I make for dinner? Who will take Joey to the dentist at 3:00 PM? and so on. When things are planned and people are informed of their responsibilities and lists of things to be done are available, things run much more smoothly. When there is no planning, the environment can be chaotic with everyone running around looking for (and asking for) things. For example, Where's my lunch? There's no more cereal. Who has the hair dryer?

In addition to planning things to be done, organizing one's working environment is important. Keeping the desk and files organized so that you know where everything is means that materials can be located at a moment's notice. Keeping an appointment book so that you know what has to be done (and with whom) is an excellent everyday organizational tool. At home, things should be equally organized so that everything has its place. That way, people know where things are and are not constantly looking for things they need at the last minute when they are under pressure to leave.

Making and keeping ongoing lists is another method of keeping organized. Making lists saves enormous amounts of time and frustration. With a list, when the time comes to do something, it is simply a matter of getting out the list and following through on what needs to be done. With no list, people try to think of things under pressure and this leads to frustration, stress, and a poor outcome because things are frequently forgotten, omitted, or not done before time runs out.

Lists to make are those that contain tasks and chores that need to be done or things that need to be bought, such as a grocery list posted where everyone in the home can have access to it. When an individual uses something up, the item is added to the list for that week. Other lists include shopping lists for various other items (department store, clothing, or hardware store items), lists of chores to be done, lists of what to bring to a picnic, what will be needed for a child's birthday party, what needs to be brought to the tax accountant, and so on. When planning a vacation, make a list of what needs to be packed. People who travel frequently can make lists of the standard things they need on each trip. Then, rather than thinking through what is needed for every trip, a person need only refer to the list and make minor adjustments (such as seasonal items) as needed.

While planning and organizing are important factors in the reduction of stress, things do not always go according to plan. Flexibility is needed from time to time to accommodate unforeseen and unavoidable circumstances.

Time Management

While organizing things in one's life and environment is important, it is equally important to budget and organize one's time. There are only so many hours in a day and the number of things one wants to do has to fit within these hours. When people plan ahead and have a time frame in mind to do a particular task, the day runs much more smoothly and everything is likely to get done. For example, if a person wants to go grocery shopping and get the laundry done in the same afternoon, he has to allot time accordingly. Making realistic time estimates and allowing some time for unexpected delays (stores are usually busier on Saturdays than weekdays) is necessary.

Other Lifestyle Stress Management Tips

Overcommitting oneself to doing more things than can possibly be done within a limited period of time is a significant cause of stress. People who overcommit themselves need to learn to say no to others making excessive demands on their time. Overcommitment sets people up for stress as they struggle to meet their extra commitments in addition to their regular responsibilities. It also causes worry in that people tend to constantly think about whether or not they will be able to meet an extra commitment and whether others will be disappointed or upset with them if they don't. There is only so much that can be done in a day and when people commit themselves to doing more than can be reasonably expected, they are cheating themselves and their families of valuable time and causing themselves additional stress.

Keeping a sense of humor about oneself and life in general is a good stress management technique. Laughter and humor can be powerful antidotes to stress. They can diffuse stress and any potentially explosive emotional situations.

When a person begins to feel overwhelmed with things as one could in situations of change and stress, one needs to take things in a step-by-step manner, breaking down tasks or situations into small, manageable parts. This makes the task easier to cope with as opposed to trying to manage everything at once.

In times of stress, social supports can be valuable. Simply talking out stressful situations with family and close friends can release a significant amount of stress and thus be quite beneficial.

Proper training for a job or other area of endeavor is also necessary to control stress because, with proper training, people feel competent. Not enough training or a lack of skills in an area where one is expected to perform keeps people stressed and on edge. They don't know if they are doing the right thing and are constantly worrying about it or fearing reprimands from their superiors. When a person has the proper skills to perform a task, she is more confident of the situation and is likely to feel less stressed as a result.

There are many books available that address each of these areas of lifestyle management in much greater depth. There are also seminars as well as counselors (dieticians, time management consultants) who can be consulted for information on how to make improvements in any of these areas.

Relaxation Techniques

There are several forms of relaxation techniques that have been proved successful in the management of stress. A brief summary of the more common ones follows. The summaries are given simply to provide an awareness of the types and methods of relaxation available. There are many books on the market that explain and explore these techniques in more depth, and they should be consulted for further information and guidance.

Meditation

Meditation is a relaxation technique traditionally linked to the Buddhist religion and Eastern cultures. Meditation is a mental exercise that people do to gain control over their thoughts. They accomplish this by continually focusing their attention on an object, sound, or body process (breathing). In the process, they block out all negative and stressful thoughts. Meditation has both physiological and psychological benefits. The mind is used to relax the body.

Today, meditation is used successfully as a stress management technique by people in many Western countries. More than one million people in the United States have had training in meditation techniques. While transcendental meditation is the most popular form of meditation in the West, it is only one of many.

Autogenic Training/Relaxation

Autogenic (self-generating) training is a form of self-hypnosis in which exercise that focuses on bodily sensations of heaviness and warmth are used to relax the body. A series of (self) instructions is given to the body telling it to relax. Autogenic training was developed earlier this century and has been used successfully in helping people with chronic illness better cope with their pain. Today, it is the most popular relaxation method in Europe.

Progressive Relaxation

Progressive relaxation is a technique used to produce relaxation of muscles and nerves in the body. Because there is a link between tense muscles and tense emotions, the more relaxed the muscles, the more relaxed the mind. This relaxation technique is sometimes referred to as Jacobsonian relaxation because it was developed by Edmund Jacobson, a physician. He originally used the method with hospital patients who exhibited features of muscle tenseness while lying in their beds. Progressive relaxation consists of a series of exercises in which muscles are contracted and then relaxed. This is done with various muscle groups throughout the body where tension resides. Progressive relaxation is particularly beneficial for people who experience a great deal of muscle tension or "bracing."

Biofeedback

Biofeedback is the process of using scientific instruments to measure or monitor a person's bodily functions such as heart rate, breathing rate, muscular tension, or moisture produced on the skin. Measurements of these functions are taken and the results are provided to the person who then uses the information to learn to exercise greater control over his or her bodily processes. For example, if a person's rate of breathing or heart rate is high, by concentrating and focusing on it, he can learn to bring the rate down. Biofeedback is used to train people to exercise greater control over their bodily processes, thereby producing relaxation.

The equipment needed for biofeedback is often expensive and not always readily available so this method is not used as widely as other techniques on a daily basis. However, people can access biofeedback equipment through clinics, hospital settings, and in universities.

Generally, all of the relaxation techniques outlined here have both physical and psychological benefits. Some of the physical benefits generated are: a decrease in muscle tension, decrease in serum cholesterol, a slowdown in respiration rate, slowdown in heart rate, increased blood flow to the arms and legs, and increase in alpha brain waves (a sign of mental relaxation).

Some of the psychological benefits are reduction in emotional arousal, feelings of inner calm, lessening of anxiety and depression, decrease in fatigue, increased resistance to stress, greater self-actualization, improvement in sleep behavior, and reduced fear and phobias. Because the body is in a state of both physical and mental relaxation, it is in a state that is opposite to the fight-or-flight response.

Relaxation techniques also help to reduce the negative effects of various illnesses such as headaches, hypertension, insomnia, indigestion, ulcers, lower back pain, hemorrhoids, and diabetes. The result of using a relaxation technique on a regular basis is a decrease in the amount of stress one experiences.

Changing the Way You Perceive Potentially Stressful Situations

Stress results from the perception of events and not the events themselves. People who can learn to perceive potentially stressful events differently can reduce or eliminate stress in their lives. Although people do not have control over many life events that affect them, they do have control over how they feel about them. Because people have control over their thoughts, they have control over how they perceive things. As a result, people have a greater degree of control over stress than they might otherwise believe. Whereas stress generated by unexpected and inescapable life events is unavoidable, most stress is within a person's control. People who are unable to stop stress in their lives are unable to stop thinking thoughts that provoke stress. For those experiencing a great deal of change, the negative thoughts often center on the fears and uncertainty regarding the change taking place.

Stress sometimes results from perceptions of physical harm, but most of the stress we deal with today results from perceptions of emotional harm. Examples include fear of failure, having to deal with a threat to one's ego or self-esteem, or having others wrongfully interfering in one's life. The mere perception or anticipation of unpleasantness or discomfort can arouse the autonomic nervous system and result in emotions such as anger, fear, insecurity, anxiety, worry, despair, apprehension, helplessness, frustration, feeling rushed, and feeling overwhelmed. These emotions in turn create physiological arousal such as an increase in heart or respiratory rate, muscle tension, and an increase in serum cholesterol.

One of the most effective ways to manage stress is to use one's thinking processes to intervene early (when stress first takes hold) in order to stop the stress response from occurring or progressing any further. The physiological changes that occur in the body upon the perception of a threat can be stopped by arresting emotional arousal. The emotional arousal can be stopped by changing one's perception of a situation or event, by not perceiving it as stressful. If a person can recognize and stop the negative or inappropriate thought processes that first come to mind when a stressful event is perceived, a person can stop the stress response from progressing. In the book *Stress, Sanity and Survival,* Woolfolk and Richardson summarize:

> *Perceiving events as threatening to our egos or thwarting of our efforts leads to harmful emotional arousal. This is the problem of stress—not outside situations or other persons, but our ideas about them and what they mean to us. Most of the ideas that produce stress can be boiled down to a few key mistaken beliefs about ourselves and the world. These beliefs are emotionally charged and highly evaluative. They lead us to make cruel and impossible demands upon ourselves and others. They are the root cause of the hurry, frustration, and growing sense of hopelessness that often characterize overstressed lives.[2]*

Changing the way one perceives situations or events means looking at them in a realistic and rational manner without catastrophizing them, blowing their significance out of proportion, or having "what if" thoughts. Few events that affect an individual in daily life are catastrophic or terrible, but people continually project this kind of thinking into their perceptions of everyday events, thereby causing themselves a great deal of unnecessary stress. Consider the perceptions of the following two people who are experiencing the same potentially stressful event:

Brad and John both have appointments with their respective attorneys, located in offices in the downtown section of a large city. Both Brad and John leave home in the suburbs in plenty of time to arrive at the attorney's office on time. Ten minutes into the drive, they both end up in a traffic jam. The throughway is reduced to one lane because an accident has occurred. Brad and John perceive the situation in different ways:

BRAD: "Oh no! a traffic jam. Damn! Now what am I going to do? I'm going to be late and I'll miss my appointment. What if the attorney leaves before I get there? What if he thinks I forgot to show up? What if he can't fit me in because I am late?" Then he begins to bang his fists on the dashboard of the car, saying things like, "Come on, come on. Get this traffic moving!" Then he sticks his head out the window several times in an attempt to see if a tow truck is coming. Then he complains that there should be a better way to clear throughway accidents. While waiting for the traffic to clear, he is angry, nervous, frustrated, and fidgety and cannot stop thinking of what the consequences will be if he is late.

JOHN: John sees the traffic stopped ahead and says, "Oh no, a traffic jam. Damn! I guess I'm probably going to be late for my appointment. Well, I did leave myself enough time to get to my appointment and there's nothing I can do about this unforeseen event. I'll get there as soon as I can. The attorney will probably understand as I'm sure this has happened to him on occasion. Hopefully, he will be able to fit me in when I get there. If not or if he has already left the office, I guess I'll have to reschedule the appointment and make the trip again another day." Then he flips through his cassette tapes looking for one of his favorite ones to play while he waits for the traffic to ease up.

Brad is feeling stress in the situation because of how he is perceiving it. He feels it would be terrible to miss the appointment and the consequences would be negative. He has no trouble imagining all the possible terrible consequences that could result. But by thinking about it more rationally and realistically, he would realize it would not be the end of the world if he missed his appointment. It would be inconvenient, yes, because he might have to wait longer to see the attorney or he might have to come back another day. That is certainly inconvenient but it is not terrible and does not warrant a high stress response. (If Brad reacts in this highly stressed manner to being late for an appointment, imagine how he might react to a major stressful situation.) The circumstances Brad is faced with (a traffic jam due to an accident) cannot be helped. There is nothing Brad can do about it. Becoming upset about it is not going to make the tow truck get there any earlier. Banging his fist on the dashboard isn't going to make the traffic clear any faster and isn't going to get him to the attorney's office any sooner. Brad needs to look at the situation more rationally and realistically, and he needs to recognize that the situation is out of his control and therefore can't be helped. He might just as well remain calm and try to relax until it is over.

John also is not happy with the traffic jam but he soon recognizes that the event is beyond his control. He intervened to stop the emotional arousal once he realized he had no control over the traffic jam. He did not allow himself to become stressed over the situation as a result. Unlike Brad, John views the situation as inconvenient but not terrible. Because he thinks of it in that way, he does not allow a stress response to progress. He recognizes that getting stressed about the traffic jam isn't going to help him get to his appointment any earlier. He prepares himself to accept the inconvenience it may cause and then finds a pleasurable way to wait out the traffic jam.

It is impossible, in the limited space of this chapter, to provide a full discussion on how to change one's thinking patterns from negative, inappropriate, and stress-provoking ones to more appropriate positive ones. Chapter 5 addressed the topic of thinking patterns and self-talk in more detail. The purpose in raising the point here is to make the reader aware that a person's thinking, perceptions, and interpretations of events can make a great deal of difference in the amount of stress she experiences and that, with effort, it is possible to change the way one thinks, perceives, and interpret events if one chooses to do so.

Controlling Stress

Like everything else, learning to control stress is easier said than done. Many people talk about the need to control stress but then do little about it. That may be because they don't know where to begin or because they don't really realize the negative and far-reaching effects that stress can have on their lives and bodies. Some people may not take the need for stress reduction seriously until something critical happens (heart attack) and forces them to deal with it. Some people understand on an intellectual level that they need to control stress, but they can't get a handle on the emotional side. Still others cannot identify their stressors so it is not surprising that they fail in their attempts to cope with stress.

Learning to control stress requires commitment. It requires consistent, focused effort and it is hard work. It requires practice and more practice. Old habits and ways of thinking that took a lifetime to form do not typically disappear overnight. But they can be changed permanently and successfully. Even if a person is able to reduce the stress in their lives by 30, 50, or 70 percent, there are substantial benefits to be gained as opposed to doing nothing. People who commit themselves to doing something about stress discover the rewards are numerous and affect many areas of their lives in a beneficial manner. They are much healthier and happier individuals as a result.

If you want to control stress in your life, you have to make a conscious effort to do so. There are many resources available to help you learn about stress and how to control it. These include books, articles, audiotapes, videos, seminars, and courses as well as consulting with counselors, social workers, psychologists, and so on. Some suggestions on how to get stress under control include the following.

First, to control stress, you need to be aware of your stressors, that is, you need to be able to clearly identify what it is that causes you stress. If you already know what your stressors are, you need to be sure that you are doing all that you can, from a preventive point of view, to keep stress under control. You need to examine your thinking patterns and the way you perceive stressful situations to determine if your thoughts and perceptions are contributing to your stress in any way. Then you need to focus on ways to stop stress during the arousal phase to prevent it from progressing.

If you are not aware of what your stressors are, make an effort to find out. For example, get a notebook and keep a diary of the things that cause you stress for a period of time (such as two weeks). Jot down all the stressful events or things that cause you stress during the course of a day on the left side of a page. On the right side, across from the stressful event, write down why the event was stressful. For example, left side—Sunday morning preparing brunch (nervous, under pressure). Right side—worried about whether I would have food ready on time for the guests I invited.

After you have completed your diary over the course of two weeks, go back to the beginning and review and analyze your notes to see what you can find out about your stressors. Ask yourself questions such as: What kinds of situations appear to be causing me stress? Under what conditions do I most often feel stressed? Why do I feel stressed? Determine if there is a pattern to the occurrence of stress in your life (e.g., I seem to be stressed most often in situations where I am short of time).

When you have determined what your stressors are, ask yourself if there are any preventive measures you can take that would reduce or eliminate the stress you feel in these situations. Review the lifestyle management strategies presented earlier in this chapter to look for clues and potential answers. If you determine that there are things you can do beforehand to reduce stress (e.g., I should allow myself more time from the start when I am doing things so that I don't always run short of time), then you need to plan to do those things (I'll have to stop overcommiting myself, or do fewer things during the course of the day, or get up earlier each day, or go to bed later).

Once you are aware of your stressors and have determined if there are things you can do on a preventive level to reduce stress, you need to examine your thinking patterns and the way you perceive things to see if they are contributing to your stress in any way. Review the information presented on stress and perception (stress begins in the mind, stress can be controlled, changing the way you perceive potentially stressful situations) presented earlier in this chapter as well as the material in Chapter 5 on mistaken beliefs, shattered illusions, self-talk, and developing a positive attitude. If you feel that your thinking patterns or perceptions are responsible for your stress, you need to work on changing them.

Then, once you find yourself in a situation where you are feeling stress, you need to work on stopping the stress response from progressing. For example, the next time you are faced with a stressful situation, as soon as you begin to feel stress, stop and ask yourself why you think you are feeling stress and what you think the cause is. Ask yourself if your thought patterns in relation to the stress are appropriate. Are you perceiving the situation in a rational and realistic manner? Ask yourself if there are some stress management techniques you can use right now to defuse the stress you are feeling (such as relaxation techniques). Ask yourself what you can tell yourself using self-talk that would help you to control stress at this moment. Determine whether there is anything you could have done on a preventive level beforehand to eliminate or reduce the stress you are now feeling. If there is, make a point of doing it next time.

Once you decide to do something to reduce or manage stress, you need to work at it, bit by bit, one step and one day at a time. You need to stick to it and practice. You can experiment with various strategies and choose those you find most comfortable and those that are most effective or generate the best results for you. As you regularly practice using your preferred stress management strategies, you will get better and better at curtailing stress over time. After a while, you will find yourself blocking the stress response from progressing almost automatically in many situations that formerly caused you stress. It may take several weeks, months, or even a year before you become proficient at it, but then the skills you develop are yours to keep for life and so are the benefits.

While this chapter on stress is limited in scope, its purpose is to help the reader understand the link between change and stress (change is a major cause of stress) and stress and illness (stress can lead to illness as well as other problems). An equally important purpose of the chapter is to make the point that stress can be controlled and that during times of change, people need to find ways to cope with and control the stress that usually accompanies situations of change to avert or minimize its negative affects.

chapter seven

Change and Loss

Change and loss are closely related. Almost every change we experience involves a loss because change inevitably means leaving something familiar behind and dealing with something new or different. Because loss is so often associated with change, it is important to understand the relationship between change and loss, how people react to loss, and the process of adjusting to loss as part of the process of adapting to change.

Experiencing Loss Is Difficult

Experiencing loss is a normal part of living since life is comprised of a series of attachments and losses. All of us experience losses of various kinds throughout our lives. Some of the losses are great and others are small. While minor losses can be irritating (loss of sunglasses, camera), they are relatively easy to deal with. However, people usually find it difficult to cope with significant losses (death of a loved one, loss of health) because they disturb the routine, structure, stability, and security of everyday life. Losses can also be painful because of the emotional impact they have on the meaning and significance of our lives.

We spend a great deal of time and we focus a great deal of energy in our lives doing things, acquiring things, and forming relationships that are important to us. Because of their importance, they become part of the purpose, meaning, and structure of our lives. They, in fact, become a part of us and we tend to take them for granted as a result. When we face the loss of something that is important to us, we are actually giving up (or losing) a part of ourselves including the physical and emotional energy we have invested over time. When we experience the physical loss of a thing, person, or ability, we also experience *the loss of what it meant to us in our lives on an emotional level, including all of the experiences we had with it in the past, the significance and/or purpose it had in our lives, and the structure it gave to our lives.* When we experience a significant loss, feelings of emptiness or a void once filled by the object of loss is created within us. These feelings can cause a great deal of emotional and psychological pain. In fact, experiencing a major loss can rock the foundations of our lives and shake us to the core.

People have always had to contend with losses in their lives but, in generations past, there were fewer losses in kind and number. Because people of the past didn't live as long as we do today and because they lived more stable and structured lives (lived in the same community or house for long time, had the same job or profession for life, stayed married to the same person for life), they experienced fewer losses than people of our time. Today, the rapid and ongoing changes occurring in our society in the area of technological innovation and development (discussed in Chapter 3) have led to an increasing number of changes in our personal lives. For example, today people move a great deal more than they used to, change jobs (and careers) more often, divorce and remarry more often, and need to replace outdated skills and technology more often than was the case in the past. For almost every new situation we find ourselves in as a result of these changes, there are usually associated losses. For example, in divorce, we experience the loss of a spouse, friend, and lover as well as the loss (end) of a partnership. Loss of control over things in our lives is also a significant form of loss and one we are experiencing more and more each day because of continual changes in our environment. As change continues to be a dominant part of our culture and lives, so must the practice of experiencing loss.

Even when people are prepared for a loss, they are often not prepared for the number and kind of changes it brings to their lives. Some losses, such as the loss of a job, can set into motion a series of additional losses (loss of home, loss of self-esteem, loss of financial independence). Loss of potential can also be experienced as a loss (loss of fertility, being passed over for a promotion, broken engagement). Even a positive change can involve loss. Marriage, for example, is a wonderful occasion to celebrate. But even this positive event has loss associated with it. For example, in marriage, a person leaves behind (or loses) an old identity, that of being a single, unattached person, to gain a new identity, that of being part of a couple or partnership. A person leaves behind (or loses) an independent lifestyle for a new one that is more restrictive.

Sometimes a gain can be a loss. When a person gets a job promotion, she is usually happy to receive the honor and looks forward to the challenges it will bring. However, leaving behind a job, even one that is considered to be less rewarding, still requires leaving behind (or losing) an old routine, boss, coworkers, and friends associated with that job to develop new ones in the new position.

The degree of difficulty a person has adjusting to a loss depends on the severity of the loss and the relationship of the loss to the self. In her book *Letting Go with Love,* Nancy O'Connor, a psychotherapist, explains the most difficult kinds of losses.

> *The closer the relationship (of a loss is) to the self, the more disruptive the loss. The most profound loss is (facing) the death of oneself, or a radical change in your body, such as losing your eyesight, a limb or a deteriorating physical illness like cancer, multiple sclerosis or others which affect physical appearance and stamina.*
>
> *The second most severe type of loss is the separation from significant people in our lives by death, divorce and abandonment. Physical attacks such as mugging or rape can be emotionally devastating, depending on the individual and on the circumstances of the event. A physical accident that requires a long recovery is also a severe loss to the self.*
>
> *The third level of losses requiring adjustment to new ways includes the normal developmental changes in life. Some examples are adolescence, starting or ending school, moving, marriage, age related changes in your body like losing hair, reduced energy or becoming a grandparent.*

The fourth area is loss of important objects, money, hopes, aspirations or expectations as well as changes in the social environment such as a Supreme Court decision that may affect your life, or giving up a pet project.[1]

Losses Change Lives

Losses can change lives dramatically. Many people who have suffered a major loss concede that their lives were transformed or forever changed by it. Significant losses can change the direction and routine of one's life as well as a person's life plans and view of the future. For example, a person who has been involved in a car accident and has suffered some paralysis has to give up his aspirations to continue a successful career in athletics. A woman who always dreamed of having a large family with many children of her own changes her whole view of the future when she marries and finds she will be unable to bear children. See Figure 7.1 for more examples of personal losses.

While a loss can be dealt with on an intellectual or material level, the greatest impact of a loss is usually felt emotionally and psychologically. For example, a person who suffers a loss through a robbery may not be too concerned about the loss of material possessions (compact disc player, television) because they can be replaced. What is of more concern is the sentimental value of some of the things that were stolen and the unique meaning they had in a person's life (grandmother's engagement ring). That loss of meaning cannot be replaced. There is also the psychological aspect—the fear that a robbery generates in people, prompting thoughts such as "What would have happened if I had been in the house at the time the robbery took place?" Likewise, there is a sense of being violated, the feeling that strangers were rummaging through personal belongings in one's home.

On a psychological level, suffering a significant loss forces us to change the way we think and behave. It teaches us how vulnerable we are. When things we thought would never happen to us happen, it shocks us into reality. It forces us to reexamine our views of life and the world from a new perspective. For example, Brenda, a forty-five-year-old woman who was diagnosed with breast cancer, had the lump on her breast removed and was assured that the cancer had not

The following are examples of kinds of personal losses. They are listed by category for organizational purposes. Some of the losses listed can fit into more than one category.

Loss of Relationships/Social Life

◆ Loss of spouse/partner (through death, divorce)
◆ Loss of friendship (through moving, death, disagreements)
◆ Loss of relatives—parents/siblings/aunts/uncles/cousins/in-laws (through death, remarriage)
◆ Loss of one's child (through divorce, adoption, death)
◆ Loss of ability to socialize (chronic illness)

Loss of Health/Ability

◆ Loss of health (serious illness/chronic illness)
◆ Loss of part of one's body (through accident/disease)
◆ Loss of ability to work (retirement, disabling illness)
◆ Loss of functional ability such as hearing/sight (from old age, disease, accident)
◆ Loss of athletic ability (disease, accident)

Loss of Potential

◆ Broken engagement
◆ Loss of fertility
◆ Passed over for promotion
◆ Not accepted to graduate school
◆ Business failure
◆ Abortion
◆ Miscarriage

◆ Retirement
◆ Loss of a significant opportunity

Loss of Material Things/Possessions

◆ Home (through financial adversity, disaster, moving into a nursing home)
◆ Car (through accident, repossession, theft)
◆ Money (bad investment, job loss, robbery)
◆ Significant personal belongings (robbery, fire, natural disaster)

Psychological Loss

◆ Self-esteem (business failure, divorce)
◆ Freedom (through illness, having a baby)
◆ Security (through loss of job, financial downturn)
◆ Status (scandal, job loss/demotion)
◆ Self-confidence (resulting from job loss, becoming disabled)
◆ Loss of control over life (because of illness)
◆ Loss of mental health

Other Loss

◆ Loss of religious faith
◆ Loss of authority (demotion, job loss)
◆ Loss of way of life (moving to city from country)
◆ Loss of important goal or dream in life

Figure. 7.1. Examples of personal losses.

spread. As a result of having to deal with the loss, from that moment on, Brenda began to view life from an entirely new and different perspective. Although she may have been pronounced free of cancer at the end of her surgery and treatment, she now lived with the uncertainty that the cancer might return at any time in the future. When she was first diagnosed, she considered the possibility of a premature death and thought about the implications it would have on her family. Being spared from the ravages of a malignant cancer for the moment, she realized how fragile and precious life is and how lucky she was to be alive. Life took on a whole new meaning for her. Her priorities and her values changed. She discovered how important her relationships were with those she loved. Material things lost their importance. Things that she used to consider problems suddenly seemed so trivial. All the opportunities she had put off for the future (taking a trip to Europe) and all her efforts to make do with things (old refrigerator) in order to save for the future were viewed from an entirely new perspective. She was no longer prepared to postpone the pleasures of everyday life for an uncertain future. She decided she was going to begin living each day to the fullest. Because the psychological impact of the loss was so great, Brenda is not likely to ever revert back to her former way of thinking again, even if she lives to be 100 years old.

People who have suffered great losses (a disaster such as fire, earthquake, a major car accident, a major health setback) and survived often become much stronger people as a result of their experiences. Although these people hope they will never have to face a similar loss again, having endured such great loss and survived, they feel they can survive anything. They become much more confident about their ability to deal with any problems that may arise in the future. Thus, life is changed by losses and it can never go back to exactly the way it was before.

Death

When we think about loss in the traditional sense, we often think of life's greatest loss: death. Of all of the major changes that people have to deal with, death is one of the hardest to accept. We frequently hear of deaths in news reports and in the community. And while we can empathize with other people who experience the death of a loved one, it is not the same thing as experiencing it firsthand. When an emotional bond or attachment has been formed with another person, the finality of death is hard to accept. Knowing that you can never see the person again, talk to them, touch them, apologize to them: these emotional bonds are very hard to break. When the emotional bond is one that has been in existence for a long time or a lifetime, it is even more difficult. People don't get over the death of a loved one overnight. It takes a long time because the death of a loved one is one of the most difficult of changes to accept and adapt to. Even when people do recover from the sorrow and pain that the death of someone close brings, it doesn't mean they no longer miss them. The loss just becomes less painful emotionally as time goes on.

The death of someone close disrupts our lives and the meaning of our lives. From the time of the death and on, there is a void or feeling of emptiness in life that is left by the person who has died. A person with whom you shared so much of your life, your joys, sorrows, your milestones, your accomplishments, and disappointments is no longer part of your world, only part of your memories. Most people never imagine the death of a loved one would be as hard to accept and deal with as it is. They never thought they would feel the emotions associated with it as intensely as they do. Emotions are complex. The grief is intense and the adjustment is hard to make.

A parent's death, for example, can have a significant impact on a person even though the person is thirty or forty years old when it happens. The sense of loss is great. With the loss of parents, the people who gave you life are no longer there. A lifelong relationship is severed. The bond with the people you have known the longest is gone. There is a sense of aloneness that accompanies the death of a parent, a sense of being orphaned, a sense of having lost part of oneself. There is a feeling of emptiness and a feeling of being disconnected from the past—like having one's roots pulled out. When parents die, your connection to the world is lost. Parents are our link to our ancestors and to our culture. Parents also provide us with a home base we can always return to. When they die, we cannot go home anymore. People then realize that the past is gone and they are now at the head of the next generation and will carry the torch from there on in. Losing a parent makes a person feel truly grown up and totally responsible for themselves.

A parent also has a unique role in a person's life, one that can never be replicated by anyone else, and it is gone with death. A parent is a parent for life. A parent has shared all your joys and sorrows, your milestones, accomplishments, and disappointments since birth. A parent gave you life, fed you, clothed you, nurtured and cared for you from birth. A parent is someone you can always look to for advice and direction. They love you unconditionally and always look out for your best interests. They don't judge you and are always there to listen, to comfort, and to provide support. You can always count on them, no matter what. With the death of a parent, an important support system is lost as is a source of unconditional love. The death of a parent can cause us to face our own immortality, often for the first time. We realize that if our parents can die, so can we. Death then becomes a more realistic probability.

While there are certain universal feelings that almost every child feels upon the death of a parent, a parent's death means different things to different people, depending on the nature of the relationship that existed between child and parent. For many, it is a time to reassess or reaffirm one's values, goals, and direction in life that is often predicated upon an assessment and review of a parent's life once he or she is gone. The death of one parent often causes us to change the nature of the relationship we have with the surviving parent as well as with siblings (for better or worse). For those who had a less than happy or satisfactory relationship, a parent's death means they finally have the freedom to make changes in their lives that they previously avoided (consciously or unconsciously) for fear of parental upset or disapproval (such as finally ending a bad marriage, changing one's field of work). For others, it means they no longer have to prove themselves to their parents.

Death is associated with feelings of sadness and grief. People who have lost a loved one through death go through intense periods of bereavement and mourning following the death. Grieving and mourning is a natural part of life, a normal and universal response to a significant loss. Grieving occurs when people's ability to adapt to a new reality is overwhelmed. The purpose of bereavement and mourning is to help people accept and cope with the death. Grieving helps people to confront the loss they face and helps them to break the strong emotional ties they had with the person who died. Grieving also helps people to cope with the void a person's death has left in their life. It is a process that involves working through the pain and sorrow they feel in response to the loss they have suffered. Grieving helps people come to terms with loss and helps them accept and adapt to the new reality of living without their loved one. It helps them let go of the past and find new meaning in life and the new reality they face. The process of grieving and mourning is part of the process of healing. Grieving and morning are necessary to help the mind heal itself so that life can continue. Fortunately, grieving is a process that has a beginning and an end.

Losses Need to Be Mourned

*J*ust as people need to mourn the loss of a loved one when there is death, similarly they have to go through the process of mourning other significant losses in life. Many changes we experience in life are accompanied by loss. All meaningful losses need to be mourned. Mourning helps people adapt to loss. As change continues to escalate in so many areas of our lives today, people will be faced with the need to mourn losses more and more frequently as time goes on.

With loss comes feelings of sadness for the thing or person or situation that must be left behind. We have formed emotional and psychological attachments to those people, things, and situations over time and need time to adjust to the severing of those attachments. We need time to mourn the loss and to adjust to all the things the object of loss meant to us in our lives—to the significance, purpose, and role it had and to the breakdown in structure and loss of continuity it may create in our lives as a result. We need time to mourn the loss of meaning and to assess and accept the impact of the loss on our lives. And we need time to adjust to the new reality we face as a result of the loss.

The degree to which a loss is felt depends on the importance or significance of the loss to an individual person. The more time invested in the thing, situation, or person lost, the greater the pain and sense of loss. For example, if a person had the same job with the same company for twenty years or more, it is much more difficult to leave than it is for a person who had a job with the same company for only a year or two.

Generally, the greater the significance of the loss, the more time to recover from it is needed. When a loss is anticipated or expected, it is somewhat easier to cope with because a person starts preparing for it emotionally and psychologically in advance. By the time the loss actually occurs, the grieving process is well under way. When a loss is unexpected, people have more difficulty coping because they are taken completely by surprise and there is no time to adjust or to prepare themselves for it psychologically in advance. Loss that cannot be recovered is particularly difficult because of its finality.

Just as people are healed by the grieving process following a death, so the mourning process is needed to heal us from any significant loss. Acknowledging and accepting a loss and experiencing and dealing with all of the emotions and problems that result from loss are needed. Mourning a loss and healing oneself is a psychological necessity. It is a process that must be undertaken in order to prepare oneself to move on with life. The old ways must be left behind to rebuild and restructure life according to the new reality. A person's thinking, interpretation, and perspective of life must be revised or reformulated to reflect the new reality that results from the loss. Loss must be grieved and acknowledged so that life can continue and healing can take place.

The Process of Mourning a Loss

*T*he process of mourning is unique to the individual. People mourn their losses in different ways over different lengths of time. However, there are feelings that are experienced to some degree by almost everyone during these times, and there is a process that most people go through to deal with loss.

When people initially face a loss, many times they are struck with feelings of disbelief and denial. They can't believe what is actually happening and they can't believe it is happening to them. They feel overwhelmed, shocked, and stunned. Sometimes it doesn't seem real or possible and it doesn't seem to register. As they first begin to deal with the loss, people become self-centered, thinking not only about the loss itself but about the effects it will have on their lives. They review the areas of their lives that will be affected and begin to think about the impact of the loss on each of them.

As they begin to realize the impact of the loss on them, people become overwhelmed by feelings of disorientation, emptiness, confusion, uncertainty, and anxiety about the future. Typical thoughts include, "How will I cope? or How will I ever get over this?" For a time, it may feel as if they will never be able to cope and never be able to get over it. People are so distraught at this time, they can't see how they will recover. The future looks bleak and a sense of hopelessness often sets in. They may feel that everything they have done in their lives up to the time of the loss is meaningless because of the occurrence of the loss.

Feelings of guilt may then emerge. Thoughts such as, If only I had . . . What if I would have. . . . With feelings of guilt, people sometimes try to change or correct their past actions in retrospect by trying to second-guess what might have made the loss avoidable.

Resentment can also set in. As a person suffering loss looks at others around her and sees their fortunate circumstances, she looks at them with resentment. Examples of typical thoughts include, "What are you worried about, you still have your job . . . You still have your health . . . You still have your husband," and so on. Other feelings that surface at this time are thoughts such as, "Why me?" A person tries to make sense of why she has been affected and why she must suffer while it appears that others do not. During this process, people can become critical of the people and circumstances related to the loss.

There are also feelings of anger. Anger can stem from several sources. It can come from the feeling of unfairness of having to experience the loss. It can be focused on those who may have caused the loss (doctor, boss, criminal). Sometimes people become angry at themselves by thinking thoughts such as, "I should never have trusted him" or "I should have known better." It is also common for people to get angry at God as a result of experiencing a loss ("Why are you doing this to me?" and "What did I do to deserve this?"). People suffering a loss can become angry with and resentful of others who do not understand the pain they are going through. This is particularly so if others make glib or inappropriate remarks or try to minimize the impact of the loss on their lives ("You're still young" "You can have another baby"). People can also get angry at the world as a result of a loss ("How can all of you people drive around, go shopping and go about your affairs as if all is well and normal? Don't you know what has happened? Don't you realize that I lost my husband yesterday?").

Feelings of vulnerability generated as a result of the loss can bring about fear and anxiety. People begin to worry and preoccupy themselves with what they might lose next. These feelings are particularly acute in the period following the loss and they diminish over time. Feelings of vulnerability and fear lead people to view the world and others irrationally or through clouded glasses for a period of time. For example, if a person has just experienced a divorce, as soon as she sees another couple arguing or fighting, she becomes convinced that the couple is also destined for divorce. If a person has experienced the death of a loved one, he becomes preoccupied with losing others he loves. He may even believe that he might be next to pass on even though he is young and healthy. At this time, people tend to project the circumstances that caused their loss onto other people or other circumstances in their lives, and they convince themselves that there are many more tragedies awaiting them just around the next corner.

During the time that these feelings, thoughts, and emotions are being felt in individuals experiencing loss, they have trouble functioning on a rational basis, particularly when their emotions are at a peak. Their judgment is not good because they don't see anything objectively. Their thoughts are clouded with emotion and they tend to see everything from a wounded-person point of view. Consequently, they do not always act or speak rationally for a while after a loss has occurred.

As a result of loss and the intense emotions that surround it, people can suffer physical symptoms during the grieving process. These can include various aches and pains, low levels of energy, fatigue, headaches, the inability to sleep, and loss of appetite. They can also experience psychological symptoms of depression, anxiety, loss of interest in life, lack of ambition, and withdrawal from others.

Grieving is a difficult and painful process of adjustment, but it is healthy and necessary to experience before one can recover and life can go on. If we deny grief, we deny the importance that the object of loss had in our lives. After a significant loss, people struggle to put their lives back together and to make some sense of it. As Peter Marris, an English social scientist, states in his book *Loss and Change,* "Loss disrupts our ability to find meaning in experience. . . . Grief represents the struggle to retrieve this sense of meaning when circumstances have bewildered or betrayed it."[2]

For people to recover successfully from a significant loss, they need to restore some structure to their lives and reestablish a sense of continuity. They need to revise their understanding of life. They need to generate a new sense of meaning and purpose in their lives by reinterpreting it from the perspective of the new reality they face and by letting go of the loss. These things are accomplished through the process of mourning.

In time, as people work through their feelings and try to make sense of what has happened, they come to accept the loss. The pain, confusion, and other feelings attached to the loss eventually dissipate and become less intense over time. Then gradually, as people recover, they begin to integrate the reality of the loss into their lives and learn to live with it. The grieving process is then complete. It has a beginning and an end.

People are preoccupied with their losses for varying amounts of time. The length of time it takes for a person to recover depends on factors such as the degree of emotional attachment to the person, place, or thing, the degree of disruption the loss brings to a person's life, the type of loss endured (death, car accident), the circumstances surrounding the loss (forced, chosen, violent), whether the loss was anticipated, the personal coping skills a person has developed in the past to deal with difficult personal circumstances, whether a person had previous experience with this type of loss, and the kind and amount of social support available. Preoccupation with loss is very intense in the early days, weeks, or months following the loss and it declines with time. Accepting loss does not mean forgetting about it. It means letting go. The acceptance of loss and intensity of emotions and grief associated with it subsides gradually. Time eases emotional pain. In many situations involving loss, time is the only healer.

When we face the loss of something or someone important to us, it is normal to wish that the pain and grief would go away so that things can get back to normal. It is only natural for people to want to avoid the pain, sorrow, and emotions associated with loss. But since loss must be recognized for life to continue and the mourning of loss is necessary for healing to take place, loss and grief cannot be ignored or wished away. They must be felt. They must be experienced. Resisting grief can lead to physical or emotional breakdown or both.

Feelings and emotions regarding loss cannot be put on the back burner to be dealt with at a later time. A person cannot resume living his life acting as if nothing has happened and everything is fine because then healing cannot take place. Nor should a person make himself so busy and involved with things after a significant loss that there is no time to think about it. The feelings associated with loss do not go away because they are ignored, denied, or resisted. The mourning process cannot be short-circuited. There is no shortcut. There is no way of skipping over it. When that is done, feelings are sent underground where a tremendous amount of harm can be done in the long run and the amount of time needed to heal can become significantly prolonged. Grief and emotions that are suppressed can stay underground and fester. Then, out of the blue or at a later time (usually the next crisis), they can come out with even more intensity. Feelings of anger and bitterness can simmer and stay with a person for years, causing great unhappiness and misery, possibly for the rest of his life. Depression can set in. When feelings associated with grief are suppressed, they can also lead to alcohol or drug abuse.

Emotions concerning loss must be felt, expressed, and dealt with. They cannot be intellectualized. The process of grieving is largely emotional, not intellectual in nature. A person cannot accept what has happened on an intellectual level and not deal with it on an emotional level. It simply does not work. A wounded person must heal. When there is no opportunity to heal (because grief is denied or there is not enough time to mourn), the pain is unresolved. In her book *Living Through Personal Crisis*, Ann Kaiser Stearns, a clinical psychologist and counselor, explains:

> *Mourning remains a process we must all go through. It simply isn't possible to go around it without jeopardizing recovery and healing. . . . The more fully a person grieves in the early months, the more relief the person will feel as*

time goes on. Healing involves being willing to hurt more in order to hurt much less . . .

Unresolved pain keeps us from being complete, content people. . . . All of us have both the right and the responsibility to take our losses seriously. Grief, when ignored or denied, can do us in, harming us in dozens of ways. Facing our losses is part of how we find our freedom again. That's how healing begins.[3]

During the process of mourning, people need to feel the pain, the hurt, the anger, and guilt in order to heal. That does not mean that a person should walk around with a long face, wallowing in self-pity, and do nothing but think of the loss all day and every day. Rather it means accepting and tolerating the feelings one has at a given moment, whatever they happen to be. For example, if a person feels like crying, she should cry. If a person feels angry, he should express that anger. Confronting grief rather than avoiding it shortens the length of time necessary to heal.

Mourning Is Difficult in Our Society

While the process of mourning is necessary to recover from situations of significant loss, it is difficult to do in our society for several reasons. For one, our society and culture do not have many recognized customs and rituals for dealing with loss (such as wearing black) as is the case in other cultures and societies around the world. In these other cultures, there are formal rites, rituals, and established traditions to mourn losses (such as death, the loss of crops, passage into adulthood) that are followed and recognized by all members of these cultures. Mourning is regarded as a natural process, a necessary part of life, and a custom expected of anyone who suffers a loss. Members of these communities provide support to help individuals deal with their losses. Ceremonies and rituals in these cultures provide acceptable ways for people to openly express their emotions, and they specify formally the amount of time to be spent in mourning rituals. Mourning is not a process that is looked down on in any way and people who mourn are not considered weak or self-pitying.

In our society, grieving and mourning are difficult because they are not readily accepted by people. Aside from paying last respects at funeral homes and attending funeral services to mourn the dead, there are few rites or customs of mourning that are known and recognized. Our society, in modern times, is largely focused on the pursuit of happiness and pleasure. Loss and death do not receive any significant recognition as a normal part of the life cycle in North American culture today. Loss, and the pain and suffering that go with it, are not things people want to hear about or talk about. Thus, they try to avoid any discussion concerning significant losses, especially death.

Before the twentieth century, many people died in their homes. The family of the deceased person was responsible for preparing the body for viewing and, in many cases, for the actual burial itself. When there was no clergy available, people had their own ceremonies in their homes and at the graveside. Relatives of the deceased person received people who wanted to pay their last respects into their homes. Children witnessed much of what went on. Because people died at a younger age and died more frequently of disease, few people reached adulthood in those days without having experienced or witnessed death and the rituals associated with it. The sight, sound, and smell of death were commonplace. Thus people of those times were more familiar with what was expected of them at the time of a death as well as with the grieving process that followed a death.

People find it difficult to be around others who have suffered losses today because they aren't comfortable being around a person suffering loss. They may feel embarrassed or awkward. They don't know how to respond to grieving people and they don't know what to say to them. They don't know how to act or react to the emotions (outbursts of crying, anger) that are expressed in response to a loss. In many instances, they react inappropriately (by not allowing a person to talk about a loss or death, by continually changing the subject, or by telling a grieving person not to cry when they need to do so). It is easier to avoid a person who is coping with a loss because then people don't have to deal with any of this.

People are also reluctant to be around those suffering a loss because it frequently reminds them or brings back memories of their own experiences with loss. People are then forced to face their own fears associated with death or loss all over again. It also forces them to face their aloneness and the inevitable fact that someday they may face the same loss themselves.

Individuals suffering a significant loss, particularly for the first time, often don't know what to expect of themselves after a loss. People in our society tend to be unfamiliar with the process of grieving. So even when they are experiencing it themselves, people question whether the emotions they are experiencing are appropriate and whether what they are feeling is normal because they don't know how they are supposed to feel. They also wonder about things such as how long the pain will last, when it will go away, and how they can expect to feel over time.

Another reason it is difficult to mourn in our society is because people who do not shed a tear and who are viewed as strong in these situations are admired for their stoicism. While this might be good for appearances, it is not necessarily good for psychological health. As we discussed earlier, people who attempt to avoid the feelings of hurt and pain and who resist the grieving process for appearances (or other reasons) usually end up causing themselves more pain and problems in the long run. One of the greatest obstacles to healing from a loss is the suppression of emotions associated with loss and the resistance and avoidance of the pain and distress associated with it. Our culture erroneously values emotional restraint.

And then there are the fast trackers, workaholics, and over-achievers in our society. Being goal and success driven, many of them consider mourning a waste of time. As a result, they may not spend enough time on it because they see no sense in it (when you're dead you're dead, what's done is done).

People are also afraid to mourn their losses because of what others might think of them. They are embarrassed to express grief. This is particularly so with men and boys who have been socialized not to cry in our culture. Our culture often negates the importance of people's emotions when they have experienced a significant loss. Those who suffer losses are often expected to be back to themselves in a few weeks; otherwise they might be viewed as having a weak character or indulging in self-pity. People can't recover from losses, particularly major losses, overnight. They can't be expected to snap out of it quickly. It is simply not possible and it is not a good strategy to follow for psychological health. People need time to accept and adjust to their losses and they must do so in their own time and in their own way.

There are times, however, when the mourning process can go on too long (over two years) or people can't seem to make much progress in getting over a loss. In these cases, a person may have to seek counseling to help him over the hurdle and get him moving along to the recovery stage. Psychologists and other counselors are trained to identify the obstacles that are blocking the path to recovery. They can be of great assistance in helping people to heal.

Loss Can Lead to Personal Growth

While loss is often thought of strictly in negative terms, people often use the lessons they learn from adversities involving loss to transform their lives and make them better. Coping with a major loss can lead to personality changes, new interests, new values, new lifestyles and attitudes, a new philosophy of life as well as new behaviors. Loss can also lead us to ask questions about the meaning of life and thereby lead to tremendous personal growth over time. Ann Kaiser Stearns summarizes the process of personal transformation through loss in her book *Living Through Personal Crisis:*

> *Loss has a way of changing our lives dramatically. Even the form of our thoughts about the future undergoes tumultuous alteration. So do we ourselves become transformed. Many of the changes will be positive life awakening experiences. Some of the transformations will profoundly enrich our lives. However, that is definitely not how life feels to us in the first six months or longer. . . .*
>
> *When we lose part of ourselves—through surgery, an illness, an accident, an act of assault, the loss of a dream or the loss of a loved one—the persons we are capable of becoming must be resurrected in new form. As we learn from the loss something of value that benefits ourselves and others, our loss is transformed. An event that takes away something precious becomes an event that gives us something new. . . . Even if we wished to remain the persons we previously were, it's simply not possible. . . . Our losses change us and our life course. The reality is unavoidable that one can never again be the same. There is often great sorrow in this reality. There is also relief. Thank goodness, I often think to myself, that things can never more be the same. I definitely would not like to be the person that I was in the past. While I'm sorry that certain losses have happened to me, I'm not sorry that sorrow has transformed my life and*

*made me spiritually and emotionally richer. I've learned too much that's too
precious ever to go back again.*[4]

Coping with Loss

*I*n times of loss, people become disoriented and confused. They
don't know how to go about their daily lives while coping with the
loss. During these times, the best strategy for people to follow is to
stay with the routines and keep to the intact structures of their lives,
insofar as it is possible, so that much of the familiarity and stability
they had in their lives before the loss is maintained, thereby providing some security. Once the period directly following a loss has
passed, people need to get back into their regular activities and their
normal routines as soon as they can. This is in spite of the fact that
they may not feel like it, may not have any energy to do so, and may
lack the needed concentration. Work and routine provide a sense of
normalcy in people's lives and provide a means of distracting some
attention away from themselves and the loss. Even though a person
may not be able to fully deal with the demands of life in the manner
they previously did, healing will take place.

Because of the stress involved in dealing with loss, there can be
a decrease in the effectiveness of a person's immune system, causing
an increased susceptibility to diseases (as explained in Chapter 6).
Therefore, it is important to take extra care of one's physical health
during times of loss even if one doesn't feel like it. Getting an adequate amount of sleep, keeping up physical exercise and activity, eating regularly, and maintaining a good diet (nutritionally) is necessary
to retain maximum stamina when the body needs it most. Avoiding
any excessive emotional stress and seeking medical advice and care
when needed are also important.

The postponement of important decisions until after the period of
greatest mourning following a loss is also a good idea, whenever possible. People don't think rationally for a while following a significant
loss, and they can make decisions about important matters that they
may later come to regret when they return to a more rational state.

Seeking support and reassurance from family and close friends
in times of loss and talking about the loss with them is important.

Expressing feelings and emotions with people you trust can be therapeutic. Someone who is a good listener and who will not try to divert your attention away from your problem, a warm and caring person who does not minimize your experience, is unobtrusive, isn't afraid of your emotions, isn't afraid that you're going to fall apart, and does not give unwanted advice is a good choice. Joining a support group, if one is available, can also be a tremendous source of support. In support groups, the type of loss you experienced is discussed with others who have experienced similar losses and are coping with similar feelings and problems. Ways to cope with the loss are shared among members. Social support group networks are also useful in helping people to deal with the effects of stress related to loss and grieving.

Getting over a significant loss requires courage, strength, and patience and it takes time. You need to believe you will recover and you need to give yourself time to do so. You will know that you have recovered when you can face reality and can accept the loss both intellectually and emotionally. As you recover, your physical and mental health will improve.

Depression Related to Loss

It is not unusual for a person undergoing a significant change or loss in their life to experience an episode of depression. The symptoms of depression include feelings of sadness, hopelessness and anxiety, feelings of guilt or worthlessness, loss of interest in food, sex, and activites once considered pleasurable, changes in sleeping patterns (insomnia), fatigue, loss of energy, inability to concentrate, indecisiveness, unexplained muscular pain and other vague complaints, and suicidal thoughts. Depression often accompanies loss when the loss is significant. The depression that follows a specific setback or loss is referred to as reactive or situational depression. It results from a specific identifiable cause (the loss). This depression, as opposed to other types of depression such as chronic depression or biologically based depression, is not usually permanent and with time and adjustment to the loss, it disappears. Time is the most valuable healer in cases of reactive depression.

Reactive depression needs to be monitored over time, however, because it can lead to chronic depression. If a person is not dealing well with the mourning process and the depression goes on beyond the normal period of mourning, a person may need to seek counseling or medical attention in order to help them recover and to prevent the depression from becoming a permanent problem.

part three

Strategies for Managing Change

chapter eight

Strategies for Managing Change

As change continues to occur in our environment and personal lives, we need not sit helplessly by allowing it to disturb and overwhelm us. You *can* make your life more change adaptive. You *can* become more comfortable living with change and you *can* learn to cope with change more successfully. The purpose of this chapter is to tell you how by presenting a series of twenty-five management strategies you can use in your daily life and in your encounters with specific changes.

Whether you want to learn to live more comfortably with change in general or whether you want to learn some strategies to apply to a specific change you are facing, there are numerous change management strategies that can be used to help you adapt to change while minimizing the negative effects and maximizing the positive effects of change. Becoming familiar with the strategies discussed in this chapter will equip you with the knowledge and skills you need to deal with change more successfully in your life. The strategies presented are general ones and need to be adapted to specific situations to be more meaningful. Many of the strategies overlap in nature and not all of them are appropriate for all situations involving change.

1. *Acknowledge and Accept the Inevitability of Change*

Change is becoming more and more pervasive in our society as time goes on and it is occurring at an increasingly rapid rate. As such, change simply cannot be avoided in our environment and in our personal lives. No one is exempt. That being the case, to become more comfortable with change, one of the first things you need to do is to formally acknowledge and accept the fact that change is a predominant characteristic of our society and modern times, that it is going to continue to occur, and that it is going to continue to affect you. From a personal point of view, you need to understand and accept that things are going to continue to change *whether you like it or not and whether you approve or not.* Many changes, particularly those resulting from new developments in science and technology, are not going to disappear or slow down because you don't like them, aren't ready for them, don't have time to deal with them, or fear them. You also need to realize that disliking change or ignoring or denying change is not going to make it go away.

If you are a person who naturally dislikes change, has difficulty adjusting to it, or finds it uncomfortable, you need to acknowledge that fact so that you become consciously aware of it as such. Then you can make an effort to do something about it. Make a commitment to yourself that you are going to be less resistant, more open-minded about change, and more flexible in the way you think about it in the future. Then practice doing so. At a future time when you encounter a situation involving change, stop and examine your immediate response to it. Check for negative thoughts and rigid thinking patterns and do so every time you encounter change until you are able to automatically and regularly respond to change situations in a more positive manner. It is helpful to begin doing this with minor changes at first, working up to more substantive ones over time. For example, you go into your local grocery store to do your weekly shopping and find that some of the food items in various aisles are being rearranged. Your first reaction to the change might be: "Those so-and-so's! There they go changing things around again. Why don't they leave things alone so we can find them. Now it's going to take me an extra half hour I can't spare to find what I need. Why do they have to aggravate people like this!"

In this situation, you need to use self-talk to stop yourself from thinking negatively about the change (because you know you naturally dislike change). You might say something to yourself like: "Here I go again getting upset and frustrated with a change. I know that this is my natural tendency because I am a person who finds change difficult to deal with, but I'm going to stop these negative thoughts and give myself a chance to get used to the new arrangement even though I may not like it. After all, there must be a reason why they are making the changes. Maybe the new arrangement will have foods grouped more logically so things will be easier to find. Since these new aisles are the reality I face, my grocery shopping is going to take longer than usual the next few times I go into the store. So until I get used to the new layout, I will have to allow myself a little extra time when I go shopping and I'll try and learn the new location of a few items each week until I get used to it. If it takes me a month or two, so be it." Remember, it is *you* who will be frustrated and distressed if you do not adjust to or accept the newly arranged grocery aisles, you and no one else—not the store manager, not the clerk, not the cashier. The store manager, for example, in this case is not likely to say to himself, "I better not change the groceries in these aisles because Mrs. Smith won't like it and will become frustrated when she sees I've had them changed." Once again, although we cannot always control change, we can control how we feel about it.

Many kinds of changes that affect us are out of our control and must be accepted because nothing can be done about them (such as death of a loved one). But not all change is out of one's control and not all change is inevitable. In fact, the outcome of change is frequently indefinite or uncertain. Thus, when we say people must accept change, it doesn't mean you can't fight it in circumstances where you do have some control over it or can influence the outcome. If you feel that a change will have a negative impact on your life or those close to you, take the opportunity to fight it and fight it hard! Examples include fighting the government's decision to locate a toxic waste dump in your community or fighting your daughter's decision to drop out of college. However, once you have done all you can to affect a change and a final decision has been made and there is nothing further you can do to influence the outcome to your liking or advantage, *then you have to work at accepting the outcome, adjust-*

ing to it, and integrating it into your life as best you can. Not doing so at this point will only result in great distress to your physical, mental, and emotional well-being.

And finally, accepting change does not necessarily mean you have to like it or agree with it but rather that you are prepared to deal with the reality of it. You may not like having to do something differently on your job, for example, but if you don't do it, you will have no job or will have to look for another. That is reality.

2. Acknowledge and Accept the Uncertainty of the Future

*P*eople's lives have always been affected by change, but for nearly all of recorded history, most of them have been personal in nature (marriage, illness, death). In the past, technology and society changed at such a slow pace that people had time (years and decades) to adjust. Thus, in past generations, a person could set a life course and make long-range plans for the future and have a reasonable chance of attaining them. For example, fifty years ago, a high school–aged boy might have decided that to earn a living after graduation, he would work in his father's print shop and learn the trade with the hope of taking over the business and running it as his father had for decades before. This was possible because in the past, things did not change much technologically or socially from the time a person was born until the time he died.

Today, while we still have to deal with many personal changes, there are more and more societal and technological changes to cope with, many of which are affecting our personal lives. In addition to that, a growing number of those changes are beyond our control or imposed without our consent. As a result, we can no longer set out a life course or make long-range plans for the future and anticipate that they will work out as such. Rather, we have to accept the growing lack of control we have over things that might affect our lives and our future. We cannot anticipate how changes occurring in society and technology today will affect us five, ten, or twenty-five years from now. No matter what experts predict and no matter how authoritative they are, no one really knows for sure what will happen in the future. We do not know what new developments there will be, nor can we foresee the scope of their influence in any field of endeavor. The development of just one new process or product can totally revolutionize society and change the way things are done in the future just as many have done in the past (e.g., electricity, the computer). Thus, we need to learn to live with more uncertainty in the future and we should plan for it accordingly. We need to be open-minded and should keep thinking flexible and plans fluid. We need to have alternatives in mind and we need to allow for change when we make plans. We cannot see things in terms of having only one outcome and we cannot put all of our eggs into one basket as the adage goes because many things don't work out as anticipated as a result of unforeseen or unanticipated changes or events.

Likewise, we need to stop thinking about the future solely in terms of it being a continuation of the present. We can no longer assume that what existed in the past and present will exist in the future. People tend to assume that the world as they know it will go on indefinitely into the future. Of course, things from the past and present may well extend into the future. But at present, we do not know and cannot predict with any certainty which aspects are likely to stay the same and which will change.

3. Learn about Change and the Process of Adapting to Change

*I*f people are to learn to live with change and learn to manage it successfully in their lives, they need to learn as much as they can about change and how it affects them personally and about the process of adapting to change. The more one understands about change, the better equipped one is to deal with it successfully on an intellectual, emotional, and behavioral level.

People undergoing significant change in their lives experience a wide range of emotions, thoughts, and behaviors. They don't feel normal (or as they usually do) and they wonder if what they are feeling is normal. They want to know how long their feelings will last, why they are feeling the way they are, and what to expect next. They worry about how to cope with change and they want to know how others survived similar changes in the past. Through the process of educating oneself about change, these questions and concerns can be addressed and normal behaviors associated with change can be identified. This can significantly reduce anxiety and fear. Being able to recognize the range of emotions associated with change situations can also help you to understand why you feel the way you do. Knowing that other people who experienced similar changes survived them successfully can provide a sense of confidence, inspiration, and hope about your own ability to cope with your situation.

Becoming aware of the process of adapting to change is also important because it provides an overview of what to expect (behaviors, thoughts, and emotions) as you are confronted with having to adapt to a significant change. It allows you to see the overall picture, the beginning, the end, and steps in between. You can see the entire adaptation process at once. This overview can serve as a reference or roadmap, indicating where you have been, where you are, and where you have to go to complete the process. You can focus on the particular step you are experiencing at any given time and you can use your knowledge of the steps involved to prepare for those ahead. You can also review the process at any time to monitor and assess your progress throughout the entire adaptation process.

Recognizing that fear of change is normal and that it is a universal reaction to change is also helpful. Understanding the reasons why people fear or resist change can help you to understand your own fears and resistance to change. It can provide an awareness of why you are reacting as you are in your situation and may provide insight into what it is you actually fear about your particular change. When you understand the reasons you fear change, you can begin to work on overcoming them. When fear cannot be identified, it exists as general anxiety and, as such, is much more difficult to come to terms with.

Another important reason to learn about change is that being aware of things or situations that can help or hinder adaptation to change can help you to exercise some control over the situation insofar as it may be possible. You can take advantage of things or do things that may positively affect the adaptation process, for example, and can avoid doing things that are known to have a negative impact on it.

And finally, if you are aware of the relationship of stress, loss, and mistaken beliefs to change and you understand how they can affect you during times of change, you can determine whether they may be affecting you in your particular situation. If you determine that they are, you can then take action or corrective measures to help you better cope, or you can take measures to buffer yourself against the negative or ill effects.

4. Plan for Change

Change is easiest to make when it is planned or prepared for in advance and when it is done on a voluntary basis. Thus, whenever it is possible to plan for change, take the opportunity to do so. Planning for change gives you some control over change in that it allows you to anticipate, prepare for, and work at making a change in your own way, in your own time, and at your own pace. When people are aware that a change has to be made and they plan for it, the process of adapting to change is much easier, more organized, and less stressful.

Changes that are easiest to plan for are those that are predictable and foreseeable and can be easily identified and anticipated. They include customary life events such as retirement or one's last child leaving home as well as changes occurring in one's environment that become increasingly obvious over time. For example, a person working in an office where people are being laid off recognizes that those with only a little less seniority than he has have been given notices. A person alerted to this situation should anticipate that he could well be next in line for a layoff and might begin to look for another job or at least begin to make plans as to what he will do if he too is laid off.

Oftentimes, people are aware that a change has to be made or they can perceive that a change is coming. But rather than preparing, planning, and dealing with it as they should, they resist the change, ignore it, or stonewall it, putting it off for as long as they can. These people think that by doing this, the change might go away on its own, or they will be able to avoid it somehow, or they will make it easier on themselves by putting it off. However, when people wait for the axe to fall or until change is upon them, they make it more difficult on themselves in the long run for several reasons.

First, they may have built up a lot of resistance to the change and this can be a problem to overcome when it comes time to do so.

Second, because they have not thought about the change, they have not developed plans to deal with it and they find themselves unprepared. As a result, they are disorganized and scrambling around doing things under pressure at the last minute. People who do not prepare for change often find that they end up with little control over the change situation. They end up with no choice in the amount of time they have to make the change, for example, and with no choice as to how the change will be made. This creates feelings of frustration and stress. In addition to this, because they have not thought about the change ahead of time, they are often not prepared for it psychologically and emotionally, compounding the difficulties of adjustment even further.

Of course, not all changes can be planned for. Some happen unexpectedly, forcing people to adjust to the change afterward. Under these circumstances, a person has no way of preplaning or preparing herself for the change. Rather, she must cope with it as best she can after the fact. Unexpected changes are usually the most difficult to adapt to for this reason.

How to Plan for Change

Not all changes are predictable and not all changes can be planned for in advance. But planning for change whenever possible does have significant benefits as we have just discussed. The following are ten ways people can plan and prepare for change.

a As soon as you are aware that a change is imminent, begin to plan for it and deal with it as soon as possible. Don't put it off. You will have more control over the change if you can adjust to it in your own way, at your own pace, and in your own time. This will avoid a great deal of frustration, stress, and anxiety in the long run.

b Make periodic assessments of your life (work, family, home life, relationships, personal development, finances) and try to determine and identify any significant changes that you think may need to be made in any of these areas over the months or year ahead. The ability to look ahead and assess what is coming can be beneficial in planning for change.

c   If you are in a period of your life when you are not coping with any significant change, take the opportunity to make changes you have postponed from the past or to prepare for change(s) you anticipate will come in the future. This will reduce the chances that several changes will build up over time and then need to be dealt with all at once, causing you to become overwhelmed with too much change. It will also allow you to plan for and make the change in your own way and at your own pace.

d   When you have identified a change, determine the kind of change it is. Is it a permanent (structural) change such as a husband retiring or a temporary (cyclical) change such as a son moving back home from college after graduation until he finds a job? Identifying the type of change will help you plan for it in the most appropriate way.

e   Educate yourself about the change you are about to experience. Get books from the library, read articles from magazines, check the Internet and World Wide Web for information, and talk to other people you know who have experienced a similar change. This can provide you with useful information on what to expect, how you might feel, and how you might best prepare for the change. For example, if you are having surgery, you can read about the operation or procedures involved, the options available to you, the length of the recovery period, and how you can expect to feel afterward. In most cases, the more psychologically prepared you are for change (in that you know what to expect), the less stressful and less traumatic the experience.

f   Change is easiest to make when it affects just one area of life at a time (such as job). If you need to make a change in a specific area, don't put it off or postpone it unless you are already overloaded with changes in other areas of your life. Take advantage of being able to focus on making changes in that one area while the others are in a state of stability.

g   Make a list of the specific tasks associated with the change that need to be done. Organize the tasks into a timeline and develop a plan as to how you will go about doing them. Break big tasks down into smaller steps. Then begin working on your plan. For example, if you are moving, make a list of the things that need to be done such as packing, calling utilities to disconnect services, arranging a moving date, arranging a farewell party for friends or business associates. Indicate the date and time when you will do these things and then do them.

h Prepare yourself psychologically and emotionally for the change by thinking about the implications of the change and how it will affect you and your life. Remember, emotions are usually the most difficult part of change to deal with. They need to be accorded as much time or even more time than the other tasks involved in the change. For example, if you are going to have a baby, recognize that it will probably be tough during the first few months because you will have to get up in the middle of the night for feedings, the baby will probably cry a lot, you may feel uncomfortable or frustrated because you don't know exactly what you are supposed to do in various situations, your freedom may be restricted for a while. (Also recognize that things will get easier as time goes on, as they do for most other people.) By thinking about the probable circumstances and feelings in advance, you can begin to get used to the idea and thus prepare yourself for the change psychologically and emotionally.

i Assess the impact that the change you are experiencing will have on others in your life and then plan to deal with it. When change is experienced by one person, it usually affects others in his environment. For example, if a person is married and has a family, his spouse and children are going to be influenced by many of the changes affecting him. If, for example, a move to another city is necessary to secure a job, children will have to leave their friends and school while the working spouse may have to leave his or her job and find another one at the new location. While change is difficult for the person affected, it can be equally difficult for others around them because the change is out of their control. When planning for change, the needs and feelings of these people need to be considered and dealt with as they too need time to prepare and adjust.

j   While it is important to plan for change, the best made plans can be disrupted by unforeseen conditions. Therefore, in planning for change, avoid making rigid plans. Because things don't always go according to plan, being flexibile allows you to deal with unforeseen or unexpected circumstances more easily if they arise.

5. *Avoid Making Too Many Changes at Once*

As we discussed earlier, when a person experiences too many changes (even positive ones) within a short period of time, there are often negative consequences such as stress, physical illness, and psychological distress (anxiety, depression). Medical researchers have documented a definite link between people undergoing multiple changes in their lives and the onset of illness. People who sustain a great deal of change within a limited period of time experience lowered personal resilience and resistance and have a high probability of becoming ill (even seriously ill) within two years of the change period. This happens because people coping with multiple changes don't have enough time to work through the process of adapting and adjusting to change for each individual change they are experiencing. They are so caught up and focused on trying to cope, on conducting the tasks and tending to the details of what needs to be done, they are unable to properly assimilate each of the changes into the structure and meaning of their lives. The process of adapting to change takes time and it cannot be done overnight. It involves working through a series of steps that allows a person to let go of the old and accept the new on a behavioral, emotional, and intellectual level.

Since the implications of enduring too many changes at once are clearly negative, it is obvious that people need to limit the number of changes they experience simultaneously in their lives. They also need to avoid planning for multiple changes whenever possible. Since change is easiest to make when it affects just one area of a person's life at a time, it would not be wise, for example, to decide to go back to school, have a baby, and build a new house in the same year. Major changes need to be spaced out over time to allow them to be properly assimilated and integrated into people's lives. If you recognize that you are already coping with significant change in your life, *do not overburden yourself with additional change* that could erode your emotional and physical resilience and cause you to become exhausted or ill. Place a moratorium on further change until you have resolved those before you.

Conversely, when you find yourself in a period of little change in your life, that is the time to make change for the sake of change or changes that have been put off from the past or plans for change you anticipate will become necessary in the future. Making changes during these periods of little change will reduce the likelihood that a number of them will build up over time and then have to be dealt with all at once. It also allows you to have some control over the manner and pace at which the change will be made, thereby making the change adaptation process a more comfortable and less stressful experience. By monitoring the number of changes you are experiencing at any given time and spacing out significant changes, you can reduce the distress that comes from making too many major changes all at once.

Structure and Stability Are Essential

*H*aving structure and stability in life is important, particularly during times of change. In fact, the amount of structure and stability there is in one's life is a good predictor of a person's ability to withstand change. Structures serve as a base, a foundation, a footing upon which people organize and build their lives. Structures contribute significantly to one's sense of purpose and belonging as well as to one's sense of continuity in life. The presence of structure also helps people to feel secure and in control of their lives. (See more detailed discussion of structure on pages 31–32 and elsewhere in Chapter 2.)

Structures in people's lives are like roots of a plant or a tree. People have to have structures to keep them firmly anchored in their lives much as a tree needs a system of well-developed roots to keep it nourished and firmly anchored in the soil. A tree can bend in the wind, lose its leaves, sustain damage to its bark, and weather the elements. With its roots firmly established in the soil, it survives and remains in place despite the stresses it encounters from the elements or any passing storm. It will be able to recover from almost any type of damage inflicted on it over time because the roots can nurture and initiate new growth and enable damaged matter to recover or be repaired.

In contrast, when a plant has no roots, like a tumbleweed, it will roll around aimlessly in unknown territory, never knowing where it is going, where it will end up or what hazards lie ahead. It is at the mercy of the elements. The wind can blow it around at any time and put it in harm's way in an instant. It may or may not recover from the stresses and wounds it sustains.

People with structure and stability in their lives, like the tree, are better able to sustain change because their roots are well anchored, that is, the structures in their lives are stable and firmly in place. They feel secure and in control of their lives as a result, and they are prepared to weather a change even though their feelings of security and confidence can be temporarily shaken by it. In fact, numerous studies indicate that older people with structure in their lives live longer and are healthier than those without it.

In contrast, people without structure in their lives are like the tumbleweed. They don't know where they belong, where they are going, or where they will end up after a change. There is no sense of continuity or purpose. They feel uncertain, insecure, and at risk and that their lives are out of their control. This makes it difficult for them to withstand change because change amplifies these negative feelings even further, resulting in negative consequences that can be difficult to overcome. Having an unstable life and not having many structures in place puts people at a tremendous disadvantage when it comes to being able to withstand change.

When people experience major change in their lives, they usually feel insecure, anxious, and that their lives are out of their control. Under normal circumstances, people cannot live with these feelings for long periods of time without suffering negative effects such as stress, anxiety, and burnout. Structures, as well as the routines and traditions associated with them, can help to buffer people against the negative effects of change by providing a sense of stability, control, security, continuity, and purpose. Doing things such as getting back into a regular routine as soon as possible after a major change, keeping familiar things around you during times of change, adhering to and carrying on traditions, and keeping a sense of purpose and continuity in focus are examples of ways to further strengthen the structure and stability around you in times of change.

People who are comfortable with change and who can withstand a great deal of change in one area of their lives (such as a job) have some stability and structure in other areas of their lives (strong marriage, strong religious beliefs or values); otherwise they would not be able to cope well. When a person is faced with significant change in one area of his life, the structure and stability of that part of his life is threatened in some way. However, if the structure in other areas of his life is stable and intact, a person is likely to withstand the changes with minimal negative effects. The stability, security, and structure of other parts of his life will keep him anchored and help him retain some security and some control in his life while changes in the targeted area are taking place. Change is easier to make in a specific area of one's life when the other areas are stable and secure. Therefore, whenever you can, take the opportunity to make changes under these conditions. For example, if your marriage or spousal relationship is strong and going well and an opportunity comes up to make job changes, then do so at that time. The stability and security of the relationship will serve as an anchor and support for you and will help to reduce insecurities and balance out the uncertainty of the new job until you adjust to the changes required. If your marriage is in difficulty or falling apart, that is not the time to initiate changes on the job front. Rather, allow the stability of the job to act as an anchor in your life until the relationship problems are resolved.

If we are to live more comfortably and successfully in our society today, we need to have stable and solid structures established and in place in our lives at all times to help us weather and survive change on a continual basis. In the past, people's lives were more structured and stable so they were better equipped to withstand change when it came. Unfortunately, in modern times, more and more structures or anchors in our lives are eroding or disappearing. Traditional structures such as the nuclear and extended family, close-knit communities, religion, having a set of solid values and beliefs, and having lifelong friendships have been weakened by the stresses of modern life and current lifestyles. This puts us as at a great disadvantage as a society. At a time when we have more change to deal with than ever before in our history, we have fewer structures than ever to support us as we make those changes. In a climate of rapid and continual change, it is important that, as a society, we acknowledge and understand the important role of structure in our lives and that we work to increase it in as many ways as we can.

7. *Maintain Good Mental and Emotional Health*

*I*n an age of unprecedented change, we need to develop as many advantages as possible that will enable us to withstand increasing amounts of change in our environment and personal lives. Maintaining good mental and emotional health can provide a significant advantage in this regard. People with good mental and emotional health are better equipped to withstand the stresses and strains of change. Psychological wellness enables people to deal effectively with the problems and stresses of daily life. Psychological wellness also promotes resilience in individuals. Resilience is the ability to bounce back and return to normal after one's life has been disrupted. The more resilient a person is, the better prepared she is to withstand change.

Almost all of us have some psychological or emotional weaknesses, but for the most part, we are able to manage them and live with them every day and lead productive and happy lives. From time to time, life may throw us a curve ball (such as an event brought about by change), testing our mental and emotional resolve. While one's health in this area might become strained or temporarily weakened, in time, one usually recovers. Ordinarily, under these circumstances, there is no cause for concern because these things happen to all of us from time to time over the course of our lives.

However, when a person does not recover from an emotional or mental setback in life, when a person has existing emotional or mental weaknesses that interfere with the ability to have a happy and productive life, when an existing problem becomes worse over time, or when the number of problems increases over time, a person then finds himself unable to function comfortably in daily life. It is then that something must be done to improve or correct the situation, particularly if he is to survive in today's environment of continual change.

In times of change, if your mental or emotional health is already impaired for whatever the reason, you are at a disadvantage because you already have existing unresolved problems that are likely to be aggravated with the introduction of a change and the stresses that accompany it. The change may also create additional or new problems that may be difficult to cope with on top of existing problems. In fact, in some cases, having to cope with a new change could become the straw that breaks the camel's back. In this case, a person already on the brink of not being able to handle any further emotional or mental distress becomes overloaded and has a mental or emotional breakdown as a result.

People with good mental and emotional health are better prepared to cope with the stresses and strains of change because they don't have existing or unresolved problems already weighing heavily on them. Thus, when change occurs, they are in a better position to withstand the mental or emotional distress that comes with it. Since dealing with the emotional aspect of change is often the most difficult part of the process of adapting to change, being in good shape psychologically and emotionally when a change comes along is a tremendous advantage.

If you are suffering from any kind of psychological or emotional distress, don't allow it to continue to plague and burden you and put you at a disadvantage in life. Not only will it compromise your quality of life, but it will also weaken your ability to withstand change. Most problems can be overcome or at least kept under control with a recognition of the problem and with effort or assistance to overcome it. There are many treatments, cures, and methods available. For whatever the reason or from whatever the source, if you experience significant discomfort such as ongoing anxiety, too much stress, depression, fear, insecurity, unrelenting anger, poor self-esteem, or any other feeling that causes you significant uneasiness, make a conscious effort to resolve it. Learn what you can about it. Read about it and begin working at overcoming it. There are many resources available that you can use (books, tapes, videos, seminars). If you can't or do not want to do it on your own, seek the help of professionals trained to assist in these matters (psychologist, counselor, social worker). Chapter 9 provides further information and suggestions on obtaining professional help and assistance.

Psychological and emotional problems can come from a variety of sources including change. Even if the distress stems from something that happened long ago, it is best to confront it and deal with it. You cannot change the past, so learn from it and then let it go. Many people enter adulthood carrying some emotional baggage from their childhood years. People often don't recognize or feel the impact or implications of their childhood circumstances until they reach their twenties and thirties when it becomes increasingly evident. Regardless of the source, emotional or mental distress should be identified and dealt with so that life can go on, healing can take place and the future can be brighter and healthier all around.

To maintain good mental and emotional health, it is important and necessary to deal with mental and emotional distress and problems on an ongoing basis throughout life. When problems are dealt with as they arise, there is little likelihood that they will build up over time and become a time bomb waiting to explode.

And finally, in modern times, we need to recognize that *mental and emotional health are just as important as physical health.* We need to look after our minds and emotions as much as we do our bodies. And, of course, if you maintain good mental and emotional health on a regular basis, not only will your quality of life improve but you will be better prepared to cope with change when it comes along.

8. Build and Maintain Social Supports

*F*riendships, relationships, and social supports are important components of a healthy and happy life. There are many benefits to maintaining a network of strong friendships and social supports. Spending time with friends brings us a great deal of pleasure and is a good way to release stress, relax, and have fun. Social scientists say that friends are integral to maintaining good overall health and many studies show a strong relationship between social connectedness and personal well-being. People with strong support networks are healthier than those without them. On the other hand, isolation and a lack of friendships and connectedness to others is detrimental to a person's well-being, fostering stress, disease, and early death. In fact, a lack of social connectedness to others can be as dangerous a risk factor to poor health as are smoking, high blood pressure, lack of exercise, and other similar well-known risk factors.

Experiences and emotions generated by the process of adapting to change can be difficult to handle. It is mentally and emotionally tough for people to survive a significant change if they are alone, feel isolated, or have little social support. During times of change when there is confusion, anxiety, uncertainty, pain, and sorrow, and when people are overwhelmed by what they face, they often turn to others for support, encouragement, or advice. Caring family members and a network of trusted friends and other relatives can be a tremendous source of comfort in difficult times even when they do not actually understand or are not familiar with the difficulties of the change being experienced. The fact that people are there for an individual, that they are concerned and care about her matters a great deal and can have a significant impact on how well a person copes over time. People experiencing the disorienting effects of change need to spend time with individuals who will be compassionate and understanding and who will listen to them. Being able to express thoughts and feelings to those they trust can help to relieve stress, tension, anxiety, uncertainty, and other negative emotions associated with change.

Many people today have inadequate social support systems for any number of reasons. First, people have less and less time for developing friendships and socializing because they are too busy with work, making a living, raising their children, and trying to get ahead in a competitive world. They increasingly struggle to find time to spend with their spouses and children, let alone friends and relatives. Sunday dinners with the family and regular face-to-face visits with friends and relatives are becoming less common because of the lack of available time. It takes time to maintain a social support system and that is what people don't seem to have enough of today. Family units and extended families are also much smaller today than they were in the past and there are fewer people available within a family to rely on for support than was traditionally the case. People also move more frequently from city to city or to different parts of the country because of their work and are less able to maintain ongoing relationships with friends as a result. When family members or friends live at a distance, there is less contact in the form of communication and visits because of the distance, time, and expense involved. And, lastly, people may have inadequate social support systems simply because they do not recognize the value and importance of having friendships and socializing with others in our increasingly stressful world. They may feel, for example, that spending extra time working or trying to get ahead is far more important and profitable than wasting time on socializing or friendships.

If you have a strong network of caring and supportive relatives and friends whose support has helped you through a major change or life crisis in the past, you already recognize the importance of having and maintaining friendships and social connections with people who give meaning to your life. You also know how much power they have to help you heal. Since people with established friendships, relationships, and a good social support system are better able to withstand the stresses and strains of change, it is important to have such social connections established and in place well in advance of when you need them. If you don't have a strong social support system or didn't think it was important to have one in the past, take time to build one now. You need to make time for friends and socializing and you need to recognize that they are important. Like everything else, friendships have to be nurtured if they are to develop and grow. You cannot build trusting and meaningful relationships overnight or with people you see once a year.

It is also important to balance supportive relationships among both friends and family members. You cannot rely solely on family members because sometimes those family members may also be affected by the same change as you (death of another member of the family) and may be in need of support themselves. At other times, it simply may not be appropriate to talk to or seek support from family members because of the nature of the change involved.

9. *Develop a Positive Attitude toward Change*

Developing a positive attitude toward change is one of the most important things you can do to learn to live with it more successfully. Change involves coping with and adapting to new and different circumstances. People naturally feel a sense of anxiety and stress when faced with change because it often means dealing with unknown, unfamiliar, and unpredictable situations. In times like these, a positive attitude can be an important coping tool.

As we discussed in Chapter 5, having a positive attitude does not mean pretending that everything about a change situation is all right. Rather, it means making the best of things when change occurs and looking for the positive things that can come from it. To make the best of things, you need to focus on the gains and benefits of a change rather than dwell on the failures and losses associated with it. Of course, there are negative feelings and emotions associated with many changes and they need to be felt and expressed. The pain and suffering of a loss, for example, are not easy to deal with. But rarely does a change occur that does not result in something positive in the end. The benefit gained can be material or spiritual, or it can involve personal growth, progress, or opportunities for the future. There is always something positive to be found in these situations even if it is the fact that things can't get any worse. Of course, with some changes, the outcome is purely positive and there is no need to look for it because it is obvious.

Change is here to stay and that is the reality we face in modern times. That being the case, we might as well make the best of change when it happens; otherwise we will find ourselves in a state of continual frustration and misery in the future. While you acknowledge the losses, failures, or other negative aspects associated with a particular change, make a conscious effort to find something positive or worthwhile about it. Look for the good that can come of the situation rather than dwell on the negative aspects. For example, Bob, a family man with a wife and three kids, lost his five-year-old small business because of financial problems he faced when a large retailer moved into town and took away much of his business. There were many negatives associated with this change as anyone can imagine: loss of a job, financial loss, loss of self-esteem, depression. However, in the long run, Bob found the outcome of this change was positive because he ended up getting a five-day-a-week, nine-to-five job after his business was closed. As a result, he had more time to spend with his wife and growing children and had more time to pursue hobbies he couldn't even think about when he was working six days a week and twelve hours a day for himself in his business. While Bob surely did not like to experience failure, in this case the failure was an opportunity for change and improvement for Bob even though it didn't come about in a positive manner.

Use self-talk, whenever possible, to help focus your thoughts on the positive during times of change. Remember that how a person interprets events through his perceptions and his beliefs and what he chooses to think about the events determine his reaction to change. Positive and appropriate self-talk can be a powerful tool in controlling negative thoughts and maintaining a positive mood and outlook.

10. Don't Be Afraid of Mistakes and Failure

People experiencing change often find themselves in unfamiliar circumstances, doing things they have never done before. In coping with and adjusting to these new situations, it is inevitable that some things will go wrong, that mistakes will be made and failures will occur. This is a natural outcome of change and it is to be expected. After all, if a person has not experienced or done something before, how can she possibly know how to do it precisely and how can she expect the outcome to be perfect?

The thought of making mistakes or experiencing failure causes great anxiety among people and it is one of the major reasons why people fear change. Because the notion of success and winning is glorified in American culture, permeating almost every aspect of life in our society, it is unfortunate that many people who make mistakes consider themselves failures for having made them. But while no one wants to make mistakes or experience failure, making mistakes is an important part of the process of learning, growing, and maturing.

Change almost always involves taking risks and making mistakes. Most successful people are successful because they are not afraid of failure and of making mistakes. Many successful people have scores of mistakes and failures behind them. In fact, they often become successful only after numerous failures. Complete and total success in life is not normal. It is the exception rather than the rule.

One of the things that makes people successful in the long run is that they learn from their failures and mistakes. They understand that failure, handled properly, can be a tremendous learning experience and a great opportunity for personal growth. They understand that failure is not an obstacle to future success much as success is not a guarantee against future failure. Thomas Edison, Alexander Graham Bell, and many other famous inventors had years of ongoing failures behind them before their inventions were successfully developed. Abraham Lincoln also had many years of continuous failure in his life and yet he went on to become one of America's greatest presidents. These successful people did not give up or wallow in self-pity because of their mistakes and failures. Rather they learned from them and went on to try again.

As change continues to escalate in the future, we will be faced with more of it in our lives. More change to adapt to means the possibility of making more mistakes and having more failures. This is a natural outcome that cannot be avoided. So when you find yourself having to deal with a change, do not be afraid of making mistakes. Understand that things will often go wrong before they go right. Give yourself permission to be imperfect and to make mistakes. You need to take risks with change. If you take risks, sometimes you will succeed and sometimes you will fail. Accept whatever happens. If you make mistakes or suffer failure, learn as much as you can from them and move on. Don't get bogged down dwelling on the negatives, and don't let fear paralyze you and hold you back from forging ahead with change and life.

And finally, don't allow failure that has occurred through no fault of your own to negatively affect you. You do not have control over many changes that affect you. Sometimes things happen that you wish had not. But if there is nothing you can do about it, you have to adjust and make the best of it. Keep your self-esteem and self-confidence intact by not taking these negative changes personally.

11. Face Problems: Don't Avoid Them

No one likes or wants problems in their lives and few people like to deal with them. But problems are a part of life and they are certainly part of the process of adapting to change. Many situations involving change have problems that need to be resolved associated with them.

Often they are problems people have not had to contend with before. When problems arise, they have to be dealt with if the change adaptation process is to be successfully completed.

All too often, however, problems are not dealt with because people have a natural aversion to them. Many find it easier to deny they exist, resist them, ignore them, or wait for them to go away. However, when problems are not resolved, they seldom disappear. If they do, it is only temporarily. Although a person may feel some immediate relief at deciding not to deal with a problem, it usually leads to more problems and greater distress in the long run. By not solving a problem when it arises, it often gets worse over time and becomes more difficult to deal with in the end and keeps people in a state of continual distress in the interim.

When people run away from problems, they often compound them because they still have the original problem to contend with in addition to new ones that are created by avoiding the original one. For example, a person resorts to drugs or alcohol to escape from a problem she does not want to face. However, by abusing drugs and alcohol to handle the problem, she creates another one, addiction. This leads to other problems such as poor health and job loss and the original one is still not solved. Unresolved problems can accumulate and build over time, creating a snowball effect. What at one time may have been a single problem can easily turn into five or ten of them.

When problems are not dealt with, they also create underlying stress. Because the problem is not solved, it is still hovering in the background. People then worry about it, which creates stress. Stress then increases over time as the problem remains unresolved. Another reason people avoid dealing with problems is they are afraid they will fail or make mistakes resolving them. Problems also take time and effort to resolve, time and effort people would rather spend doing other things.

Blaming others for a problem is another way some people divert attention away from facing or solving a problem. But blaming others or saying that something is not one's fault doesn't solve the problem. For some individuals, things always have to be someone's fault. In reality, however, someone is not always at fault. Blaming others for problems simply shifts the responsibility for owning the problem elsewhere. It does nothing to solve the problem. Blaming others for problems and shifting responsibility to others also creates victims. People who are victims feel they do not have to take responsibility for solving a problem because it is not their fault the problem exists. By becoming victims, people give up control over some part of their lives. Losing control leads to more stress, anxiety, and feelings of insecurity.

There are many people waiting for the day when their problems will be over with and they will be happy. Unfortunately, they do not realize that that day will never come. While there are certainly periods in life when problems are much fewer in number and severity, problems in some form will always be with us. Like many things in life, they tend to come and go in cycles.

When problems arise, or when you become aware of a problem during the process of adapting to change, it is best to deal with them as soon as you can. Don't focus your energy on finding excuses or finding ways to avoid them. Don't deny or pretend a problem doesn't exist. Don't look for an escape and don't delude yourself into thinking they will go away if you put them off. You need to face them and deal with them head on, one at a time, as they occur. Taking responsibility for your problems is a sign of maturity.

If you face a problem and deal with it, it is under your control. When you have control, or at least some control, you are in a better position to manage and deal with a problem because you can make some choices about how, when, and where it will be resolved. Even though the outcome may not be exactly what you want or expect, having some control over a problem reduces the amount of insecurity, uncertainty, powerlessness, anxiety, and fear you may feel about it.

While there are many ways to solve problems and many problem-solving models that can be used as a guide, most include these few simple steps:

a Identifying and defining a problem
b Finding the cause of the problem (when applicable)
c Generating possible solutions
d Evaluating solutions and deciding which is best under the circumstances
e Implementing the most appropriate solution

Use these steps (or other available problem-solving models) as a guide to help you solve problems. Don't be afraid of making mistakes. In fact, expect to make some. When problems appear overwhelming, break them down into manageable pieces and deal with them one step or one piece at a time. Anticipating problems whenever possible can make them easier to deal with because it allows you time to plan ahead and prepare for them. It also allows you to prepare yourself psychologically and emotionally, thereby reducing some of the stress and uncertainty that would otherwise be associated with it. Allow yourself time to deal with problems. Most cannot be resolved overnight.

People who learn to face and deal with problems no longer fear them. While they don't like having problems anymore than anyone else, they know they can handle them because they have done so many times before. These experiences give them the practice and confidence to handle other problems whenever they come along.

And finally, if you need further assistance in problem solving, there are many resources available to help. These include library books, videos, audiotapes, professionals (such as psychologists, counselors, social workers, and clergy), consultants, support groups and formal organizations. Do not be afraid to use these resources if they can make things easier for you.

12. Have a Sense of Humor

A sense of humor can do wonders for a person trying to cope with change. Being able to laugh at oneself and at the absurdity of life provides immediate relief from the stresses, frustrations, and pressures of dealing with change.

Laughter releases physical and mental tension and anxiety. It is an outlet for hostility and anger and a defense against depression. Laughter decreases the production of stress hormones, leaving people more relaxed. It causes chemical changes in the body that provide an increased sense of well-being. Thus, having a sense of humor helps to build immunity to stress.

When you are faced with stress and problems that result from change, remind yourself to lighten up and find something to laugh about. Laughing at yourself in stressful times can reduce the level of stress you feel. Search for humor in situations where everything seems to be going wrong. Look at a stressful event or what might otherwise be considered a calamity with a sense of humor. If you can find humor in something, you can survive it. Turn pain into laughter whenever you can.

When you are feeling overwhelmed by a change, use humor as a temporary escape. Get some comedy movies to watch or view a situation comedy on television. Read a funny book or listen to comedians on audiotapes. Tell jokes or humorous stories about past events or make light of your present problems. Then later in the day or week when you are once again facing reality and you need to break tension or release frustration or stress, think of something funny, laugh, and let your thoughts lighten your burden and bring a smile to your face. Let humor be a friend in times of change.

13. *A Solid Core of Personal Values Is Important*

While personal values are part of the structure of one's life (as discussed in strategy 6), they are important enough to be considered a strategy in their own right.

Values are ideas or concepts that people think are important in life. They include ethics (justification of conduct or how people behave) and morals (the question of what is right or wrong). Values are standards of conduct or worth that people try to support or live up to. Values can be used as standards to help us judge and determine whether conduct and things (objects, ideas, people, manner of behaving) are right or wrong, good or bad. They can also assist us in evaluating whether certain kinds of actions are proper and worthwhile as opposed to those that are not.

Why do we need to maintain a strong core of values in order to be able to cope with change? Values are an important part of the structure, framework, or foundation of our lives and, as such, can act as an anchor or support for us during times of change. They do this by providing us with a sense of continuity, stability, and a sense of control. Values can serve as guideposts and can give us direction as to how to respond or adapt to change. They can also furnish us with the confidence to do so. Values provide us with a base from which to evaluate new or changing circumstances and allow us to fit change into the meaning of our lives more comfortably. If you have a strong core of values and understand why you have them, when change comes along, they will be part of your psychological support system.

If you do not have a solid core of values, part of the framework of your life is missing. This weakens the structure and when change comes along, it is threatened. A lack of values leads people to feel disoriented, fearful, uneasy, helpless, and out of control when confronted by significant change. Because they lack the footing, the orientation, the guideposts, the clear sense of direction, it is more difficult for them to react and know what to do. They don't have a firm sense of stability, continuity, and purpose that helps to maintain psychological equilibrium. All of this makes it difficult to make judgments and take action. Also, if there is no distinct feeling for what is right or wrong, good or bad, just or unjust, people can flounder psychologically trying to deal with a change and trying to make sense of where the change fits in their lives.

The discussion of values in today's society is not easy because there are so many values that people hold simultaneously, yet many of them are in conflict with each another. People think differently on a wide range of issues and it is tolerated within certain limits. In cultures past and present, values were more uniformly held by the general population and value judgments were much easier to make as a result. However, in discussing our current values, the question inevitably arises, "Whose values are right and which values count"?

In terms of adapting to change, unless the change involves the issue of values directly (it challenges one's values or proves them wrong), other people's values do not matter. When you are trying to cope with change, it is *your* core of values that is going to help you because you developed them over time, you believe in them and are committed to them, and you are prepared to live by them. They are going to guide you and give you strength as a result. Other people's values or those that conflict with yours cannot help you and therefore do not matter. For example, a forty-three-year-old woman finds herself faced with an unplanned pregnancy. Her other children are in their late teens, and having a baby at this time would change things dramatically for her and her family. She must decide how to deal with this change in her life. If she has a strong core of values, the decision will be made easier. For example, if she believes that abortion is wrong, she will try to carry the baby to term and will make the necessary adjustments to her life and family willingly because she knows she is doing the right thing. By contrast, if the woman opts for an abortion because she feels having a baby would be too dramatic a change in her life, then she will make that decision and live with the consequences knowing that she did the right thing for herself and her family. Both of the values underlying the decision made by this woman conflict but are nonetheless accepted in our culture. At the same time, however, they are also vehemently opposed by segments of the same population. Regardless of how anyone in society views her decision, her values will give this woman a clear sense of direction on how to adapt to the change she was facing. She is unlikely to regret the decision she made as a result.

However, a woman who does not have a solid core of values in this position will have a more difficult time with this change and decision. She is much more likely to anguish over it, not know what to do, and is more likely to worry about the consequences of her actions in the future. She may later have regrets about her decision because she does not have the guideposts and convictions that the other woman had on which to base her decision.

If you are having difficulty coping with a change, consider whether your values have a role to play. Are they helping you because they are solid and giving you direction, or are they hindering you because they are unclear and lack definition? In the past, when values were more homogeneously held, they were easier to identify. With so many choices and acceptable values in society at present, a person can easily be confused as to what his or her values are. People today also don't spend much time thinking about values because they are too busy. So it often takes being confronted by a significant change to bring them to light or to the forefront of one's life.

In order to help you come to terms with a change you may now be facing, you need to undertake action to clarify your values if you determine that they are in doubt or not very well defined. To do this, you need to think about them, analyze them, talk about them, and discuss them with a friend, family member, or confidant. Read about values and how to clarify them. Visit the library or bookstores. Take time to introspect and to reflect so that you can identify with certainty what your values are. This will give you some direction with which to respond to your change. You may find that you have clear values but didn't realize it because you've never really stopped to think about them. This exercise will then serve as a means of reinforcement for you. On the other hand, if your values are not obvious or apparent, by spending some time defining them, you will be much better prepared to deal with your current change as well as those you will face in the future.

14. What Can I Learn from This Change?

Whether the outcome of a change is positive or negative, there is always something to be learned from it. Before you put a change behind you, you need to think about what you have learned from it. Identifying and assessing your successes and failures and examining your losses and gains are part of the process.

Some of the things we learn from change become apparent as the change unfolds and progresses. Often, however, the things we learn from significant change are not obvious or evident at the time the change is taking place. That is because while the change is in progress, our attention is focused on dealing with it or getting through it. We are caught up in the emotions that accompany change and we are busy trying to cope. But when the process is over and we can look back at the change more objectively, lessons and messages become evident. For example, losing a loved one through death is a very painful experience. While a person struggles to resume life without the loved one, she will not likely find anything positive or anything to learn about change at that time. Losing a loved one is definitely a negative experience. However, when the process of healing begins, the loss may generate some positive insights. For example, it may make her realize how important relationships are in life. As a result, she may make a deliberate attempt to strengthen the relationships she has with other loved ones and she may make a point of not taking her relationships for granted anymore, thus enriching her life experiences.

As well as the practical things that can be learned from experiencing change, there are also lessons of a more spiritual or philosophical nature such as those about life. Significant changes can provide new insight into some aspect of life, forcing us to reinvent how we think about it. Having illusions shattered or discovering that beliefs we had about life are mistaken helps us to rethink, reshape, and redirect our lives so that they become more meaningful in the future.

If we do not reflect on what can be learned from each significant change in our lives, if we say good riddance, forget about it entirely, or consider it only bad luck, or if we focus our efforts solely on assessing blame and determining who is at fault, we may be doomed to make the same mistakes over again in the future or we may be unable to grow wiser and more mature as individuals. There is no doubt that many times, change causes great pain and difficulty. But it is from that pain and difficulty we often learn the most and thus experience tremendous personal growth. That growth can have a positive impact on the direction, quality, and meaning of our lives in the future.

After a significant change, you need to ask yourself some important questions such as, What can I learn from this experience that might help me in the future or with the next change I face? What can I learn from this situation that will help me grow as an individual—that will make me a better person, that will make life more meaningful? What have I learned about myself from this experience? What is life trying to teach me? Give yourself time to reflect on life and to get over the change event. Experience is a valuable teacher and much of what is learned from change experiences can be applied to life in general. And remember, what you learn will not necessarily end when the change does. Some lessons may not be evident until long after the change is over. People often have insights years afterward that would have not been possible if the change had not occurred.

15. *Work at Overcoming Fear of Change*

*F*ear of change, like fear of anything else, can have a negative impact on people over time by causing a great deal of mental and emotional stress and anxiety. Fear of change also keeps people from doing many things in life. When people continually look for ways to suppress change and when they spend a great deal of time and effort doing things that enable them to avoid change, they cannot live life fully as it was meant to be lived. They also cannot grow and mature as individuals.

When older people are asked about what their biggest regret in life is, the answers frequently focus on what they didn't do as opposed to something they did. Many regret that they failed to seize the moment when an opportunity arose or when they had the chance to make a change. All too often the reason given for those missed opportunities was fear (as well as a lack of confidence).

Fear is a natural and universal reaction to change. In fact, dealing with the fear that a potential change generates is often worse than having to actually make the change itself. Regardless of the reasons for fearing change (discussed in Chapter 2), it is important to recognize that you can overcome a great deal of fear associated with change, if you make an effort to do so. Fear can be conquered or at least kept under control. There are many strategies that can be used to overcome fear of change.

First, become aware of the nature of change. Recognize that it is disruptive, that it creates uncertainty, insecurity, pain, and so on. The more you know about it, the less you will fear because you know what is involved and what to expect. Then you need to identify what it is you fear about a change. When a fear can be identified, you can begin to work at diffusing or overcoming it. When a fear cannot be identified, it exists as general anxiety and is much more difficult to come to terms with as such. If you are aware of the reasons why people fear change (such as it is disruptive, threatens our security, puts us at risk for failure and making mistakes, causes uncertainty about the future and a loss of control), you are in a better position to analyze, identify, and understand your own fears. This in turn will enable you to begin to work on overcoming them. For example, if you are afraid of a change because you are afraid of making mistakes in a new situation, you need to acknowledge that what you fear in your case is making a mistake. Then deal with it from that point of view. A good place to begin is to acknowledge that making mistakes in times of change is normal and that you might make mistakes because it is natural to do so in new and unfamiliar circumstances. Use self-talk to help you deal with the fear. Tell yourself that you are going to do your best to ensure that you don't make a mistake but if you do, it won't be the end of the world and you will deal with it at the time.

Educate yourself about your specific change by reading books, watching videos, attending seminars, consulting with knowledgeable people, and so on. The more you know about what to expect in your situation, the less fear you will have of the unknown because when the unknown is revealed, it is no longer a mystery and therefore no longer something to be afraid of. You might also want to educate yourself about the topic of fear by reading books on it and finding more ways to overcome it.

Examine your beliefs, expectations, and perceptions of the changes you face to determine if they are realistic and rational and to determine if they are contributing to or causing your fears. For example, in your perception of the consequences of a change, are you blowing things up all out of proportion, making mountains out of molehills, and creating unnecessary or additional fear as a result?

Use self-talk to eliminate negative ideas or fearful thoughts or to keep them under control. Use it to boost your self-confidence about your ability to deal with the fear and to keep stress associated with fear of change under control.

Stop worrying about what might happen as a result of change. You can't control the outcome of change in many circumstances and worrying about it isn't going to force the outcome to your liking. Fearing what might happen is therefore nonproductive and a waste of time. It increases anxiety and fear needlessly.

And finally, perhaps the greatest thing you can do to overcome fear of change is *to resolve to live with whatever happens as a result of change*. If you can do that, you will be able to let go of the fear and live a less stressful life: one without phantoms of fear constantly hovering over you. Resolving to handle whatever happens as a result of change and having the confidence to do so is a sign of maturity.

16. Handle Change in Manageable Pieces: One Step at a Time

As we recognize and become aware that a change is upon us, we begin to think about what it will mean to us in our lives. As we contemplate change and all of its implications in their entirety, they can seem completely overwhelming to us at first. It can appear impossible to have to cope with or even a hopeless situation. We don't know what to do first or where to begin. As a result, we can become discouraged and overwhelmed with negative thoughts about how we will cope before we even begin to deal with it. This is particularly so when a change is unexpected or involuntary.

If you feel overwhelmed by all that needs to be done or all that is involved in a particular change, you need to call a temporary time-out period during which you must try to remove your emotions from the situation and look at it as objectively as possible. You need to recognize and accept that you can't do everything that needs to be done all at once. It is not humanly possible and you shouldn't attempt to do it. You need to tell yourself that you will be able to make the change if you handle the change one step at a time or in smaller, more manageable pieces. Using this approach, whenever possible, will help you to cope with change more easily and successfully over time.

Once you decide that dealing with a change one step at a time is the best approach to use in your circumstances, you need to examine the situation and evaluate what needs to be done overall. Make a list of the tasks involved and prioritize them in order of importance (or urgency). Have a trusted friend or relative help you with this task, if appropriate and if you so desire. You need to attend to those things that must be done immediately and leave other less significant things for a later time. Break large tasks down into smaller, more manageable ones that are easier to handle. Organize and divide tasks involved in order of priority and work at them one at a time. Eventually, you will get everything done.

17. Learn to Accept Reality

While all of us have ideas and visions about the way we would like things to be in our lives, in reality, things don't always work out according to our plans or as we anticipate. Change sometimes forces our lives in a direction different from the one we envisioned for ourselves. Oftentimes change does not happen in a manner we would like or at a time we prefer. Other times it destroys our future plans and dreams.

While we can fight change, attempt to influence its outcome, or try to prevent it from occurring when it is appropriate to do so, many times there is nothing we can do to affect a change. Many of the changes in our lives, our society, and environment are beyond our control. When change comes into our lives and there is nothing we can do about it, we have to accept it and learn to live with it.

While we may not like the reality change brings into our lives, we cannot pretend the reality is different than it is. While it is difficult to let go of our expectations about what we feel life should be, *we have to learn to accept things as they are in reality instead of how we want them to be.* The world simply cannot be how we want it to be no matter how long we wish it were so. Ignoring reality and longing for the way things should be inevitably leads to frustration, cynicism, disappointment, disillusionment, depression, and general unhappiness.

Accepting reality doesn't mean we can't have hopes and dreams for the future. It does mean that we have to give up illusions, inflated expectations, and images of perfection about life in a culture and environment where we are constantly bombarded by them. For example, we have to ignore false messages promoted in the media that tell us that we can have it all or we can have what we want. We need to realize and accept that perfection doesn't exist and we should stop measuring the outcome of things in our lives according to standards of perfection. We need to stop thinking about the way things should be, ought to be, and are supposed to be in life instead of how they actually are.

If you learn to accept things as they are in reality, your expectations of life will become more realistic. As a result, you will be less likely to become disappointed, disillusioned, and dissatisfied with life. You will also have less difficulty accepting and adjusting to change.

18. Maintain Routines

A person's ability to cope with life depends on the existence of consistent, predictable, and reliable structures (relationships, job, religion) in one's life and environment and the daily routines and patterns of behavior associated with them. Structure and routines are closely related. Structure gives us a dependable and consistent frame of reference for making decisions and judgments about things, and it allows us to organize our lives and develop behavioral routines to deal with everyday events. Structures as well as the routines and traditions associated with them provide us with a sense of stability, control, security, continuity, and purpose.

When something new or different comes into our lives in the form of a change, it disturbs the way things are, disrupting our routines and patterns of behavior and interrupting the smooth functioning and normal flow of events we are used to. This causes disorientation and uncertainty. To counter the uncertainty and disorientation you may feel during times of change, you need to maintain as many of your usual routines as possible. Following routines will give you a sense of stability, familiarity, predictability, a sense of normalcy and continuity, and a feeling of control over your life while change is occurring around you. It will also help to reduce anxiety and stress associated with change. Because change is disruptive to regular routines, sometimes it is not possible to adhere to them during a period of change. You should, however, get back into a regular routine as soon as you can afterward. If routines have been disrupted in only one area of your life as a result of change, try to maintain your routines in the unaffected areas to add some stability to your life until the adaptation process is complete.

19. Examine Your Beliefs for Validity

As we discussed in Chapter 5, people often have mistaken or irrational beliefs about themselves, others, or life in general. These faulty beliefs can undermine or hinder a person's ability to successfully adapt to change (as well as make it difficult to deal with problems in general).

Also discussed in Chapter 5, one of the most significant findings in the field of psychology over the last few decades is the discovery that *individuals can choose the way they think*. If individuals can choose the way they think, they can change the way they think. Thus, if a person's thinking patterns and beliefs are flawed and generating negative consequences in their lives, including the inability to adapt to change successfully, they can change them. Inaccurate ways of thinking about life and mistaken or irrational beliefs need to be identified and replaced with more appropriate and positive thinking patterns. Remember, it is not what happens to us in life that causes us distress and turmoil but rather *what we tell ourselves about what has happened* through our beliefs, thoughts, and perceptions of events. Developing more appropriate ways of thinking can significantly improve one's quality of life as well as dramatically improve one's ability to cope with change.

If you are having difficulty adapting to a specific change in your life or in accepting change in general, you need to examine whether your beliefs (as they relate to the change) are having any kind of negative impact. To do this, consider the circumstances of the change you face and then determine whether your beliefs about the circumstances (in light of the change) are realistic, rational, and factual. For example, look for evidence of validity by asking yourself if there are facts to support your beliefs about the change. Think about whether your expectations (under the circumstances) are realistic or whether you have been living under illusions (e.g., believing that what happened could never happen to you). Consider whether your beliefs are based on how things are supposed to be or ought to be rather than how things are in reality. Determine whether your expectations are based on standards of perfection rather than on reality. To help with this task, review the material presented on this topic in Chapter 5.

20. *Get Stress under Control*

Most people are aware of the negative consequences that stress has on individuals. As we discussed in Chapter 6, stress can have many negative effects on people's mental and physical health and on the quality of their lives. Change is a major source of stress in our lives. Since stress accompanies so many of the changes we experience, being able to manage stress is a great advantage when it comes to being able to live with and adapt successfully to change.

Since there is a relationship between change and stress in that change causes stress, when we talk about learning to manage change, we also need to talk about managing stress. If a person cannot handle stress well, she will not be able to cope with change well. A person whose life is already overloaded with stress may be unable to cope when a significant change comes along that brings with it even more stress. This can result in a physical or mental breakdown. On the other hand, if a person has stress under control in her life and is then faced with more stress as a result of a change, she is less likely to be overwhelmed by the stress. That is because she will not have a great deal of stress already existing in her life because she has developed the skills to manage it.

If you want to be able to live more comfortably with change, you need to take stress management seriously and get stress under control in your life. Take time to assess your ability to manage and deal with stress and make improvements where they are warranted. Stress can be effectively managed. Identify and examine your stressors and find ways to handle them more effectively. Since change is increasing in our society and our lives, we can conclude that we will likely experience increased stress from it in the future. Chapter 6 contains a more detailed discussion of ways to reduce and control stress. There are also many resources available (books, tapes, seminars, courses, and professional counselors) to help you learn to control and reduce stress.

21. Mourn Your Losses

*A*s we discussed in Chapter 7, all meaningful losses in life need to be mourned. Just as people are healed by the grieving process following a death, so it is needed to heal us from significant loss. When we face the loss of something important to us, we are actually giving up part of ourselves. We need time to assess the impact on our lives and we need time to adjust and adapt to the new reality we face. Mourning a loss is not an option. It is a psychological necessity. We cannot heal and move on with life if we do not mourn our losses. Loss must be acknowledged so that healing can take place. If you experience a change involving a significant loss, be sure that you find and take the time to mourn the loss. When losses are mourned as they occur, people are in a better position to cope with change when it comes along. We should also note that as change continues to escalate in our society and our lives, we will be faced with the need to mourn losses more and more frequently in the future. For more detailed information on the process of mourning, review the material presented in Chapter 7.

22. A Sense of Control Is Necessary

One of the most disturbing and frightening aspects of living with change is living with the loss of control that often accompanies it. When people experience a major change, they often lose control of their lives or some part of it. When people feel they have lost control, they feel powerless, helpless, anxious, uneasy, apprehensive, frightened, and threatened as they do not know where change will take them and how it will affect their lives. Under normal circumstances, people cannot live with these feelings for long periods of time without suffering negative consequences such as stress, anxiety, and burnout.

Structure and predictability in life are needed for people to feel secure. When people are in familiar and comfortable surroundings, when they can depend on things, and when they are able to predict the outcome of their behaviors and actions, they feel they have control over their lives. Structure, routines, and a sense of control make people feel stable and secure.

Since structure, routine, and familiar surroundings give people a sense of control in their lives, it is important to preserve and maintain them during times of change. When things are changing around you, you have to feel you have control of something. Try to maintain control over the areas of your life that may not be affected by change and do not engage in any behaviors that will lead to further loss of control in your life or that will undermine the control you still have, insofar as it is possible. Doing so will only increase insecurity, stress, fear, and anxiety to your detriment.

23. Use Positive Self-Talk

Self-talk can have a profound effect on how people feel, how they handle events in their daily lives, and how they cope with and react to change. We have suggested using positive and appropriate self-talk as part of various other management strategies throughout this chapter and in other parts of the book. Using positive self-talk will be recognized here as a strategy in itself because it is one of the most important and beneficial techniques a person can use to cope with the stresses and uncertainty of change.

To review what self-talk is, when people encounter various situations including those involving change, they mentally evaluate the situation and instruct themselves how to feel about it, using a silent inner voice. How a person thinks about, interprets, and talks to himself about how to react to a particular situation is self-talk.

Change means facing new situations, uncertainty, and the unknown. It means making mistakes, losing control, and feeling insecure. Change creates stress, anxiety, and loss. What you say to yourself and how you instruct yourself to feel and react in these circumstances has a significant effect on how you will feel and how well you will be able to cope with a change. If you use positive self-talk as you face or deal with a change or change-related circumstance (e.g., "I know it will probably be difficult but I can do it if I remain calm and take things one step at a time"), you are more likely to maintain a positive mental and emotional outlook and will be able to get through the change in a more successful and positive manner. However, if you use negative self-talk as you face a change (e.g., "It's no use. It's hopeless. I can't do this. I'm never going to be able to make it. I can't stand it"), you will likely remain in a negative emotional and mental state and may even experience additional feelings of distress (depression, anxiety, hopelessness) over time as a result. Your physical health could also suffer and you will not get through the change as easily.

Positive self-talk can be used in a wide variety of circumstances generated by or associated with change. For example, it can be used to calm oneself down and to reduce the fear, anxiety, and uncertainty associated with change. It can be used to control negative thoughts about change. Positive self-talk can be used to boost your self-confidence and to reinforce your ability to handle various situations you encounter in times of change. You can use it to control stress generated by change as well as to prepare yourself to face an unfamiliar or uncomfortable situation. You can use self-talk to help you focus your thoughts on the positive aspects of change and, most important, you can use it to maintain a positive attitude throughout the entire change/adaptation process. This will significantly improve your chances of coming through the change comfortably as well as emotionally and mentally intact.

Whenever you find yourself facing a change, make a point of analyzing your thoughts, thinking about the change, and evaluating your situation using positive self-talk. Avoid talking to yourself negatively about it. Turning negative into positive self-talk can contribute immensely to the improvement of your mental and emotional outlook and quality of life in general. And once again, while we cannot always control the things that happen to us, we can control our thoughts about them and therefore how we feel about them using our silent inner voice. For a more detailed discussion of self-talk as well as how and when to use it, review the information presented in Chapter 5.

24. *Keep Traditions Alive*

*T*he need to maintain continuity in life is important as it provides people with a sense of identity, of where they come from, and where they are going in life. It enables people to feel a sense of purpose and meaning and provides a feeling of stability.

Change often disrupts the purpose and meaning of our lives in some way. When familiar structures and patterns of behavior in people's lives are disturbed by change, the sense of continuity in life is shaken. When change disrupts or calls into question a source of meaning or purpose in our lives, it causes disorientation, confusion, and anxiety.

Traditions, that is, the passing down of ideas, customs, beliefs, and stories from generation to generation, play an important role in the continuity of our lives. The way we celebrate life's important events and holidays, the way we do things within our families, are part of our identity and they give us a sense of who we are as well as a sense of belonging. Traditions add to the meaning of our lives and our personal history. In some ways, traditions are our link to the past and future. Traditions are predictable and familiar to us and help us to feel secure. They become part of the structure and routines in our lives over time.

In times of change, we need to keep our traditions alive whenever it is possible to do so. When things are changing all around us, some things need to stay the same to keep us anchored. Following traditions provides us with a sense of stability and security and allows us to maintain continuity in our lives. As a general strategy, to help us better withstand change in general, following traditions can help to buffer us against some of the negative and disorienting effects of change.

25. *Have Confidence in Yourself*

When people initially face or experience a significant change, they often feel overwhelmed by it and worry about how they will be able to deal with it. Typical thoughts include, "How will I cope? How will I ever get through this? What am I going to do now? I'm afraid. I can't handle this. What's going to happen? I hope I can do it." Feelings of insecurity, uncertainty, and apprehension challenge self-confidence and self-esteem.

In times of change, you have to remind yourself that these reactions to the prospect of change are perfectly normal, part of human nature. You also have to bear in mind that these feelings and reactions can be overcome. To do so, try to temporarily set aside your emotions and look objectively at the change you are facing. Remind yourself that you have the ability to get through the change because you have the knowledge, resources, and skills to do so. Boost your self-confidence by thinking of as many of them as you can. For example, understanding the process of adapting to change will make you aware of what you will face, and this will provide a good idea of what to expect emotionally and intellectually throughout the process. Identifying and understanding the reasons you fear your particular change can help you to keep fear under control. Recognizing the range of emotions associated with change will help you to understand why you feel the way you do about it. Obtaining resources and learning about your specific change by reading books, viewing videos, listening to audiotapes, attending seminars, joining support groups, and talking to others with similar experiences, for example, will provide you with further knowledge of what to expect in your particular situation. Being aware of how change can cause stress can enable you to take measures to keep it under control. Learning strategies to help you cope with change will help you to get through the change/adaptation process more easily. Knowing you have caring friends and family members to help you through your change can be reassuring. Maintaining a positive attitude can help to sustain confidence and a sense of hope throughout the change process. And using self-talk as a companion to talk your way through the process and to boost confidence along the way can be of significant benefit as well.

To increase confidence even further, you might also think about all the thousands or millions of people in the world who have experienced a change the same as or similar to yours and survived. They, too, were anxious and frightened and felt insecure but survived and went on to live happy and productive lives. If thousands or millions of others survived, so can you despite the interim difficulties. You might also think about people who endured difficulties or pain even greater than yours associated with change (e.g., lost entire family in plane crash) and survived. Thinking of them can also provide hope and inspiration.

And finally, there is always outside help available (psychologists, counselors, social workers) if you need assistance or are having difficulty coping with a change on your own. These people have been professionally trained to help those in your situation. They can boost your confidence by helping you get through a change and by providing support for you along the way.

chapter nine

Getting Help and Support

*T*he experiences and emotions generated by a major or significant change can be difficult to handle alone. People undergoing
change often need support to help them accept, adjust to, and cope
with their new situations. There are a variety of resources available
that people can use for help and support. In this chapter, we review
four major sources that you can call on during times of change: self-
education, talking to friends and family, joining a support group, and
seeking professional help.

Self-Education

*P*robably the most important thing people can do to help prepare
themselves for change is to learn as much as they can about it. This
includes learning about the nature of change itself, the process of
adapting to change, and the specific change they are faced with. Self-
education is important because it allows people to help themselves
adjust to change. When people are knowledgeable about change,
they are much better prepared to deal with it because they know

what to expect in the way of thoughts, behaviors, and emotions. This in turn reduces or eliminates much of the mystery, anxiety, fear, and uncertainty associated with it. People are then able to better focus their energies and attention on positive and productive behaviors, feelings, and strategies related to change rather than on fear and other negative emotions.

When people learn about change, they gain knowledge about how change affects them. This knowledge enables people to understand the feelings and emotions they experience and helps them understand why they feel the way they do. When people are aware of the stages and steps involved in adapting to change, they know what to expect and are better prepared to cope with the entire process. When people are informed about the pitfalls they may encounter in adjusting to change, they are better able to avoid them. When people are aware of strategies for dealing with change successfully, they are in a position to cope with change more successfully. When people are alerted to the companions to change (stress, loss, and mistaken beliefs), they can determine if these factors have a negative impact on them in their personal circumstances, and they can take appropriate measures to minimize any potential negative effects.

People can educate themselves about change using a variety of resources. There are many books, magazine articles, journal articles, videos, and audiotapes available at libraries, bookstores, and through mail order on a wide range of topics relating to specific changes (such as first year of marriage, diagnosis of chronic illness, looking after an aging parent, preparing for the birth of a child). Similarly, there are seminars, workshops, and courses that people can take to learn about the changes they are experiencing. These are provided through national organizations and various local agencies as well as through community colleges, churches (or other religion-based organizations), and community education programs. Talking directly to other people (who have experienced similar changes) for information on things such as what to expect and how to cope is another way to educate oneself. Once again, the more you learn about change, the better prepared you are to help yourself deal with it.

Talking to Friends and Family

*H*aving close and trusted friends to be with and to talk to can be a tremendous source of comfort, encouragement, and support for people experiencing significant change. This is the case even when friends and family members may not actually understand what you are going through. The fact that they are there for you, that they are concerned and care about you is reassuring and a source of strength and support in itself. When you can count on people to be there for you when you need them, the burden and stresses related to change can be lightened. People with well-established friendships and good social support systems are better able to withstand the pressures and difficulties associated with change for this reason. Friendships can have extraordinary power to help you heal.

While experiencing the disorienting effects of change, you need to be around people and spend time with people who are accepting, understanding, and supportive of you. You also need to talk about the change and what you are going through with a person or people you can confide in. Being able to talk about the change and being able to express thoughts and feelings about it to those you trust is a good way to release a tremendous amount of tension, anxiety, insecurity, fear, and other negative emotions that can build up. Talking about what you are going through allows you to mentally unload some of your stress and burdens and allows you to vent any pent-up negative emotions associated with the change and thereby improve your mental and emotional state. At times in your discussions, you may find yourself repeating or expressing the same stories and thoughts over and over again to others. This is a natural tendency during times of change as it helps you to psychologically work through and come to terms with the reality of the change you face.

Whether the person you choose to talk to is a close friend or family member, there are qualities that make some people better confidants than others. While the ability to be a patient and good listener is probably the most important, there are other desirable traits. For example, choose people who are not embarrassed or who do not feel uncomfortable with your emotions or tears, people who accept you without judging you, who can be trusted with your secrets and confidences, and who do not give unwanted advice.

When you feel vulnerable and need support during times of change, spend time with others you trust even when you don't feel like talking. The mere presence of those who care about you can be reassuring in itself. When you do feel like discussing things, avoid talking to people who make you feel worse about the situation by doing things such as judging or condemning you ("I told you not to marry that jerk"), making you feel guilty ("Think of what this will do to Mark"), belittling your feelings ("Oh, you'll snap out of this in a couple of weeks"), or changing the subject when you try to talk about or express your feelings about the change. People who are uncomfortable with your emotions or who do not understand the psychological need to express your thoughts and feelings may try to avoid discussion of the subject, change the subject, or shift the focus away from the subject whenever you try to discuss the change. These people feel they are doing you a favor by preventing you from becoming upset. But their thinking is misguided and you should not frustrate yourself trying to discuss things with them when they cannot meet your needs in this regard.

Joining a Support Group

A support group is a group of ordinary people who have similar problems or changes to face and who meet on a regular basis to support and help each other through the stresses and difficulties of the circumstances they find themselves in. Because each member of the group is experiencing the same type of condition or change, they can easily understand and relate to each other. A support group provides a forum for people to discuss their feelings and what they are going through with others who understand. When you join a support group, other members understand your feelings, frustrations, fears, and stresses because they have similar ones themselves. A support group also provides a forum for people to share knowledge such as new research findings, new treatments, and useful resources relating to their circumstances.

Joining a support group can be beneficial in many ways. First, simply knowing and spending time with other people who understand your situation is reassuring. It helps people who are experiencing change to feel that they are not alone, that there are others who are experiencing similar circumstances and are able to cope. Many times only a person who has experienced a particular change can truly understand what another person in the same situation is going through. Second, talking about the difficulties in an environment of acceptance among others is a good way to release tension and stress associated with the change. Next, people are less fearful and less stressed when they face problems in the presence of others as opposed to facing their difficulties completely alone. People in support groups can also gain practical advice from others on ways to overcome or to successfully deal with problems. They can also learn about the failures or difficulties of others and thereby avoid some pitfalls they may be unaware of as a result. Those who have been members of a support group for a long time can provide guidance to new members by relating their experiences about dealing with change over time. And finally, when people share their own experiences and advice with others who are in turn helped by it, their self-esteem is raised because they feel they are making a worthwhile contribution to the lives of others in the group.

The number of support groups or self-help organizations formed to help people with various problems has grown tremendously in recent years. As a result, there are literally thousands of active support groups across the country and there are groups for almost any major change or problem one can think of. The range includes traditional groups such as Alcoholics Anonymous and Parents Without Partners, groups that deal with various medical problems and diseases (arthritis, migraine sufferers, parents of children with serious diseases), and those for people suffering from grief and bereavement. Support groups can be located in the yellow pages of the telephone book, through information pamphlets found at local community centers and libraries, by recommendation of professionals (psychologists, doctors), and through recommendations of people who have belonged to a support group in the past. There are also national and state level self-help clearinghouses that can be of assistance by providing you with information on specific kinds of support groups in your area. Information can be obtained by calling the clearinghouses listed below.

National Clearinghouses

National Self-Help Clearinghouse, New York, 212-354-8525
American Self-Help Clearinghouse, New Jersey, 973-625-9565

State-Level Clearinghouses

Alabama, Birmingham area, 205-251-5912
Arizona, 800-352-3792 (in Arizona only); outside Arizona,
    602-231-0868
Arkansas, Northeast area, 501-932-5555
California, San Diego, 619-543-0412; Los Angeles, 310-305-8878;
    Modesto, 209-558-7454; San Francisco, 415-772-4357; Sacramento,
    916-368-3100; Davis, 916-756-8181; Macon, 217-429-HELP
Connecticut, 203-624-6982
Illinois, 773-481-8837; 312-368-9070; Champaign area only,
    217-352-0099
Iowa, 800-779-2001 (in Iowa only); 319-356-1343
Kansas, 800-445-0116 (in Kansas only); 316-978-3843
Massachusetts, 413-545-2313
Michigan, 800-777-5556 (in Michigan only); 517-484-7373
Missouri, Kansas City, 816-822-7272; St. Louis, 314-773-1399
Nebraska, 402-476-9668
New Jersey, 800-FOR-M.A.S.H. (in New Jersey only); 973-625-3037
New York, New York City, 212-586-5770; Long Island, 516-626-1721;
    Westchester, 914-949-0788, ext. 237
North Carolina, Mecklenberg area, 704-331-9500
North Dakota, Fargo area, 701-235-SEEK
Ohio, Dayton area, 937-225-3004; Toledo area, 419-475-4449
Oregon, Portland area, 503-222-5555
Pennsylvania, Pittsburgh, 412-578-2450; Scranton, 717-961-1234;
    Lehigh Valley, 610-865-4400
South Carolina, Midlands area, 803-791-2800
Tennesee, Knoxville area, 423-584-9125; Memphis area, 901-323-8485

Texas, 512-454-3706
Utah, Salt Lake City area, 801-978-3333
Virginia, Tidewater area, 757-340-9380

American Self-help Clearinghouse web site: http://www.cmhc.com/selfhelp

Other Helpful Information Hot Lines in the United States

National Health Information Clearinghouse, 800-336-4797 (U.S. only)
National Organization for Rare Disorders, 800-999-NORD (U.S. only)
Alliance of Genetic Support Groups (genetic illnesses), 800-336-GENE (U.S. only)

Canadian Self-Help Clearinghouses

Calgary, 403-262-1117
Nova Scotia, 902-466-2011
Toronto, 416-487-4355
Prince Edward Island, 902-628-1648
Vancouver, 604-733-6186
Winnipeg, 204-589-5500 or 204-633-5955

Seeking Professional Help

*T*raditionally, when people experienced significant change that caused them distress or problems, they sought the help and support of their families, friends, and clergy (or other religious figures). Today, because of changes that have occurred in society over the last few decades (such as changing family structure, reduced religious involvement, more mobility), these traditional sources of help and support are no longer feasible or available to a growing number of people. As a result, more and more people are seeking counseling and advice from mental health professionals such as psychologists, social workers, counselors, psychiatric nurses, and other therapists whose job it is to help people with change and transitions in their lives.

Not long ago, there was a stigma attached to consulting professionals for assistance with personal problems. Today, that stigma is fast disappearing as more and more people are consulting professionals for assistance with their personal problems and are using the services of professionals to get the advice and information they need to help them through periods of change. People are recognizing the importance of maintaining good mental health and the value it has on the quality of their lives.

Individuals may seek professional assistance when faced with a change because they don't know how to help themselves or they are too distressed to deal with it on their own. They may not have any social supports (family, friends) nearby that can help them through a change or they may not want to involve family or friends for whatever reason. Some people may realize there is something wrong in their lives but they cannot diagnose what it is and for that reason turn to professionals for help. Another reason some people seek professional assistance is because they are busy and do not have the time to research about change or the problem they have. Instead, they consult a professional who can readily provide them with information, advice, coping strategies, and suggestions that will enable them to begin working on solving a problem or coping with a change within a short period of time.

A growing number of employers today are providing mental health care insurance benefits for their employees much as they provide employees benefits for physical health care. They recognize that mental well-being is as important as physical health and that employees with good mental health are happier and more productive than those without it.

What can psychologists, counselors, and other mental health specialists do for people experiencing change or difficulties associated with change? How do they help? Psychologists, counselors, social workers, psychiatric nurses, and therapists are trained to help people cope with changes and transitions in their lives. It is something that they do every day. Psychologists and therapists are people who can look at your situation or problem objectively because they do not have the emotional attachment to your situation that you do, and they are not emotionally attached to you. With their objectivity, training, and experience, they can identify problems that you may not see and can provide practical commonsense advice and suggestions on how to overcome or solve a problem or cope with a change or transition. They do this by suggesting a range of methods and coping skills that you can use and by helping you develop skills and strategies that are best suited to your circumstances. Psychologists and counselors can also tell you what kinds of behaviors and thoughts are normal for people in your situation and why you are feeling the way you are. They can also provide you with ongoing support and encouragement and monitor your progress and keep you on track once you embark on a course of action or recovery. All this is done with complete confidentiality.

The way psychologists and counselors help people is by talking, by discussing things with you, and by listening to you talk (psychotherapy). Because they are objective, they are able to look at your situation and assess your thoughts and emotions relating to it. They can spot and identify conditions that may be causing you problems or contributing to your distress. For example, they can detect erroneous thinking patterns, incorrect perceptions, and mistaken beliefs. They can help people see the errors in their thinking and help them put things into proper perspective. They can identify bad emotional habits and help people recognize the sources of stress in their lives. Part of the mental health professional's job is to understand troubling emotions and circumstances, where they come from, and how they affect people.

A psychologist, social worker, counselor, or other therapist is someone you can talk to freely, someone who will listen, who won't judge you, condemn you, belittle you, or provide unwanted advice. Simply being able to speak to them freely about your thoughts and emotions can provide relief in itself and can release a great deal of stress, tension, and other negative emotions associated with change.

Most people who seek the help of mental health professionals are satisfied with the help and care they receive. They find that psychotherapy does work and makes a positive difference in their lives by providing relief, by helping them cope with their situations, and by helping them resolve their problems.

When choosing a mental health professional to work with, competence and personal chemistry are probably the most important factors to consider. Check the person's experience and qualifications. Be sure that they are licensed or certified to practice. If you do not feel comfortable with a therapist or feel you aren't making any progress, do not hesitate to seek another. To find an appropriate therapist, ask for referrals from your family doctor, clergy, local universities (psychology department), hospitals, psychotherapy training institutions, friends, or former clients of therapists or look in the yellow pages of the telephone directory. You can also contact national professional organizations (for mental health care providers), or state or local chapters of these organizations to find out about service providers in your local area. Information can be obtained by calling the numbers listed below.

National-Level Organizations

American Psychological Association, 202-336-5800
National Association of Social Workers, 800-638-8799
American Association for Marriage and Family Therapy (number to
    call to request a free copy of *The Consumer's Guide to Marriage and
    Family Therapy*), 202-452-0109

State-Level Psychological Associations

Alaska, Anchorage, 907-344-8878
Alabama, Montgomery, 334-262-8245
Arkansas, Little Rock, 501-614-6500
Arizona, Scottsdale, 602-675-9477
California, Sacramento, 916-325-9786
Colorado, Denver, 303-692-9303
Connecticut, East Hartford, 860-528-8550
District of Columbia, Washington, 202-336-5557
Delaware, Claymont, 302-478-2591
Florida, Tallahassee, 850-656-2222
Georgia, Atlanta, 404-351-9555
Hawaii, Honolulu, 808-394-0388
Iowa, Knoxville, 515-828-8845
Idaho, Boise, 208-331-4141

Illinois, Chicago, 312-372-7610
Indiana, Indianapolis, 317-686-5348
Kansas, Topeka, 785-267-7435
Kentucky, Louisville, 502-894-0222
Louisiana, Baton Rouge, 504-344-8839
Massachusetts, Boston, 617-523-6320
Maryland, Columbia, 410-992-4258
Maine, Augusta, 207-621-0732
Michigan, Farmington Hills, 248-473-9070
Minnesota, St. Paul, 612-489-2964
Missouri, Jefferson City, 573-634-8852
Mississippi, Jackson, 601-982-7675
Montana, Billings, 406-252-2559
North Carolina, Raleigh, 919-872-1005
North Dakota, Bismarck, 701-223-9045
Nebraska, Lincoln, 402-475-0709
New Hampshire, Concord, 603-225-9925
New Jersey, Livingston, 973-535-9888
New Mexico, Albuquerque, 505-883-7376
Nevada, Las Vegas, 800-288-6772
New York, Albany, 518-437-1040
Ohio, Columbus, 614-224-0034
Oklahoma, Oklahoma City, 405-879-0069
Oregon, Portland, 503-253-9155
Pennsylvania, Harrisburg, 717-232-3817
Rhode Island, Pawtucket, 401-728-5570
South Carolina, Columbia, 803-771-6050
South Dakota, Sioux Falls, 605-332-3386
Tennessee, Memphis, 901-372-9133
Texas, Austin, 512-454-2449
Utah, Salt Lake City, 801-278-4665
Virginia, Winchester, 540-667-5544
Vermont, Montpelier, 802-229-5447
Washington, Edmonds, 425-712-18852
Wisconsin, Madison, 608-251-1450
West Virginia, Scott Depot, 304-757-0458
Wyoming, Laramie, 307-745-3167

Canadian Psychological Associations

Alberta, Edmonton, 403-424-0294
British Columbia, Vancouver, 604-730-0501
Manitoba, Winnipeg, 204-784-9617
Nova Scotia, Halifax, 902-422-9183
Ontario, Toronto, 416-961-5552
Quebec, Montreal, 514-738-1881

State-Level Associations of Social Workers

Alabama, Montgomery, 334-288-2633
Alaska, Juneau, 907-586-4438
Arizona, Tempe, 602-968-4595
Arkansas, Little Rock, 501-663-0658
California, Sacramento, 916-442-4565
California (Los Angeles only), 213-935-2050
Colorado, Denver, 303-753-8890
Connecticut, Rocky Hill, 860-257-8066
Delaware, Claymont, 302-792-0646
District of Columbia, Washington, 202-371-8282
Florida, Tallahassee, 850-224-2400
Georgia, Atlanta, 770-234-0567
Hawaii, Honolulu, 808-521-1787
Idaho, Boise, 208-343-2752
Illinois, Chicago, 312-236-8308
Indiana, Indianapolis, 317-923-9878
Iowa, Boise, 515-277-1117
Kansas, Topeka, 785-354-4804
Kentucky, Frankfort, 502-223-0245
Louisiana, Baton Rouge, 504-346-1234
Maine, Hallowell, 207-622-7592
Maryland, Baltimore, 410-788-1066
Massachusetts, Boston, 617-227-9635
Michigan, Lansing, 517-487-1548
Minnesota, St. Paul, 612-293-1935
Mississippi, Jackson, 601-981-8359

Missouri, Columbia, 573-874-6140
Montana, Helena, 406-449-6208
Nebraska, Lincoln, 402-477-7344
Nevada, Las Vegas, 702-791-5872
New Hampshire, Concord, 603-226-7135
New Mexico, Albuquerque, 505-247-2336
New Jersey, Trenton, 609-394-1666
New York City (only), 212-577-5000
New York, Albany, 518-463-4741
North Carolina, Raleigh, 919-828-9650
North Dakota, Bismarck, 701-223-4161
Ohio, Columbus, 614-461-4484
Oklahoma, Oklahoma City, 405-239-7017
Oregon, Portland, 503-452-8420
Pennsylvania, Harrisburg, 717-232-4125
Rhode Island, Providence, 401-274-4940
South Carolina, Columbia, 803-256-8406
South Dakota, Spearfish, 605-642-0711
Tennessee, Nashville, 615-321-5095
Texas, Austin, 512-474-1454
Utah, Salt Lake City, 801-583-8855
Vermont, Montpelier, 802-223-1713
Virginia, Richmond, 804-643-1833
Washington, Seattle, 206-448-1660
West Virginia, Charleston, 304-343-6141
Wisconsin, Madison, 608-257-6334
Wyoming, Cheyenne, 307-634-2118

Conclusion

And so, we come to the end of this book on change but certainly not to the end of change itself. It will go on and on into the future, driving us, transforming us, shaping our world, and framing our destiny. Where will it take us? What will it bring to each of us? How will it affect our lives, our culture, and our world?

No one knows what kinds of changes face us tomorrow. No one can anticipate how much change lies ahead. No one can predict where it will come from or what form it will take. But we can be fairly certain in predicting this: Tomorrow will be different from today because of change. If we are to survive and flourish in a future of continuous change, we have to prepare ourselves for it. This book, it is hoped, has helped make a contribution in that regard. But there is much more research and work that needs to be done in this area before we can attain a state of significant readiness.

We have to begin to study all facets of change, particularly as it relates to human adaptation, with much more vigor and intensity to fill the immense vacuum that currently exists in the literature. And we need to educate ourselves about it. Knowledge about change and how it affects us needs to become as common and widespread among the public as awareness is of good nutrition, preventing dental decay,

241

or heart disease. The leaders and policy makers in our society must also learn about these facets of change. Then they can employ strategies and structure the environment in the institutions and establishments they represent (schools, business, government) so that people in their care will benefit from the positive effects of change to the greatest degree possible and be protected from any adverse effects.

What we cannot do is continue to blindly forge ahead with our personal lives and with our history without developing a greater understanding of change and its effects on humans. The price we may have to pay someday for our inattentiveness and laxity in this area may prove too high in terms of our physical and mental health and well-being. There are too many questions about change and its effects on people that have yet to be answered. And there are even more questions that have yet to be asked. Consider these examples:

More change in the future means the need to mourn more losses, deal with more stress, experience more uncertainty, disorientation, anxiety, insecurity, and loss of control. How much more can we safely endure?

As the average life span increases, people will be faced with more change over the course of a longer life. Will they be able to tolerate it without sustaining any harmful effects?

How do we prepare for an era of hyperchange? What can we do to maximize the positive effects and benefits of change and minimize the adverse effects? Is there a point at which the negative consequences generated by change outweigh the benefits created by it?

Are we experiencing the phenomenon Alvin Toffler refers to as "future shock"? If not, how close are we to that point now? As Toffler states in his book:

> "It is quite clearly impossible to accelerate the rate of change in society . . . without triggering significant changes in the body chemistry of the population. By stepping up the pace of scientific, technological and social change, we are tampering with the chemistry and biological stability of the human race. . . . There are discoverable limits to the amount of change that the human organism can absorb . . . by endlessly accelerating change without first determining its limits, we may subject masses (of people) to demands they simply cannot tolerate."[1]

The time has surely come to find out what those limits of human tolerance are. That time is now.

Endnotes

Introduction

1. Carl Rogers, as cited by Arlene Crandall in "The Challenge of
   Change in School Psychology," *School Psychologist*, spring 1989,
   p. 1.
2. Alvin Toffler, *Future Shock*. New York: Random House, 1970, p. 2.

Chapter 2

1. Alvin Toffler, *The Third Wave*. New York: Bantam, 1981, p. 373.

Chapter 4

1. William Bridges, *Transitions*. New York: Addison-Wesley, 1980, p.
   91.

Chapter 5

1. Ann Kaiser Stearns, *Living Through Personal Crisis*. New York:
   Ballantine, 1984, pp. 148–149. Reprinted with permission of the
   author.

2. Penelope Russianoff, *When Am I Going To Be Happy?* New York: Bantam, 1988. p. 33. Reprinted with the permission of Bantam Books.
3. David Burns, *Feeling Good: The New Mood Therapy.* New York: Avon, 1992, p. 353.
4. Robert Woolfolk and Frank Richardson, *Stress, Sanity and Survival.* New York: Signet, 1979, pp. 83, 86. Reprinted with the permission of Simon & Schuster. Copyright © 1973 by Robert Woolfolk and Frank C. Richardson.
5. Woolfolk and Richardson, p. 79.

Chapter 6

1. Thomas Holmes and Richard Rahe, "Social Readjustment Rating Scale," *Journal of Psychosomatic Research,* Vol. 11, 1967, pp. 213–218.
2. Woolfolk and Richardson, p. 73.

Chapter 7

1. Nancy O'Connor, *Letting Go with Love: The Grieving Process.* Tucson: La Mariposa Press, 1984, pp. 169–170. Reprinted with the permission of La Mariposa Press.
2. Peter Marris, *Loss and Change.* New York: Pantheon, 1974, p. 147.
3. Stearns, pp. xv, 55–56.
4. Stearns, pp. 14, 146–147.

Conclusion

1. Alvin Toffler, *Future Shock,* p. 326.

Recommended Readings

Arond, Miriam, and Samuel Pauker. *The First Year Of Marriage: What to Expect, What to Accept and What You Can Change*. New York: Warner, 1987.

Beck, Aaron. *Love Is Never Enough*. New York: Harper and Row, 1988.

Benson, Herbert. *The Relaxation Response*. New York: William Morrow, 1975.

Branden, Nathaniel. *The Power of Self-Esteem*. Deerfield Beach, Florida: Health Communications, 1992.

Branden, Nathaniel. *The Six Pillars of Self-Esteem*. New York: Bantam, 1994.

Bridges, William. *Transitions*. New York: Addison-Wesley, 1980.

Brown, Barbara. *Between Health and Illness*. Boston: Houghton Mifflin, 1984.

Burns, David. *Feeling Good: The New Mood Therapy*. New York: Avon, 1992.

Charlesworth, Edward, and Ronald Nathan. *Stress Management: A Comprehensive Guide to Wellness*. New York: Ballantine, 1984.

Eisenberg, Ronni. *Organize Yourself*. New York: Macmillan, 1997.

Eisenberg, Ronni, and Kate Kelly. *The Overwhelmed Person's Guide to Time Management*. New York: Penguin, 1997.

Elliott, Miriam, and Susan Meltsner. *The Perfectionist Predicament.* New York: William Morrow, 1991.

Ellis, Albert. *How to Stubbornly Refuse to Make Yourself Miserable about Anything—Yes Anything!* New York: Lyle Stuart, 1988.

Ellis, Albert, and Robert Harper. *A New Guide to Rational Living.* Englewood Cliffs, New Jersey: Prentice Hall, 1975.

Engler, Jack, and Daniel Goleman. *The Consumer's Guide to Psychotherapy.* New York: Simon and Schuster, 1992.

Feldman, Christina. *Principles of Meditation.* London: Thorsons, 1998.

Goleman, Daniel. *Emotional Intelligence.* New York: Bantam, 1995.

Goleman, Daniel, and Joel Gurin (eds). *Mind Body Medicine.* Yonkers, New York: Consumers Union of United States, 1993.

Greenberg, Jerrold. *Coping with Stress: A Practical Guide.* Dubuque, Iowa: William C. Brown, 1990.

Hales, Diane, and Robert Hales. *Caring for the Mind: A Comprehensive Guide to Mental Health.* New York: Bantam, 1996.

Klein, Allen. *The Healing Power of Humor.* New York: Putnam, 1989.

McKay, Matthew, and Patrick Fanning. *Self-Esteem.* Oakland, California: New Harbinger, 1992.

Meichenbaum, Donald. *Coping with Stress.* New York: Facts on File, 1983.

Meyers, David. *The Pursuit of Happiness.* New York: William Morrow, 1992.

Myers, Edward. *When Parents Die: A Guide for Adults.* New York: Penguin, 1997.

O'Connor, Nancy. *Letting Go with Love: The Grieving Process.* Tucson, Arizona: La Mariposa Press, 1984.

Paris, Bob. *Natural Fitness: Your Complete Guide to a Healthy Balanced Lifestyle.* New York: Warner Books, 1996.

Roberts, Francine. *The Therapy Sourcebook.* Los Angeles: RGA Publishing, 1997.

Robinson, Bryan. *Overdoing It: How to Slow Down and Take Care of Yourself.* Deerfield Beach, Florida: Health Communications, 1992.

Russianoff, Penelope. *When Am I Going to Be Happy?* New York: Bantam, 1988.

Schlosberg, Suzanne, and Liz Neporent. *Fitness for Dummies.* Foster City, California: IDG Books, 1996.

Seligman, Martin. *Learned Optimism.* New York: Knopf, 1990.

Seligman, Martin. *What You Can Change and What You Can't*. New York: Knopf, 1994.

Sheehy, Gail. *New Passages: Mapping Your Life across Time*. New York: Random House, 1995.

Spencer, Sabina, and John Adams. *Life Changes: Growing Through Personal Transitions*. San Luis Obispo, California: Impact, 1990.

Stearns, Ann Kaiser. *Living Through Personal Crisis*. New York: Ballantine, 1984.

Tatelbaum, Judy. *The Courage to Grieve*. New York: Harper and Row, 1980.

Toffler, Alvin. *Future Shock*. New York: Bantam, 1970.

Toffler, Alvin. *The Third Wave*. New York: Bantam, 1980.

University of California, Berkeley. *The Wellness Encyclopedia*. Boston: Houghton Mifflin, 1991.

Veninga, Robert. *A Gift of Hope: How We Survive the Tragedies in Our Lives*. Boston: Little, Brown, 1985.

Winston, Stephanie. *Getting Organized*. New York: Warner, 1991.

Woolfolk, Robert, and Frank Richardson. *Stress, Sanity and Survival*. New York: Signet, 1978.

Index